PRAISE FOR *VEGAS CONCIERGE: SEX TRAFFICKING, HIP HOP, AND CORRUPTION IN AMERICA*

"Brian Joseph courageously sheds light on the political corruption that allows the sex trafficking industry to thrive on the Las Vegas Strip. He masterfully demonstrates the violence and trauma bonding sex traffickers use to maintain control over their victims. Truly a must read!"—**Jodi Niswonger**, PhD, trauma specialist based in Las Vegas

"*Vegas Concierge* is the real deal, both the wide societal lens and the intimate, personal tale. This is intricate, it is what investigative reporting should be. Anyone who paid attention to Puffy's house being raided, who has ever wondered whether the most braggadocious parts of hip hop are true, or how Vegas really operates, well, this is the book for you."—**Charles Bock,** bestselling author of *I Will Do Better* and *Beautiful Children*

"From the glitter of the Las Vegas strip to the grit of back rooms in the hood, *Vegas Concierge* takes the reader on a journey through the wild world of sex trafficking. Pulling no punches, but taking plenty of prisoners, Brian Joseph's cinematic style reveals a stark portrait of the dangers, dramas, and (sometimes) deaths of the participants involved in that world as well as the real lives of the people behind the personas. While writers and filmmakers have romanticized that brutality for decades, Joseph is more concerned with hardcore truths."—**Michael A. Gonzales**, contributor, CrimeReads.com; former writer-at-large for *Vibe, The Source, Ego Trip* and *XXL*

"Brian Joseph cuts through the stigmas and stereotypes most often associated with sex trafficking to give us an unsettling, disturbing picture of what is really happening to countless victims in Las Vegas and all over the country. This is an important and necessary book."—**Nick Owchar,** former deputy editor and contributor, *Los Angeles Times Book Review*

"Brian Joseph has written a gutsy and courageous book that displays his old school journalistic passion to comfort the afflicted while confronting a diminished old line media." —**Dan Morain**, journalist and author of *Kamala's Way: An American Life*

"The best investigative reporting combines deep background research with human sources to help the reader understand the scope of a societal problem in ways that manifest change. This book reflects the tiresome work necessary to understand massive institutions and the dogged pursuit of a story that illuminates the depravity of sex trafficking. *Vegas Concierge* takes dead aim at the issue, and by doing so, sheds light into the darkness."—**Charles N. Davis**, PhD, dean, Henry W. Grady College of Journalism and Mass Communication, University of Georgia

"A long overdue and blunt look at the heart-wrenching life of women forced into sex trafficking in plain sight in Sin City, where women are mere pawns in the hands of rich, powerful men. A wake-up call for America." —**Joe Dunn**, former Democratic California state senator

"*Vegas Concierge* is a very provocative and troubling book. Brian Joseph's depth of research and analysis exposes a dark side of life that does not usually get discussed. This book brings the topic to the front and points out the difficulties of trying to cure it. Hopefully, it will influence others in the future to treat it more seriously." —**Dick Ackerman**, former Republican California state senator

"In *Vegas Concierge*, journalist Brian Joseph confronts a social ill that has remained in the shadows for far too long. With sensitivity and compassion, Joseph paints an authentic picture of the tragic lives of sex trafficking victims and how American society continues to fail them." —**Lou Correa**, U.S. representative

"*Vegas Concierge* starts as a deep dive into the hidden world of sex trafficking, a form of modern-day slavery. But it has an extraordinary cast of characters. Its chief villain is Mally Mall, a reality TV star and hip-hop producer who has worked with Drake and Justin Bieber. Despite his fame, Mally was, in real life, a ruthless pimp who exploited women and stole their earnings. Brian Joseph, who lost his job at the *Las Vegas Review–Journal* trying to expose the problem, courageously unearths this world with the help of Angela, who managed to escape Mally's clutches. A riveting read." —**David Heath**, investigative journalist, author of *Longshot*

"In *Vegas Concierge*, award-winning investigative journalist Brian Joseph illustrates a gut-wrenching tale spanning across America with Las Vegas at the epicenter." —**Chuck DeVore**, executive, Texas Public Policy Foundation; former California state assemblyman

"Brian Joseph had me from page one. He writes, 'Pimps are master manipulators who use psychology to bind their victims in invisible chains and control them.' *Vegas Concierge* exposes those chains to dismantle their power. Fast-paced and thoughtful, the real-life depictions read like a novel." —**Esse Johnson**, speaker

"If we want to lessen the sexual abuses of young girls that carry over to ruin the lives of so many, we need to know what this book reveals." —**Robert C. Fellmeth**, former criminal prosecutor; Price Professor of Public Interest Law and director of Children's Advocacy Institute, University of San Diego

"With a delicate balance of empathy and accountability, Brian Joseph amplifies the voices of survivors while condemning the actions of their exploiters, ultimately issuing a powerful call to action against the indifference that can perpetuate sex trafficking. *Vegas Concierge* stands as a sobering and thought-provoking exploration of the crime of our time: sex trafficking in modern America." —**Shannon Grove**, California state senator

Vegas Concierge

VEGAS CONCIERGE

Sex Trafficking, Hip Hop, and Corruption in America

BRIAN JOSEPH

ROWMAN & LITTLEFIELD
Lanham • Boulder • New York • London

Published by Rowman & Littlefield
An imprint of The Rowman & Littlefield Publishing Group, Inc.
4501 Forbes Boulevard, Suite 200, Lanham, Maryland 20706
www.rowman.com

86-90 Paul Street, London EC2A 4NE

British Library Cataloguing in Publication Information available

Library of Congress Cataloging-in-Publication Data

Names: Joseph, Brian, 1980- author.
Title: Vegas concierge : sex trafficking, hip hop, and corruption in America / Brian Joseph.
Description: Lanham : Rowman & Littlefield, [2024] | Includes bibliographical references and
     index.
Identifiers: LCCN 2024003468 | ISBN 9781538171691 (cloth ; alk. paper) | ISBN
     9781538171707 (epub)
Subjects: LCSH: Human trafficking--Nevada--Las Vegas--Case studies. | Human trafficking-
     -Investigation--Nevada--Las Vegas--Case studies. | Prostitution--Nevada--Las Vegas--Case
     studies.
Classification: LCC HQ146.L37 J67 2024 | DDC 364.15/5109793135--dc23/eng/20240426
LC record available at https://lccn.loc.gov/2024003468

For sex trafficking victims and survivors everywhere.

It might not seem like it, but some people do care.

CONTENTS

Introduction xiii

Notes on Research and Language xxi

Trigger Warning xxv

Cast of Characters xxvii

Part I 1

CHAPTER 1: Trapped. 3

CHAPTER 2: Babylon. .13

CHAPTER 3: Trust Me .17

CHAPTER 4: All Day, Every Day. 21

Part II. 31

CHAPTER 5: Sideways .33

CHAPTER 6: From the Ground Up 39

CHAPTER 7: Bring the Noise 49

Part III 53

CHAPTER 8: Poppin' Bottles 55

CHAPTER 9: Mouths to Feed 69

CHAPTER 10: It's Like That 81

CHAPTER 11: Exclusive 89

Part IV 93

CHAPTER 12: Trying to Come Up. 95

CONTENTS

CHAPTER 13: Business 107

CHAPTER 14: Broken Glass 117

Part V **125**

CHAPTER 15: Traveling Light 127

CHAPTER 16: Bad Dreams 133

CHAPTER 17: All of the Lights 141

CHAPTER 18: No Answer 153

Epilogue 171

Policy Discussion 179

Acknowledgments 185

Resources 189

Notes 205

Index 245

About the Author 263

INTRODUCTION

This is a true story about domestic sex trafficking in America. In it, you will meet real people who exemplify some of the most typical sex traffickers and sex trafficking victims in this country.[1] You will be familiar with these people. They're commonly depicted in American popular culture. But they're not always associated with sex trafficking.

Sex trafficking frequently is portrayed as something that occurs on the fringes of society, in the dark and in secret. In movies and on TV, trafficking victims often seem to be presented as foreign women, and they always seem intensely aware of the evils of their situation and desperately struggling to escape it. Traffickers, on the other hand, are depicted as brutal but mysterious men who live in the shadows and rule by violence.

This popular image of sex traffickers and the victims of sex trafficking is almost completely wrong for much of the sex trafficking that occurs in America. About the only thing Hollywood gets right is the brutal men, and even that is more complicated.

This is not a story about cuddly victims—about obvious victims. Rarely do sex trafficking victims ask for help, because rarely do they see themselves as needing help. Instead, you'll find they are leather tough and street savvy, and frequently they'll have a bad attitude or be painfully unreliable. For many people, the victims won't seem sympathetic at all, at least not at first. I say this from experience. During my research, I encountered victims who were frustrating, flakey, rude, or passive aggressive. They were sometimes unpleasant to be around. But that didn't make them any less deserving of compassion.

The villains in this story, you'll recognize them as evil. But they won't shy away from attention or hide in the shadows. They'll be bold and brazen and, in some cases, welcome the limelight.

The story of sex trafficking in America is, largely, the story of pimps and prostitutes.[2] And in American culture, pimps are funny and silly and cool, and prostitutes are "dirty whores."

Prostitution is often referred to as humanity's oldest profession. But despite its longevity, the vocation is burdened by some heavy baggage. Prostitutes, generally, are perceived as vile women. They get little sympathy because people assume they consciously and rationally choose to sell their bodies, and typically prostitutes do nothing to dispel this notion.

But almost always their stories are not that simple. Long before a prostitute enters the sex industry, she often has experienced profound personal trauma. Maybe she grew up with an abusive father, or lost her brother to murder, or bounced from one foster family to another. Whatever happened, she almost certainly suffers from painfully low self-esteem and sees sex work as her only way to make a buck. As the therapists of sex trafficking victims are fond of saying, *No little girl dreams of being a prostitute.* Under the best of circumstances—"best" being a relative term here—women frequently fall into prostitution after they've been beaten down by life.

But even then, many women don't fall into prostitution, they're pushed—by manipulative pimps who feed on their vulnerabilities and brainwash them into believing that's all they're good for. Hollywood may play pimps for laughs; see Will Ferrell's character Gator in the movie *The Other Guys* as a good example. But to its credit it does frequently portray them as violent. The term "pimp slap" is a testament to our knowledge that pimps beat the women they force and coerce to work for them. But violence is just one of a pimp's tools, and it's not even his most devastating one.

Pimps are master manipulators who use psychology to bind their victims in invisible chains and control them. "(P)impin' is psychological warfare, it's not physical combat," writes Pimpin' Ken Ivy, a Milwaukee pimp, in *Pimpology: The 48 Rules of the Game*,[3] an astoundingly explicit book about how pimps think:

> Most hoes have low self-esteem for a reason. A pimp looks for that weakness, and if it isn't on the surface, he brings that motherfucker out of them. It doesn't matter to a pimp what hoes' weaknesses are, so long as they have them. Then he uses those weaknesses to his advantage.

Yes, some pimps kidnap their victims and force them into prostitution through brutal, gut-wrenching violence, and you'll see that in this story. But you'll also see pimps deftly prey on women's emotions and past traumas, influencing them so subtly that they'll think it was their idea to sell themselves all along.

I'm not going to argue that there aren't some prostitutes out there who freely choose this lifestyle. That question always comes up whenever prostitution is discussed. That happens, and there is a vocal group of self-proclaimed "sex workers" who speak proudly about their profession. Evidence gathered by academic researchers and by law enforcement officers on the streets, however, strongly suggest that this is a niche perspective, that overwhelmingly most prostitutes are victims of at least horrible life circumstances, but more likely also the manipulation of a trafficker, whose cruel intentions we sanitize under the word "pimp."

Now's probably a good time to discuss the terms we'll use in this book. Throughout, I'll use the words "pimp" and "sex trafficker" interchangeably, because when you drill down deep enough, you'll see that they are synonyms. In American jurisprudence, pimps generally face two possible charges: pandering or sex trafficking.[4] They are essentially the same crime—soliciting customers for a prostitute and/or luring a woman into prostitution—with one critical difference. Pandering is silent on the pimp's violence or manipulations. Sex trafficking, on the other hand, proves that the pimp used force, fraud, or coercion to lure a woman into what's commonly known as The Life or The Game. (Many anti-trafficking advocates say they prefer the term "prostituted person" instead of "prostitute" because it captures the extreme imbalance of power in the dynamic with a pimp.)

If the distinction between pandering and sex trafficking seems subtle or even strange, that's because it is. Pandering was illegal long before the concept of sex trafficking was accepted, before we as a society acknowledged that prostitutes could be victims. (Sex trafficking did not become a criminal charge in Nevada until July 1, 2013.[5]) But as Pimpin' Ken Ivy makes abundantly clear, force, fraud, and coercion are fundamental to a pimp's playbook. Pimps regularly convince women to work as prostitutes by selling them empty promises, like that once they earn a certain amount of money they can retire. But no matter how much a prostitute makes, she's typically never allowed to stop. That's fraud. Pimps also frequently blackmail women into continuing to prostitute by threatening to tell their families what they had previously been doing voluntarily. That's coercion. With sex-trafficking laws now on the books, prosecutors try to find a way to charge a pimp with sex trafficking, which typically carries much harsher penalties than pandering.

So, pimps are sex traffickers. Don't let the widespread acceptance of the word or their presence in music videos or at awards shows fool you. Pimps are cold-blooded slave masters, men as cruel and evil as Harvey Weinstein or Jeffrey Epstein.

Speaking of victims, I'll also use the terms "victim" and "survivor" interchangeably when describing women who have been sex trafficked. This may be a bit of a controversial decision in the anti-trafficking community but let me explain my reasoning. Many women who were sex trafficked prefer to be described as survivors rather than victims because they don't want the stigma of victimization. For them, the term "survivor" proudly proclaims that they made it through their trafficking experience, whole and intact. I absolutely respect that line of thinking. But as I'll show time and time again throughout this book, women who have been sex trafficked are routinely disregarded by the people and institutions that should help them. I think it's important to continue using the word "victim" when describing women who have been sex trafficked because there are still wide swaths of the population who see them as worthy only of scorn. We celebrate survivors, and we should celebrate every woman who gets out of The Life. But we also need to recognize that these women are suffering, from injuries and manipulation and trauma, and it's my experience that many people just don't see that.

So, my hope is that by using the term "victim" I can hammer that point home.

I'll also concede, for anyone spoiling for a fight, that not all prostitutes are women and not all traffickers are men. But this book is about one of the most typical forms of domestic sex trafficking in the United States, and typically these traffickers are men—pimps—and prostitutes are typically women or, in some particularly awful cases, girls. Either way, some of the most typical sex trafficking victims in America don't come from far-away lands. They have common names like Jessica and Alisha, and they come from places like Seattle, Washington and Houston, Texas.

Sex trafficking occupies an awkward place in our current political landscape—even though many believe it's not a political issue. Undoubtedly, the #MeToo movement has made the eradication of sexual violence against women by powerful men both a political and social priority. But sex trafficking victims clearly are underrepresented in that movement, likely because victims are understandably hesitant to speak out, and because of society's general disdain for prostitutes.

But for a variety of other reasons, sex trafficking also is an unappealing topic for many on both the Left and the Right. I'll address both, and I'll start with the Left, not out of any political bias on my part, but simply because L comes before R in the alphabet. (That seemed like the easiest way to avoid showing favorites.)

Anyway, on the Left there is a contingent that seems to equate prostitution with abortion, in that the government should not tell a woman what to do with her body. These liberals argue that sex work can be empowering, and that society's goal should be to create a system where prostitutes can work freely and openly, without fear of shame or judgment. This line of thinking, calling for the decriminalization of prostitution, seeks to eliminate the stigmatization of sex workers and that's a worthy goal. But it can neglect to address the traumas, both societal and personal, that often lead women to sex work, or offer "off ramps" from prostitution and/or direct services to victims and survivors. It also can ignore the scourge of traffickers. Indeed, some on the Left seem to suggest that the problem of sex trafficking is overblown and that many prostitutes are, in fact, working voluntarily.

Of course, that's not to say everyone on the Left thinks that way. There are other progressives who are intensely concerned about sex trafficking and who believe jailing women and girls caught up in The Life is morally reprehensible. As you'll see in this book, perspectives on this topic often differ, even among people who are part of the same group.

Discounting the realities of sex trafficking isn't so much of an issue on the Right (although there are libertarians who believe people should be able to prostitute freely, despite the consequences). Evangelicals in particular lament the cultural conditions and wicked men who send women into prostitution. They are among the Right's biggest champions of sex trafficking victims. But their opposition to certain forms of sexual expression—like the *Sports Illustrated* Swimsuit Issue—reduces their credibility with some who seem to worry that Evangelicals are more concerned with controlling people's private sexual practices than in saving souls. At the same time, some business interests, particularly casinos, seem to view efforts to combat sex trafficking as a threat to their bottom line. These business interests don't deny that sex trafficking exists. They just don't seem to really want to deal with it. It also doesn't help that hip hop stars who have adopted the style of pimps have become pitchmen for major, household brands.

Don't get me wrong: hip hop is not to blame for sex trafficking. I am aware of nothing to suggest that the enslavement or abuse of vulnerable women is intrinsic to the culture. Rather, sex trafficking has a long history with economically disadvantaged communities and sadly that's been a part of the Black experience in America. Hip hop merely reflects the neighborhoods in which it was born. Pimping and prostitution became a part of some of those neighborhoods, so they ended up in raps. But as this book will show, sex trafficking isn't limited to just our poorest communities. It shows up everywhere, in the suburbs and among the rich and famous alike, with pimps of all races, creeds, and colors.

And make no mistake, with the internet, sex trafficking can occur anywhere in America. Much of this book is set in Las Vegas, arguably the epicenter of sex trafficking in the United States today. But this horrendous plague on our society is not limited to Sin City—where, despite what you may think, prostitution is not legal—or even to our biggest metropolitan areas. As part of my years-long research into sex trafficking, I encountered a federal case about a pimp who was busted in Rapid City, South Dakota. As you'll soon see, pimps frequently move their victims around to increase profits and evade law enforcement. One of their favorite tactics is taking their victims on cross-country road trips, where they'll traffic women out of any small town or suburb they encounter.

Despite whatever you might have seen or read, or whatever your personal experiences might tell you, this is not a problem with easy answers. This is an entrenched, complicated affliction in our society, more akin to domestic violence or drug addiction than to plantation slavery. It is grossly misunderstood and too often ignored.

My hope is that this book will help to change that.

Notes on Research and Language

Every effort has been made to make the following narrative as accurate as possible. An independent, third-party fact checker was hired to review the manuscript, as was an attorney. (These reviews were separate from reviews conducted by the publisher.) I have gone over the contents of this book thoroughly with the two protagonists and many secondary subjects to attempt to ensure its accuracy. Even individuals mentioned in the text who declined to be interviewed were given the opportunity to verify detailed information about themselves. Numerous endnotes at the back of the book provide insights into how certain facts were ascertained or offer additional context. Also, please note that only quotations that I directly read or directly heard (and transcribed *immediately*) appear within quotation marks. All other quotations appear in italics, indicating that they might not be precise reproductions of what was said or written. (I have also used quotation marks when referencing certain colloquialisms or terms specific to police work or the pimp-prostitute subculture, among other, minor phrases.)

I should note that many of the events depicted in this book occurred many years ago and that the only records of them anywhere are in people's memories. This can be challenging when dealing with subjects who have been the victims of trauma. As research has shown, trauma victims often mix up details when recounting their memories. I and the major subjects of this book, as well as several unnamed sources, have spent many hours attempting to straighten out even the most minor of details described here. Together, I am confident that we have done the very best we possibly could to present an accurate picture of events. But I also should note that the subject matter of this book is highly contentious and that several primary sources of information refused to participate in the research, are difficult to speak with freely, or were otherwise unavailable for consultation. Their lack of cooperation or participation, for whatever reason, could have affected our ability to paint a complete picture, especially in instances when I had only one source to draw upon.

A lot of thought was also put into the language used in this book, which attempts to balance the competing values of authenticity and sensitivity. Women are second-class citizens in the prostitution subculture and that is frequently reflected in the words used to describe them. Likewise, as this book will demonstrate, issues of race are deeply woven into the subculture.

To immerse readers as much as possible into the subculture, words like "bitch" and "ho," "prostitute" and "working girl," are sometimes used to describe women, but that's only in the context of how their pimp relates to them or in specific instances to drive home how dehumanizing the subculture is to women. (Some anti-trafficking advocates, for example, object to the term "prostitute" because of the stigma long associated with the word and because they believe it subtly implies that women labeled as such have freely chosen to engage with the men who harm them.)

These pejoratives are offensive. They are employed here, however, to illustrate the casual cruelty of The Life, and to reflect how many Americans unfamiliar with the nuances of sex trafficking speak about it. I do not use these words to degrade women, nor to assume that any woman in prostitution chose it. As I hope is starting to become clear, prostitution is typically something thrust upon women, not something they seek out.

Also, many minor subjects who appear briefly in the story are sometimes identified by their race in addition to their gender or other attributes. This may be controversial, as many in the writing world believe a person's race should only be identified when it's specifically germane to the matter at hand. However, in the pimp-prostitute subculture, a person's race is almost always germane (because a person's race typically determines how someone is perceived within the subculture). As such, to reflect that reality, I have elected to identify subjects' races at times when other writers might have chosen not to. That decision is not intended to offend, but rather to illustrate how race constantly looms over this subculture.

As described in more detail in the Acknowledgments, a wide range of people of different races, genders, and backgrounds reviewed this book prior to publication for sensitivity, including several people with deep expertise in the pimp-prostitute subculture and the cruelties of sex trafficking. With their help, I have tried my best to write a book that is compassionate and culturally appropriate while also reflecting the offensive realities of the pimp-prostitute subculture.

I have tried very hard not to offend in my writing here. But if I do, I sincerely apologize.

Trigger Warning

This book describes sexual violence and includes examples of overt racism and sexism. It may be disturbing and traumatizing to some readers.

CAST OF CHARACTERS

Jamal Rashid aka Mally Mall: Las Vegas pimp, hip hop music producer, reality TV star

Angela Williams (née Delgado): Sex trafficking victim, survivor

Donald Hoier: Head of the Vice Section's Pandering Investigations Team at the Las Vegas Metropolitan Police Department (otherwise known as Metro)

Brian Joseph: Author, journalist, the "I" in this book

PIMPS AND OTHER FIGURES IN THE GAME

Ocean Fleming: Violent, "gorilla" pimp with an explosive temper, sentenced to life in prison

Arman Izadi: Las Vegas nightclub promoter, pimp

Tarnita Woodard aka "Tia": One of Mally's lieutenants

April Millard: Sex trafficking victim with ties to Fleming and Mally

OTHER CRIMINAL JUSTICE FIGURES

Christopher Baughman: Star detective on Vice's Pandering Investigations Team

Warren Gray: Detective with Metro's Criminal Intelligence Section (otherwise known as Intel)

Liz Mercer: Clark County Deputy District Attorney

Al Beas: Detective on Vice's Pandering Investigations Team

Karen Hughes: Head of Metro's Vice Section

Kevin White: Ambitious, young FBI agent

Vic Vigna: Metro Vice sergeant

Media Figures

Shawn "Tubby" Holiday: Interscope Records executive

George Knapp: Investigative reporter for KLAS-TV, a CBS affiliate, in Las Vegas

Sheldon Adelson: Casino magnate, major Republican campaign donor, owner of the *Las Vegas Review-Journal* newspaper

Part I

CHAPTER 1

Trapped

ANGELA DELGADO KEPT TO THE SHADOWS TO HIDE HER BLACK EYE.[1] All around her the sidewalk surged with the chaotic energy of the Las Vegas Strip. A kaleidoscope of joyful, laughing faces flashed before her eyes, but all she felt was fear. Every nerve in her body seemed to be on fire, her senses overwhelmed by the dangers that she knew lurked beneath the gleaming lights.

Despite her diminutive, five-foot, one-hundred-pound frame, Angela considered herself tough and street smart. She'd worked as a stripper and a prostitute for a long time. She'd seen and done a lot in her twenty-two years. She thought she knew how to handle herself. But now, more than 1,000 miles away from anything familiar, she felt small and vulnerable, a child afraid of what would happen next. Her body was so tense. She hoped no one would notice her knees were shaking.

Angela had just arrived in Las Vegas that day, dragged into town by her latest trafficker, a violent street pimp who went by the name "Dallas." Buzzing into the desert in his outdated Cadillac (yes, really), Dallas had shuttled them to the Motel 6 on Tropicana Avenue, strategically placing them less than a mile from The Strip. The place was crawling with what appeared to Angela to be crackheads and other pimps and "hos," all eager to tap The Strip's endless supply of sex buyers. That's why Dallas had driven Angela here, more than 1,000 miles from Houston, to cash in on Sin City's anything-goes excess. Dallas made his expectations clear: Angela was to walk up and down The Strip and not come back until she had earned $1,000. Angela didn't need to ask what would happen if she failed to meet her quota. The days-old bruise on her face was a reminder that he meant business.

After dark, Angela had trudged west from the motel to the lights of Las Vegas Boulevard. It was a beautiful, warm evening in mid-2006.[2] Despite her racing thoughts—*What is he going to do to me? How do I get away from him?*—Angela had enough presence of mind to be wistful, if only for a moment. Here she was, in what she considered to be the capital of America's sex industry, at the peak of the field she had somehow found herself in. She wanted to enjoy the moment, to feel glamourous and sexy, like Sharon Stone's character in the movie *Casino*. Instead, she just felt ridiculous. Dallas had dressed her in what Angela considered a trashy ensemble from the clothing line Baby Phat: cork wedges, capri jeans, and a lacy, cream top, cut low to accentuate her breasts. Her ghetto look was a far cry from the chic styles Stone had rocked as Ginger McKenna.

But Angela didn't have time to bemoan her wardrobe. She needed to make money and she felt hopelessly out of her depth. The Strip stretched out before her like a mine field, threats everywhere she stepped. She had to keep an eye out for the authorities, but she didn't know how casino security guards dressed or what the local police did to target prostitutes. Every block was a different resort, with a different theme, and a different array of lights and shadows. Each time she came to a new property, she had to quickly scan her surroundings and search for anyone in uniform. It was nerve-wracking—and that wasn't even the worst of it.

Angela knew she was surrounded by other pimps and prostitutes, some obvious, others not. As many as a thousand working girls descend on The Strip every night, strolling Las Vegas Boulevard or loitering in casino lounges, lobbies, and bars.[3] Angela was experienced in the sex trade by this time, but still she was stunned by what she saw. Sex seemed to be on everyone's mind. At every corner, Latino men handed out glossy cards of scantily clad women who could be in your hotel room within the hour. Up and down The Strip, Angela saw women in short skirts and impossibly high heels, walking briskly through the crowds. These women appeared to be "ho'ing," and their ubiquitous presence seemed to embolden the men. If a woman winked at a guy, Angela saw that's all it took for him to ask if he could fuck her in the ass.

Even more frightening, however, were the big Black men[4] Angela saw following some of the more obvious prostitutes. These men chattered incessantly, seemingly trying to get a reaction out of the women. Angela recognized them as pimps who were probably trying to attract the attention of rival prostitutes, maybe beat them up and steal their money. She tried blending in, but other women walking the street sought her out. *Hey, girl,* they'd say. *How are you doing tonight?* Angela caught on that she must looked frightened and out of place, which made her a target. Pimps didn't just expect their "hos" to make them money—they expected them to recruit other women, too. Angela knew other prostitutes saw her as a prize they could take home to their pimps.

Angela searched the faces of the men. She started panicking. She had to find a buyer, right now, just to go back to his hotel room and get off the street, even if just for a moment. Yes, sex with a strange man was risky. A john could rob her or rape her, even kill her. But that risk was preferable to how vulnerable she felt.

Eventually, Angela encountered a tall, white guy in his mid-to-late 30s, dressed liked a businessman. He was drunk and walking alone, an easy mark. *Hey, baby. You need some company?*, she asked. Slurring his words, the man invited her back to his room at The Venetian. She followed him into the lavish resort, her eyes on the ground. In his room, the man handed her $500 to get comfortable, but she still felt uneasy. He gave her another $300. He wanted sex, but Angela's stomach remained in knots. He let her go even though she didn't give him "full service." Angela figured he felt sorry for her.

At the Wynn resort next door, Angela caught a glimpse of the valet area packed with flashy sports cars. She wanted to stop and stare, but she knew better. Soon enough, Dallas called her cell, one of those Motorola Razr flip phones. Angela complained that her feet hurt. *Beat your feet,* he said. Get moving.

Angela was named after her maternal grandmother, Angelina, a wild but enterprising Choctaw woman who acted as the center of gravity for the Delgado family. Angelina had nine children. Her husband was a blue-eyed Spaniard who owned a prosperous autobody shop that did work for the Houston Police Department. But tragedy struck when he suddenly died of cirrhosis of the liver. To support her large family, Angelina turned to selling drugs and printing fake immigration documents, an enterprise that generated a lot of money, but also caused problems.

When Angela was born in 1984, she and her mom lived in a house close to Angelina in a poor, Hispanic neighborhood on the south side of Houston. Her mom started having children at the age of sixteen with a Latino boy she met at a skating rink. They had three children altogether, two boys and Angela. However, at some point when she was pregnant with Angela, at almost twenty, she had ditched her boyfriend due to his cheating. Angela's mom worked as a pharmacy tech, but she depended on Angelina to pay her bills.

Angela's first memory is of someone apparently in law enforcement pulling her mom's hair through a screen door. The officer wanted information on Angelina. In June 1988, Angela's grandmother was busted for marijuana possession.[5] Angelina spent nearly a year in jail, which sent Angela's young life into a tailspin. Her father took her two older brothers and moved them to San Francisco while her mom relocated Angela to a dumpy apartment, where a walk-in closet became the little girl's bedroom. To make more money, Angela's mom quit her job at the pharmacy and became a stripper. After that, Angela said her mom left her with a series of babysitters for days at a time. Sometimes, Angela's mom would come back from her benders drunk with a trash bag full of toys. For a long while, Angela didn't have a consistent person in her life who made her feel cared for and loved. The experience slowly broke down her self-esteem, making her vulnerable to dominant, overwhelming personalities.

But Angela was not a complainer or a crier. She put on a happy face and did everything she could to get positive attention from adults. She loved their smiles. When her mother was away, Angela would sit by the window and stare out at the world, wondering when she'd see her mom again or if her dad was thinking about her. In April 1989, Angelina was released from jail, according to records, then moved into the same, run-down apartment complex. She became Angela's primary caretaker, affording her mother the chance to disappear for even longer stretches. Sometimes when her mom would come around, she'd give Angela a $100 bill, which Angela took to the corner store to buy toys for herself and the other kids in the neighborhood.

Angela's father and two brothers returned to Houston in 1992; the boys became immersed in drugs and gang culture. As she got older, hip hop was the rage, but Angela and her best friend were more interested in Hello Kitty, alternative rock, punk, and ska. They dreamed of a life outside of their depressing neighborhood. Among their favorite places to escape was a whimsical local attraction on Munger Street called the Orange Show. Built by a Houston postal worker over twenty-five years from the 1950s to the 1970s, the carnival-like landmark was a quirky mishmash of handmade folk art that provided a colorful reprieve from an otherwise unremarkable block. Still, there was only so much the girls could do to avoid the influence of the neighborhood. When they were in middle school, they hung out at a local youth center that hosted a Friday night contest where adolescent girls could show off their thongs. It was not unusual for her classmates to get pregnant. It desensitized Angela to sex at a young age.

In the late 1990s, both of Angela's brothers ran afoul of the law, picking up serious criminal charges for violent felonies—manslaughter and aggravated robbery. Eventually, both were sentenced to long prison terms in Texas. Their legal troubles deeply affected Angela, who began experimenting with LSD and ecstasy at rave parties.

Angela entered Stephen F. Austin High School in 1998. She hated it. There were fights every day and students having sex in the bathrooms. At the end of tenth grade, Angela convinced her mom to let her enroll in an independent study program, which allowed her to do her school-work from home. Angela dreamed of becoming a marine biologist—as a Pisces, she says she's attracted to the water—but in the short term she focused on saving money for her own place. At fifteen, she got a job at a $5 pizza buffet, then later became a cashier at a Kroger grocery store, then a telemarketer.

Angela graduated from high school a year early, in 2001, at seventeen, and moved out, eventually renting a tiny studio apartment with green shag carpet. She was interested in furthering her education—she attended Houston Community College[6] and a surgical tech program at Sanford-Brown College,[7]—but her main focus was on just pocketing enough money to leave the neighborhood, which to her felt like a prison. Angela didn't want to grow up to be like some of the old women she saw who had never left the south side of Houston.

One day, one of Angela's friends[8] told her that she had met an older guy and landed a great job. She invited Angela to come by and hang out where she worked. Her friend worked out of a nondescript building behind a strip club. The place—an illegal brothel—was crawling with girls in their late teens or women in their twenties. Each was assigned a room with its own theme. One had a red couch with Marilyn Monroe photos on the wall. Another was decorated in a garish, wild pattern while another was Italian-themed, with grapevines and pictures of Rome. In the back, there was a lounge with a big-screen television, a shower, and a fridge full of snacks. The place was a lot nicer than Angela's tiny apartment with shag carpet. Her friend would hang out with Angela in the lounge until a man would come by. Then she'd disappear into a room. Angela caught on that her friend was providing sexual services to men, but she didn't judge. Her mom was a stripper. Everybody's got to make a living.

Once when Angela was hanging around, the brothel's boss, Andre "Dre" McDaniels, stopped by.[9] A Black man from Kansas, McDaniels was a former drug dealer and the definition of 'hood rich. He was involved with a BBQ joint, a record label, and several illegal brothels with names like Taboo Modeling Studio North and Total Pleasures. McDaniels was relentless in his recruitment of new prostitutes. He had a white van that he would use to shuttle his girls to the mall or Burger King, where they'd pass out cards advertising openings at a modeling studio. Angela saw McDaniels give her friend $200. *He takes care of me,* the friend said. Angela was stunned—$200 was a lot of money to her.

After that, Angela's friend started pestering her to join the brothel. At eighteen, Angela started stripping and tentatively dipped her toe into

McDaniels's world. In Angela's initial forays into The Life, McDaniels babied her, allowing her to refer clients asking for full service to other girls, which some of the other girls resented. For a while, Angela moved between the brothels and the strip clubs, where she learned she could make more money selling drugs than dancing. The money was intoxicating, which led her to try moving more narcotics. But she wasn't good at it. In November 2003, she was busted with cocaine and pharmaceutical syrup and sentenced to ten years' probation.[10] Now a felon, Angela figured it would be safer working for McDaniels, where the worst charge she could catch was a misdemeanor for prostitution. Looking back, Angela would later realize that McDaniels had slowly but surely groomed her for The Life, carefully breaking her down and desensitizing her to the cruelties of sex work.

When Angela fully committed to McDaniels's network, life was a bit different. He expected her to perform full service. One time, he instructed her to meet an "old guy" behind the bleachers of a high school football stadium and pretend to be a minor. She was told to hang out with the guy for a few days and snort cocaine with him, which made her shake and puke. McDaniels set her up with an apartment of her own, but she realized nobody she worked with was happy. Her breaking point came when she asked McDaniels for some Versace towels, but McDaniels would only buy her Ralph Lauren towels you could get at Ross. Angela couldn't figure out why she was doing all this shit if all she got out of it were towels from Ross.

Angela left McDaniels and ended up at a new apartment complex, poor and depressed. She started smoking weed with a guy she met through a girlfriend. He wore nice clothes and drove a Cadillac. He said his name was Dallas.

Over shared blunts, Angela told Dallas what she did at the brothel. He didn't say much. Then one day he told her he and some friends were going on a road trip. He invited her to come along. *It won't be long*, he said. *You could make some money.* A few days later, Angela piled into Dallas's Cadillac as his friends followed in other cars. After a few hours, they all pulled over at a truck stop. In the women's bathroom, a girl from one of the other cars told Angela that she wanted to run away, that they were all headed to a track in Washington, DC. Angela's blood ran cold. A track is a stretch of road, usually in a dumpy part of a town, where prostitutes are known to pick up sex buyers. Angela knew walking the track—or the "ho stroll" as its sometimes called—was dangerous in any city. If this girl wanted to escape, Angela shouldn't be there either. *Shit*, she thought. *What have I gotten myself into?*

When they got back on the road, Dallas reached from the driver's seat and grabbed Angela by the head. *Don't talk to other pimps or hos*, he yelled. *You were out of pocket.* Angela wasn't sure what that meant, but she soon learned. Dallas liked the rapper Suga Free, who rapped about prostitution in a teaching sort of way. Dallas played his songs constantly over the radio. On the track "Happy," Suga Free chirps, "I, Step, My, Game, Up, so if you disrespect me get outta pocket and you can get fucked up." Angela came to understand that being out of pocket was one of the worst offenses a prostitute could do to her pimp. That could include talking to another pimp or rival prostitute without permission. In The Game, that was a sign of disrespect, punishable by a beating. Angela would have to watch herself.

After driving for more than ten hours, Dallas had car trouble in Steele, Alabama. He began to think it might be better to ditch the caravan and turn around. *Why don't we go to Las Vegas?* he suggested. *Fine*, Angela replied. *Just drop me off in Houston.* Dallas wouldn't hear it, but Angela wouldn't stop asking. *Take me home!* she pleaded. Around Birmingham, Dallas had had enough. He popped the trunk and pushed Angela inside. *No, please, don't!* Angela cried. Dallas slammed the trunk and continued west, back toward Texas.

Inside the trunk, it was dark and hot and stuffy. Angela cried at first and felt hurt. *Why me?* she wondered. Then she got angry and started kicking. Dallas didn't care. For the next ten hours or so, he opened the trunk just a couple of times, to yell at her. *Punk bitch. You're going to learn.* He didn't let her out, even to use the bathroom, until they reached Lewisville, Texas, a suburb of Dallas. There, they got a room at an extended-stay hotel. *I want to go home!* Angela pleaded. Dallas punched her in the face, then grabbed a wire hanger and started whipping her with it, leaving bright red welts on her back. When he was done, Dallas pulled a chair over to the door, faced it toward Angela, and just sat there, watching her.

This pattern continued for days—Dallas whipping her, then sitting by the door and watching her—the routine changing only when Dallas told her to sleep next to him or when he'd have sex with her. Angela cried the whole time. Dallas beat Angela so badly it was days before she could hide her bruises with makeup and see sex buyers again.

Later, Dallas took Angela to his mother's house, which was in a nearby suburb. He told her he wanted her to walk the track on Harry Hines Boulevard in Dallas. Then he left her in an upstairs bedroom while he spoke with his mom. By then, Angela figured the only way she'd survive was if she went along with his demands. But she was afraid to walk the track. *How can I make some money?* she wondered. There was an old desktop computer in the room. Dallas was already having her post ads online; she figured he wouldn't care if she used the computer. She hopped on the internet and started looking on Craigslist and Backpage for escort services. *Maybe they could refer me to some clients*, she thought.

Angela called several ads, but no one picked up. Then she saw a help-wanted ad for a site called Dallas Top 10, which was described as a *female-owned-and-operated adult modeling agency*. Angela knew what that really meant. She dialed the number and held her breath. A moment later, a bubbly, young-sounding woman answered the phone. *I'm Tia*, the woman said. In a rush, Angela told Tia she was looking for work and wanted referrals. Tia seemed happy to help. In a smooth, professional manner, she explained to Angela that she was based in Las Vegas and that the service split the proceeds with escorts fifty–fifty. Tia sounded smart and experienced. Over an hourlong conversation, Tia peppered Angela with questions, which made Angela think she cared about her. Angela figured Tia must own the escort service. For the next several days, Angela and Tia spoke on the phone daily. Every time, Tia would start talking business—*Hey, girl. Are you on? Can you take a call?*—but, inevitably, she'd steer the conversation to Angela's personal life. Angela thought they were friends.

After a few more days in Texas, Dallas loaded Angela back into his Caddy. There was big money to be made in Las Vegas.

Back on The Strip, Angela's feet were aching. From the Wynn, she had walked for hours, eventually arriving at Caesars Palace. Her brain felt foggy, and she didn't know what to do. Pimps frequently employ a practice known as "knock and move," with "knock" being pimp slang for convincing a woman to work for a trafficker and "move" meaning taking the woman to a new, unfamiliar place. The idea is for a pimp to isolate and disorient a new prostitute the moment she enters his stable so she can't escape. Whether he had done so on purpose or not, Dallas executed "knock and move" to near perfection on Angela. She was isolated and confused in a strange, foreign city. But she wasn't completely alone.

At Caesars, Angela ducked into a bathroom by an outdoor bar. She pulled out her phone and dialed Tia. *I'm in Vegas*, she said. Maybe it was the late hour or something in her voice, but Angela got the impression that Tia knew she was desperate. *I'll send a car to pick you up tomorrow*, Tia said.

CHAPTER 2

Babylon

ANGELA CRASHED THAT NIGHT WITH A PROSTITUTE NAMED J.[1] J. HAD some kind of prior relationship with Dallas; he introduced Angela to her, and they all shared a blunt before he sent Angela onto The Strip. But J. was no friend of the pimp; she was happy to help Angela get away from him. J. was a "renegade," street slang for a prostitute who worked without a pimp. Previously, J. had worked for a pimp for ten years as well as a legal brothel in rural Nevada, which in both instances required her to give away a huge portion of her earnings. She now said it was foolish to give any money she made to someone else. She seemed to hate pimps, and seemingly did well for herself as a renegade. She had a nice, large house, which is where J. took Angela at the end of the night.

But when J. brought her inside, Angela saw most of the rooms were empty—no furniture, nothing. The only decorations in the kitchen were rows of empty Hennessy bottles above the cabinets and fridge, which wasn't surprising, since J. wore an ankle monitor due to a recent DUI.

J. cooked Angela macaroni and cheese with onions and shoyu chicken and then the women slept until about noon, which for them was the equivalent of morning. Angela was not prepared for what happened next. Tia's ride arrived—a Rolls-Royce. Both J. and Angela were dumbfounded. *That's a nice-ass car*, Angela thought. The driver, a thirtysomething white guy dressed as a proper chauffer, opened the back door for her to get inside. Angela felt so excited, like a little kid. The big-bodied car sported televisions in the headrests. Angela had never seen anything like it.

The driver threw some hip-hop music videos on the TVs and started to drive. Angela thought that just made the ride even cooler. The drive lasted about fifteen minutes, as the Rolls headed almost directly south from East Desert Inn Road and South Nellis Boulevard in southeast Las Vegas to another one of the city's dusty, unremarkable suburban blocks.

Then Angela got her second surprise of the day: The car pulled up to a metal gate decorated with palm trees. Opening, the gate revealed a long, curved driveway backed by a mansion straight out of *MTV Cribs*. The large house was ringed by palm trees, giving it a beachy, vacation vibe that stood in sharp contrast to the rest of the drab neighborhood.[2] Angela's jaw practically hit the ground.

An Asian security guard dressed in a polo shirt, khakis, and work boots came out of the property's security station located in the second garage to talk to the driver. One of the garage doors opened, revealing more luxury cars. The driver led Angela through the garage into the mansion's kitchen. Adjacent to the kitchen was a large aquarium and to the left of that were two living rooms, one of which held a caged monkey. Animals seemed to be everywhere. A large, speckled cat that looked something like a cheetah lived in one of the bedrooms but was allowed to roam freely around the house. A few big, gray wolves were fenced in behind the garage. There was also a big yellow snake in a cage.

And that was just the beginning. There was a room with a big leather sectional couch and an enormous television. The formal dining room had been converted into a game room with a pool table and several arcade cabinets, including Pac-Man, Angela's favorite. There were even a couple of "secret" rooms, accessible by hidden doors. As she looked around, eyes wide, Angela overheard the driver and security guard talking. One of them said *he* wasn't around. Angela figured the house had to be owned by a man as the walls were plastered with paintings of topless Black women. But nobody offered any explanations about who owned the place or anything else.

Several people worked in the house, and everyone was cordial. But they were also standoffish. Angela got the impression the house staff was used to having random, stray people hanging around. An older Latina maid handed her a bowl of leftover chicken and eggs, a sort of Mexican breakfast bowl. It was yummy. Angela parked herself on the sofa and ate and watched TV and smoked a blunt.

Many hours passed. Around midnight, an aloof white woman named Jen came by the mansion and said she was there to take Angela to the escort service offices. Angela could hardly get a word out of her, but Angela noted she drove a regular car, not a fancy Rolls. Angela knew that meant she didn't truly matter in whatever operations she had suddenly found herself in.

This ride took a little longer, about half an hour, as Jen drove them to a gritty, industrial stretch of Sammy Davis Jr. Drive, just west of The Strip. There, above the Can Can Room, a no-frills, totally nude strip club, was the escort service office. Right as she walked through the door, Angela saw a big, slovenly woman working the phones. It was a small, no-nonsense office, with no decorations. Just an open office plan, with some desks, a whiteboard, index cards, and filing cabinets. But the office was busy, with women coming and going and talking on the phone. Tia came over and introduced herself. She wasn't what Angela had expected. Based on how she sounded over the phone, Angela thought Tia had to be a peppy, cheerleader type. Instead, she looked to Angela like a city girl, rough around the edges. Tia chatted with Angela about her problems with Dallas. She seemed to really care.

Then Tia gave her an overview of the escort service, how women in the office took calls from sex buyers, then dispatched prostitutes to their location. It all seemed really professional and organized to Angela, impressive even, and Tia struck a commanding presence. Once again, Angela thought Tia had to be the owner. She seemed to know everything about the place.

Someone handed Angela an independent contractor's agreement to sign. Angela didn't really understand what she was signing, but if she had read it carefully, she would have seen that it established that the escorts weren't employees of the service; they're independent contractors who rely on the service for client referrals. The agreement essentially set up a legal business front, including an explicit statement that the company would not participate in illegal practices like the exchange of money for sex. But the document's language was completely disconnected from the reality that the escorts were engaging in prostitution, as the escorts for most legal services in Las Vegas are.

Angela spent the rest of the evening just hanging out in the office, observing. It was kind of boring and weird, but also a lot for her to process. Angela saw the setup was sort of like McDaniels's lounge at the brothel. There was space for women to relax when they came back from a client to make their drops—and they made heavy drops. Angela saw women deliver a lot of cash to the office that night. It was a powerful display. To Angela, the escort service seemed to be a well-oiled machine.

But still, something was a bit off. Sometimes the women would whisper around her and at one point Angela overheard Jen talking about her to Tia. *Is she staying at Mall's?* Jen asked. Angela didn't know who Mall was, but she knew there was more going on than she was being told.

That night, Angela slept in a guest room at the mansion. The next day, Tia picked her up for lunch. Angela was disappointed to see that she too drove a regular car. *I guess she's not the boss after all*, Angela thought.

On her second evening with the escort service, Angela was shuttled back to the office, then driven out on her first client call, for $800. The client was an easy one to exploit because he was on drugs. But Angela didn't know what she was doing—working as a Vegas escort required upselling skills she hadn't developed. So, the service quickly sent out a second woman to help Angela wring all they could from his wallet.

By this point, Angela was convinced that working for the service would be much safer than walking the track. She had someone who would drive her to her clients and a network of help just a phone call away. If she was going to be a prostitute, this seemed to be a pretty ideal situation.

Still, she felt unnerved, both by the wealth that surrounded her at the mansion and the obvious secrets being kept from her. After spending another night in the guest room, Angela told Tia the following day that she wanted to be dropped off back at J.'s.

CHAPTER 3

Trust Me

ANGELA TOLD J. EVERYTHING.[1] J. KNEW ALL ABOUT THE PROSTITUTION subculture in Las Vegas. She said the mansion and escort service probably belonged to a prominent area pimp known as Mally Mall.

For a short while, Angela worked as a renegade like J., splitting the $60 cab fare with her to The Strip and catching johns on her own, without a pimp taking her earnings. Angela got the feeling that J. was testing her to see if she'd make a good roommate. Angela figured J. thought she could help with bills. (Angela understood that J. had a lot of bills, including lots of back taxes owed to the IRS.) Then J. invited Angela to go to Los Angeles, where she and some other prostitutes were planning to lure clients to their rooms in various hotels around the metropolitan area. Angela agreed to go, but again she found herself out of her depth. The women she was with knew how to market themselves on Craigslist and what to say in online ads to attract sex buyers. But Angela was unfamiliar with the market and the other women weren't in any hurry to help her figure it out. So, while her companions caught dates and pocketed cash, Angela floundered.

One day, when the women were staying at a Howard Johnson near Los Angeles International Airport, Angela borrowed one of their laptops and logged into her Myspace page. There she saw Mally Mall had commented on one of her photos, complimenting her booty. *Can I have that?* he posted. Angela pulled up his profile. He was a large tattooed man with olive skin and a shaved head. He looked like a rapper or a crime boss.

A short while later, Mally sent her a private message saying, *We should talk* and provided a phone number. Angela called. The voice on the other end sounded like a standard white guy. He didn't try to sound Black or sexy, and he had no accent and used no slang. The fact that he didn't sound ghetto relieved Angela. Mally said he was in Japan but would be coming back to the United States shortly. He told her she didn't need to stay at the Howard Johnson; he invited her to stay at his apartment in Los Angeles until he flew in.

Angela looked at her companions. J. only seemed to want her for money. Angela knew she couldn't make it in The Game without help and none of these women seemed willing to help her. She agreed to go to Mally's apartment.

Once again, a Rolls-Royce was sent to pick her up. The driver took her north from the airport to Wilshire Boulevard, one of Los Angeles's major East-West corridors. The car deposited her in front of the Legacy, a six-story, luxury rental community just east of Westwood Village, a shopping area that borders the campus of UCLA. A doorman greeted her. He was expecting her, in fact. He gave Angela a key to Mally's apartment and directed her to the elevator. Angela rode the elevator with a sense of anticipation. She slid the key into the lock and opened the door onto a living room, where she saw a Black girl sucking a fat Black guy's dick.

The pair looked up with surprise at Angela, who quickly backed out of the room and dialed Mally. *I think I'm at the wrong place!* she said. Mally started cracking up. *That's just my roommate Tubby. He works for Interscope Records*, he said, laughing as he asked for the play-by-play. Mally instructed her to go back inside and head to his room on the right. Angela crept back in, but the living room was now empty. The condo was decorated like a modern hotel room. Not as flashy as the mansion, but still nice—nicer than anything Angela was used to. She found Mally's room and dozed on his bed while watching television. (Shawn "Tubby" Holiday today denies anything like this ever happened, saying no woman ever was given a key to the apartment and walked in on him doing anything. He did confirm that he was roommates with Mally at the Legacy in Los Angeles during this time and confirmed Angela's descriptions of the condo.)

Later, Mally arrived. The bedroom was dark when he entered, his silhouette casting a shadow against the glare of the TV. At 6'2" and more than two hundred pounds with sculpted muscles and a smooth, bald head, Mally reminded Angela of Vin Diesel. He wore a black tank top, expensive-looking jeans, and Louis Vuitton sneakers. His wrists and neck were blinged out with a watch, bracelet, and chain all laced with diamonds. Angela was used to seeing pimps rocking gold and diamond jewelry, but this was different than what she had ever seen before. The quality of Mally's diamonds looked incredibly high. His aura was all wealth and luxury, and he commanded the room like a professional athlete or a professional musician. Angela was both intimidated and impressed. She found herself pausing to study his hands, his teeth, his head, his arms, his muscles. He moved like a boss.

Mally rolled a Swisher Sweets blunt and held it out for Angela to hit. The weed was really good. He started talking to her casually, like he had known her forever. Angela could tell he had an energetic, positive personality. It was infectious. He finger-combed her hair and lifted up her chin to examine her caramel-colored features, like a talent scout. *Oh, you have nice cheek bones*, he said. *We can get good pictures.* Angela was borderline creeped out.

Mally told her that he also was in the music business, which Angela thought was cool. He said that with him guiding her he could take Angela to the top of the sex industry—he would make her a "buff bitch," a coveted prostitute in The Game. He said working for him would be classier than working for a pimp, because he wasn't Black[2]—he claims to be part Egyptian and part Brazilian. He boasted that he employed a "dream team" of lawyers who could fix any legal issue she might have. Angela confessed she had an outstanding warrant for her arrest; she was in violation of her probation in Texas. Mally didn't seem worried. He said his lawyers could handle that easily. Mally also said he'd pay to get Angela a boob job, which would help her make more money in The Game.

Angela thought Mally came off like a braggart, but still she liked his pitch. She figured once again if she was going to work in prostitution, she wanted to be safe doing it. And clearly Mally had the resources to keep her safe. She agreed to join his operation.

As the night wrapped up, Mally demanded oral sex. There was nothing seductive about his request; it was all mechanical. Angela thought that since she was at his place, she should do it, even though she wasn't attracted to him. To Angela, Mally felt more like a trick or a john than a love interest.

As Angela serviced him, he told her to sing acapella on his dick. *Sing, bitch! Sing!*

CHAPTER 4

All Day, Every Day

LIFE INSIDE MALLY'S OPERATION WAS INTENSE AND ALL ENCOMPASS-
ing.[1] Angela was expected to acclimate to the culture of his network
quickly, which caused the following days and weeks to run into each
other as she scrambled to absorb a rush of new experiences.

The scale of Mally's organization was extraordinary, the amount of
money it generated astounding. At any given time, he'd have twenty to
fifty women working for him. Most were white, reflecting a common
sensibility among American pimps that white women are the most
desirable and therefore have the greatest earning potential. (As the pimp
Tayvone Banks, a Black man, once told a YouTube channel that posted
interviews with pimps, "If she ain't white, she ain't right.")

Unlike most pimps, Mally employed two tiers of prostitutes. "Priority
Girls," of which Angela immediately became one, were at the top of the
food chain. These women were assigned the best, most lucrative clients,
and enjoyed all the perks of Mally's network—including housing and
transportation. In exchange, Priority Girls lived under Mally's thumb and
had to give him an enormous cut of their earnings, either 70 or 100 percent, depending on the deal each woman worked out with him. Angela
yo-yoed between those standard percentages, changing her agreement
with Mally from time to time. Mally's stable of prostitutes typically had
ten to twenty Priority Girls at any moment. For that tier, Mally usually
drew from women experienced in The Game, women who were used to
submitting entirely to the will of a trafficker.

But Mally was greedy, and, unlike other pimps, he didn't limit himself to only women who would totally surrender to him. He also employed a second class of prostitutes with whom he'd split their earnings, fifty–fifty. These women, who might have had experience in modeling and whom Mally treated more like business associates than his "hos," didn't get to live in Mally's properties and weren't assigned the best clients. But his escort service generated a lot of leads—more than the Priority Girls alone could handle—so he was happy to make referrals to this second tier of women, for a cut of the action of course.

The activities of Mally's operation were organized every day into three eight-hour shifts: Day Shift, Swing Shift, and Graveyard. Angela found herself working a lot of double shifts, Swing and Graveyard. Initially, new prostitutes were given a $1,000-a-day quota. But as soon as they showed an ability to earn good money, those quotas went up to $2,500 or $3,000 a day. Mally pressured his girls to have sex with as many clients as possible—as many as ten a day—which conservatively could generate for him tens of thousands of dollars in a week. Mally employed a pricing model like those used by massage parlors—that is, he sold his girls by the hour, requiring them to frequently spend long periods of time with strangers. This contrasted with the experience of street prostitutes, who often are only expected to stick around until their clients orgasmed. Some of Mally's clients were wealthy, or even household-name celebrities;[2] they purchased his girls for hours at a time. The pace was grueling, and the women's bodies suffered for it.

Mally's escort service secured clients through aggressive marketing both online and in the glossy cards handed out on the corners of Las Vegas Boulevard. The ads displayed photographs of alluring women that johns could order just by calling a phone number. But Mally evidently wasn't concerned about truth in advertising. Some of his ads featured women who were no longer working for him, which created problems for the women who currently were. Before heading out on a call, Angela would be told things like, *You're a blonde named Barbie*, which would require her to throw on a wig to conceal her jet-black hair.

Still, Angela got a lot of doors slammed in her face when clients saw she wasn't the woman they thought they were getting. When that happened, Mally's girls couldn't just leave. They were expected to stay at the hotel and bullshit the client until another, more acceptable woman could be sent over. Mally's girls were never permitted to depart from the location of a client until they were cleared by a dispatcher, no matter what was going on. It didn't matter if the women were being chased by hotel security; they could not leave until they were given the green light.

And the women certainly had no choice as to which clients they could service.

Mally loomed over everything in his network. But he wasn't involved in the day-to-day operations like other pimps. Instead, those details were handled by his three female lieutenants, who not only managed the women's schedules and looks, but who also appeared on some of the corporate records associated with Mally's escort service, which went by different names on official paperwork, including Las Vegas Concierge VS1 and International VIP. Tarnita Woodard—the woman Angela knew as Tia— worked the most with Angela. But there was also Jennifer Paone (Jen, the woman who picked up Angela on her first night at the mansion)[3] and Julie Edwards (who also went by the name Julie Blevins and apparently later Julie Wasserman).[4] Jen and Tia and other working girls in Mally's network remade Angela from a "street ho" into a high-class lady of the night. They flipped her wardrobe from the trashy Baby Phat ensemble Dallas had given her to Versace, Roberto Cavalli, and Jean Paul Gaultier dresses, designer purses, and six-inch heels. They decided her hair should be no longer than shoulder-length; so she got a bob. They also showed her the benefits of having her makeup done professionally, by a makeup artist Angela would hire every night. Soon, Angela started thinking of herself as a "super ho," who only wore things like $2,500 cashmere dresses or, when she wanted to be casual, $500 Versace t-shirts.

Mally had properties all over Vegas where he'd let his Priority Girls live. But they never seemed to stay in the same place for very long. Angela, for example, at various times lived with another girl in a luxury condo at The Meridian, just east of The Strip; in a house Mally owned on Davina Street in Henderson, a bedroom community southeast of Las Vegas; and at Soho Lofts on Las Vegas Boulevard. Angela didn't like to drive, but for the women who did, they had access to a fleet of community cars—a Jaguar, a Hummer, and a Mercedes. Women could use the vehicles whenever they wanted, but it was clear the cars weren't theirs. If a woman left Mally's network, it's not like she could take one of them with her.

At one point, Mally even purchased a space that he turned into a hair salon, called the Exclusive Beauty Lounge. Like many pimps, Mally would promise his girls, particularly his top earners, that he'd buy them businesses. Several of his girls wanted to own a salon. So, to show he followed through on his promises, Mally purchased one. But he never gave it to any of the women. He kept the business in his name and used it as a place to shoot photos of the escorts.

The culture within Mally's organization was one of work—work, work, work. The prevailing ethic was if you weren't "ho'ing" you should be getting ready to "ho." Certainly not spending time talking to friends or family. Once you got into Mally's universe, he isolated you from the outside world, particularly anyone from your past life. You were discouraged from having friends, period, not just outside of his organization, but within it as well. Whenever he was around, Angela noticed Mally would try to stir up drama amongst the women, then wade in like a hero to fix things. She caught on to the fact that his game seemed to be divide and conquer. By keeping the women at odds with each other, fighting over his affections, he could control them. But Angela didn't desire Mally like the other women, so that didn't work on her.

Mally reveled in attention; all eyes had to be on him, and he always had to be the best at everything, whether it be in the gym or in the music business, or whatever. Mally was the top dog, and everyone had to constantly feed his ego. That wasn't a problem for the women who lusted after him, the prostitutes who dreamed of being the last "ho" standing, the girl who Mally would eventually retire with, maybe marry. That dream hung out there for many of the women in his stable. But not for Angela, who saw her employment with Mally as a business arrangement and nothing more. She had no romantic yearnings for Mally, which meant she sometimes found it hard to muster the over-the-top infatuation he required from his girls. Whenever that happened, he'd get surly with her and threaten to put her on the street, which he knew from grooming her was her biggest fear. Angela, however, never knew him to be violent, just incredibly narcissistic and manipulative as hell.

Mally likened himself to a sort of hip-hop Hugh Hefner and he ran his organization with the same kind of cult of personality. In his fledgling career as a music producer, he produced a couple of songs for the hip-hop group Bone Thugs-N-Harmony,[5] but not one of their name-brand hits, like "Tha Crossroads" or "1st of tha Month." He produced, for example, an obscure track ("So Good, So Right") on their 2007 album, *Strength & Loyalty*. He played the bouncy song constantly to the secret annoyance of some of the women ("Sucka-free, we see underneath all you fake thugs / From all these wack rappers, we come back to save ya'").

As a special treat, if a woman earned particularly well one week, she was invited to hang out with Mally while he got ready for the evening or when he was recording music. Once, Angela was granted this honor; she was shocked at the size of Mally's shoe closet. Like many pimps, Mally pressured his women into getting tattoos to honor him. The practice is known as branding, and it's not unlike what farmers do with their cattle. A pimp's brand shows his ownership over a prostitute. Mally often had his girls get Egyptian-themed tattoos, each one a little different. He asked Angela to get one, but she demurred.

That was about the closest thing to affection Mally would show his "bitches"—pressuring them to get branded or letting them watch him get ready. He used his Muslim heritage as a reason to deny them Christmas or Valentine's Day gifts and as a rationale for making them work on holidays. (I don't celebrate that, is what he'd basically say.) Angela heard Mally preach a lot about the virtues of Islam, but she never saw him pray, not even once. Somewhere along the way, she learned that his real name was Jamal Rashid. Mally seemed proud of his last name; the word "rashiid" is found in the Qur'an three times, all in chapter 7, and can be translated to mean "right minded." As part of his music biz marketing, Mally sometimes billed himself as "The Egyptian God of Music."

For a while, Angela thought working for Mally made her better than other prostitutes in The Game. Once she started dressing well and raking in cash, rival pimps and prostitutes started hollering at her, trying to recruit her away from Mally's network. That made Angela feel desirable, like Mally had fulfilled his promise to take her to the top. But Mally's rivals weren't enamored with his game. They insisted Angela was being fed a lie, that despite all appearances, Mally wasn't some king pimp, dedicated to The Game's integrity.

Rival prostitutes told Angela that Mally was a snitch.

Mally's escort service, with its ads and drivers and dispatchers and protocols, shielded Angela from many of the grim realities of street life. But she still was required to develop some specific skills to navigate the unique world of Las Vegas casinos. She quickly learned the value of tipping generously—valets, security guards, whomever she needed to play nice with in order to pass through any little, restricted section of a casino to reach a client. Tipping is the universal language of Las Vegas and prostitutes will tip anyone working for a casino if they will look the other way. Angela knew a prostitute who left a tip every night for a security guard in a potted plant; that was her way of staying on his good side. In return, he might warn her where Las Vegas police were conducting undercover busts of prostitutes or let her loiter somewhere she wasn't supposed to be. Angela also learned that making friends with Black prostitutes was critical. For some reason, they always knew where Vice cops were going to be working undercover and they shared it amongst themselves in a kind of underground information network. Another trick Las Vegas prostitutes discovered was to collect key cards from every casino. Security at some resorts wouldn't let you onto the elevators unless you had a key to a room. Prostitutes figured out they could defeat this obstacle if they just flashed the right-looking key to the guards; they never checked to see if the cards were active. A sure sign of a prostitute in Las Vegas is a woman with a dozen or more key cards from different casinos in her purse.[6]

Mally never concerned himself with these mundane details. Whenever he'd interact with his "hos," he'd talk to them about empowerment, self-fulfillment, about taking concrete steps to make their biggest dreams come true. Mally was a hustler like any other pimp, but his hustle was more like that of a self-help guru or get-rich-quick schemer. He'd talk about third eyes and chakras, about Egyptian spiritual symbolism. He'd burn incense, promote positivity, and do all this other hippie shit.

His act threw Angela off initially—she'd never met a trafficker who behaved like Mally, which made him seem less threatening. But it didn't take long for her to start to see through his façade. In short order, she saw him as not only manipulative, but also insecure and phony. She found his act tiring.

The last thing a pimp wants is an independent-thinking prostitute, who gets ideas of her own and jumps ship. But whatever his obvious shortcomings, Mally was canny; he intuitively understood people and how to subtly push their buttons. He may have thought the best way to keep Angela around was to give her a long leash, allowing her to leave, then welcoming her back as if nothing had happened. In that way, he allowed Angela to indulge her stubborn, freewheeling impulses while keeping her on his hook.

In late 2006, Mally allowed Angela to leave him to work for his ex-bodyguard Ocean Fleming,[7] a Crip with a broken tooth and penchant for violence.[8] Angela had quickly grown disillusioned with Mally and his bullshit, and Fleming said he had an escort service at almost the same level as Mally's. Angela figured she'd be just as safe with Fleming as she had been with Mally—maybe even more so because he was so tough. Angela once saw him shoot at a car from the street. Another time she saw him knock a guy out with one punch. Around him she felt bulletproof, like she was in the care of an untouchable mob boss.

But Fleming didn't have an escort service—Angela was his only girl—and she soon discovered the cost of working for such a violent man. One day, he brought home a blonde woman and she openly flirted with him. That was against the rules of The Game—pimps weren't supposed to fuck women who weren't paying them. Angela confronted Fleming. *Check her, or we're gonna fight*, she said. Fleming slapped her, hard, across the face—then immediately had sex with Angela, which sort of brainwashed or desensitized her to the violence. The experience left Angela dazed.

A while later, Fleming brought in another woman, a tall, Native American who was new to prostitution. Fleming had Angela show her the ropes, but Angela found the woman irritating and lazy. Angela kept ditching her on The Strip, which led her to complain to Fleming that Angela was being a poor "wife-in-law," a term prostitutes use to describe fellow women in their stable. One night, as Angela and Fleming were going to sleep in the same bed, the Native American woman began pouting that she couldn't join them. Fleming told Angela to bring her into their bed. Angela refused. Fleming slapped her again, sending her to the floor. He took off his belt and whipped her with the metal buckle as Angela curled into a ball and begged him to stop. When he was satisfied that he had made his point, he dragged a shaking and bleeding Angela by her hair into the bathroom, where he turned cold water on in the tub and threw her in. That sent Angela running from Fleming and eventually back to Mally. Thirty days with Ocean Fleming was enough for Angela.

During this time, Angela got arrested a lot by undercover Vice cops working for the Las Vegas Metropolitan Police Department.[9] Often, the crew that arrested her was led by a lanky sergeant named Vic Vigna.[10] Vigna was an infamous figure in the prostitution subculture of Las Vegas, a notorious asshole. One time, Vigna's crew nabbed Angela, a couple of other women, and a transgender woman working as a prostitute. The transgender woman had more money—$5,000—than any of the women. Vigna told them, *You are a bunch of sorry-ass hos.* Another time, a cop felt Angela up and found weed in her bra. At that point in her life, Angela never got the impression the Las Vegas cops gave a damn about her or any of the prostitutes.

Every arrest was the same. The women would be held in a cold jail cell for a few hours at the Clark County Detention Center in downtown Las Vegas. Angela would be overdressed. Other women would be underdressed. It would inevitably devolve into what Angela thought of as a "crackhead slumber party," with women asking each other, *Who is your pimp?* Somebody would tell somebody else to shut the fuck up, and then they'd all get released near the Golden Nugget casino.

The whole process was tiresome, but scary, too. Angela always worried whenever she got arrested that someone would discover she had an outstanding warrant for ducking her PO in Texas. But Angela had several fake IDs that seemed to work well. One was for a woman named Jennifer Finnerty; that ID included information that Angela was told was stolen from a dead woman from Portland, Oregon. Another was for Angelina Delgado, with a birth date that made her two years older than she was. A third was for a Tiaday Carvalho, a name Angela couldn't even pronounce.

So, like many prostitutes in Las Vegas, Angela cycled briefly in and out of jail for months, with little disruption to her "ho'ing." But her luck ran out on May 5, 2007, the night of the super welterweight bout between Oscar De La Hoya and Floyd Mayweather Jr. Events like that are huge economic drivers for Sin City, drawing larger numbers of tourists than a regular weekend. That also makes them big nights for Las Vegas prostitutes, who can see their earnings rise at a similar rate, as well as for the Las Vegas police, who often set up special enforcement measures to deal with the extra tourists.

On that night, the police set up a DUI checkpoint to catch drunk drivers. The car Angela was riding in was stopped and everyone's ID was checked. For some reason, this time the fake she used didn't work. Her real name now known, she was identified as having a warrant out of Texas and taken into custody.

This time, Angela wouldn't be released in a few hours.

Part II

Chapter 5

Sideways

FOR A LONG WHILE AMERICAN LAW ENFORCEMENT TREATED PROSTITU-
tion as a nuisance to manage, a quality-of-life crime, like panhandling or
graffiti, rather than something serious like domestic violence or sexual
assault.[1] In most US jurisdictions, prostituting is a misdemeanor, which
makes enforcement of prostitution laws a low priority for most police
departments. The TV show *Miami Vice* may have been synonymous with
danger and glamor, but in real life Vice officers focused on prostitution
are perceived by their peers as second-class cops, policing misdemeanor
crimes in a felony world.

Of course, it didn't help that for decades most law enforcement
agencies viewed prostitutes as riffraff, the equivalent of junkies or the
homeless. Prostitutes were thought of and treated like throwaway people.
They were considered to be immoral, nasty girls who worked the streets
to the shame and embarrassment of city leaders. A Vice cop's job was to
remove the blight, nothing more.

Prostitution has been a particular problem in Las Vegas, at least since
the 1970s. Las Vegas is known as Sin City, but the entire state of Nevada
is rooted in a Wild West, anything-goes, libertarian ethic.[2] (Nevada has
few laws prohibiting people from openly carrying guns and it doesn't
require firearms to be registered. It's not unheard of in the Silver State
to see someone packing in the produce aisle at your local grocery store.)
Brothels existed in Nevada almost since it became a state[3] in 1864. They
were technically illegal, but often tolerated, until 1971,[4] when Nevada
made them legal—but ultimately only in counties with a population of

33

less than 700,000, and only if those counties elected to legalize it. That makes brothels and prostitution illegal in Las Vegas,[5] but legal nearby. Just an hour west of Las Vegas, tourists can go to the town of Pahrump in rural Nye County, Nevada, and legally purchase sex in a licensed brothel.

By the 1970s, Las Vegas was transforming into the lascivious metropolis it is today and the added proximity of legal, commercial sex just upped the ante. Out of towners unfamiliar with the nuances of Nevada law thought prostitution was legal in Las Vegas and the city's powerful casinos, not wanting to lose their customers even for an hour, had little incentive to tell them otherwise. Crowds of prostitutes soon became a common sight on Las Vegas Boulevard. Tasked with fixing the mess was the Las Vegas Metropolitan Police Department, a unique law enforcement agency that was formed by the July 1973 merger of the Las Vegas Police Department and the Clark County Sheriff's Department.[6] Metro, as it's known to locals, provides police services within the limits of the city of Las Vegas as well as the unincorporated areas of Clark County. (Other Clark County cities, like North Las Vegas and Henderson, maintain their own police forces.) Metro is a police department, but it's headed by an elected sheriff. It's one of the largest police agencies in the nation.

In the beginning, Metro approached prostitution like any other police department, like a public nuisance to be eradicated at all costs. Old-timers said officers in unmarked vans would pull up to street corners crowded with prostitutes, drag everyone inside, then drive them out to Lake Mead, thirty miles east of Las Vegas. It was a callous tactic, but effective. Back then, Metro didn't care why women ended up in prostitution or who might be controlling them behind the scenes. The department just wanted them off the streets as quickly as possible.

That slowly began to change, however, as American society in general and law enforcement in particular started understanding that prostitutes are often victims of trauma and manipulation. In 1994, Metro became one of the first police departments in the country to consider that the underage girls they encountered were not "child prostitutes" but victims of a crime. They were still arrested, but an effort was made to determine how they ended up in The Life, to refer them to social services, if available, and to identify and arrest their pimps—none of which was done for adult prostitutes. It might not seem like a big change by today's standards—and, in reality, there were significant systemic obstacles to getting the girls help. But in the 1990s, it was a radical idea, and it gradually led to more enlightened policing. By 2008, Metro and many other American law enforcement agencies had overhauled their approach to prostitutes, trying to be more respectful and compassionate in their interactions with them while still enforcing prostitution laws, recognizing all prostitutes as victims, and putting a greater focus on identifying and arresting their pimps.

At Metro, the symbol of this new approach was Vice Det. Christopher Baughman.[7] Baughman grew up in poor neighborhoods in Las Vegas.[8] The son of government employees, he attended Rancho High School in the early 1990s. At 6'1," two hundred pounds, Baughman cut an arresting figure, with white splotches of psoriasis on his dark face and neck, giving him the appearance of a burn victim.

Baughman joined Metro in 1999 and in a few years became a detective in the Gang Section. There, he distinguished himself in December 2007 when, in a matter of hours, he identified one of the main gunmen involved in a confusing, fast-moving investigation of a shooting at a school bus stop. The incident, which made national news, left six people wounded and escalated from a ninth grader bumping into one of the gunmen the day before.[9] In 2008, the head of Metro's Vice Section, Lt. Karen Hughes,[10] recruited Baughman and other experienced investigators to test for a new squad she was forming, which would become known as the Pandering Investigations Team, or PIT. This team would be responsible for conducting proactive and reactive investigations involving pimps who victimized adults. Hughes was a distinguished cop herself, known for her strong but thoughtful approach to policing. She taught criminal law at the police academy and headed Internal Affairs before taking over Vice. Hughes wanted skilled investigators for PIT and Baughman had come highly recommended. She pursued Baughman aggressively, promising him the chance to make a high-profile impact on one of the most pervasive problems in Las Vegas.

Baughman seemed to relish the attention. He readily agreed to test for Vice and finished No. 1 on the transfer list. Soon he became the public face of Vice, appearing on the news when PIT made big arrests.

In March 2009, the Vice Section received a tip. It was about a well-known pimp running prostitutes through an escort service. Baughman took the lead on the investigation, which required months of extensive front-end work, including monitoring the comings and goings at the suspect's known addresses and cataloging his assets. The target was a man named Jamal Rashid, who also went by the moniker Mally Mall.

Four months later, the police department's Tourist Safety Unit received its own tip about Mally. That tip said Mally was pandering eight to ten high-end prostitutes. The tipster also said Mally had allegedly befriended a Metro officer named Jesse. Tourist Safety was often at odds with the Vice Section over how Vice addressed prostitution-related problems along the tourist corridor. Tourist Safety was based out of the Convention Center Area Command, the police substation responsible for policing The Strip. It was a relatively new unit, having been created in the early 2000s. But to some Vice officers—who couldn't think of a crime Tourist Safety investigated that wasn't already the responsibility of another unit—its duties were redundant. Officers in Tourist Safety seemed to feel Vice was not making enough arrests of pimps and prostitutes along The Strip, and that they could do a better job themselves. Without coordinating with Vice—which, by policy, had jurisdiction over all prostitution-related matters—Tourist Safety began its own, separate investigation of Mally.

On July 14, 2009, Tourist Safety sent out a "Be on the Look Out," or BOLO, bulletin for Mally to all area commands. Listed on the bulletin was an address he frequented, his criminal history, and his photo. Tourist Safety also printed up colored flyers with Mally's picture. (BOLO information typically ends up in the hands of casino security in Las Vegas. Well-connected criminals in the area would know they are under investigation if a BOLO about them is released.)

Five days later, Roger Barrera, a cop patrolling the area, stopped a suspicious vehicle around the address listed on the bulletin, near a Motel

6 and a weekly motel. The stop, in the parking garage of the weekly, resulted in the arrest of an ex-felon for possession of a firearm and also identified a prostitute associated with Mally. (The woman appeared to have been in a fight with other prostitutes before Barrera arrived on the scene.)

Later that night, after his shift ended, Barrera went to Drai's nightclub to see some friends. (He frequented nightclubs.) Drai's was known to some as a popular hangout for pimps at Bill's Gamblin' Hall and Saloon (now known as the Cromwell). There, according to Barrera, he ran into a friend of a friend, who worked as a VIP host at some Wynn casino nightclubs. While they were sitting on an L-shaped couch and drinking, a large man walked up to Barrera's acquaintance to say hi. Barrera said he didn't know who the man was until he lifted his sunglasses. Then, suddenly, he said he recognized him as the pimp from the flyer—Mally.

After Mally walked away, a panicked Barrera confronted his acquaintance about hanging out with criminals, saying that Mally was under investigation by the police.[11] As a police officer, Barrera could get in trouble for associating with a so-called person of ill repute. The acquaintance turned around and texted Mally what he had just learned. Mally then came back to confront Barrera. He tried downplaying his criminal behavior to Barrera, saying his escort business was legitimate. The two spoke for several minutes before Mally left again.

Barrera said he immediately reported to his supervisor what happened. That got him in trouble—and it changed the case's trajectory. Because of Barrera's report, the nature of the Mally investigation shifted to include public integrity concerns, not just Vice.

In law enforcement, public integrity cases generally involve police officers or local government officials. At Metro, such cases are handled by the Criminal Intelligence Section. Intel, as the section is commonly known, is a shadowy unit within the police department that also manages some criminal informants. Virtually everything Intel did was considered confidential, even to other officers within the department.

Thus, Metro's investigation of Mally became an Intel matter. Vice, however, wasn't cut out entirely. Because he was already familiar with Mally, Baughman was kept on the case and partnered with an Intel officer who took over as the lead detective.

CHAPTER 6

From the Ground Up

VICE OPERATED OUT THE SECOND FLOOR OF AN ANONYMOUS, TWO-story building not far from the Las Vegas airport, near the south end of The Strip.[1] You wouldn't know the beige building had anything to do with Metro unless you came right up to it; only a small sign by its glass front door identified it as a Metro office. Intel as well as Metro's Gang Section and its Special Investigations Section, which dealt with issues related to businesses that require licenses (like gaming and liquor), operated out of the first floor. Vice shared the second floor with the Narcotics Section and the Technical and Surveillance Section, which conducted court-authorized wiretaps and electronic and mobile surveillance for the department. It was easy to distinguish Vice's cluster of desks and offices from the other units on the floor—Vice's furniture and equipment were all hand-me-downs from other sections, reflecting its lowly status within Metro.

Still, Sgt. Donald Hoier had found a home at Vice. A Marine Corps veteran who concealed a soft heart beneath a quiet, jaded exterior, Don joined Vice in 2001 after nine years in Patrol. Initially, he had expected to stay for only a of couple years, but he came to see the section as a place where he could make a difference and help people in need. He sympathized with the prostitutes he encountered as head of one of the Vice enforcement teams responsible for arresting them. Before it was trendy, Don tried to change the culture within Vice to make it more compassionate and respectful to prostitutes, and he had some success.

Then, in 2007, Lt. Karen Hughes took charge of the section and in her he found a kindred spirit. Hughes embraced the notion that prostitutes were victims and intuitively understood that arresting working girls over and over again would never solve the problem. Don became Hughes's right-hand man and confidant as she learned the cruel realities of The Game. Hughes came to trust and respect Don so much that in September 2009, when he was forty-two, she asked him to leave enforcement to take charge of the Pandering Investigations Team, Hughes's top priority.

PIT's biggest detective, of course, was Christopher Baughman.

One day, shortly after Don started his new job as head of PIT, he poked his head into Hughes's office to check in at the beginning of his shift. In the last couple of years Don had gradually cut his hair and trimmed his beard; before he had looked a bit like John Lennon. Now, he sported a short top with a neat beard, set off by his blue eyes. He hoped his new look would play well with his superiors. Hughes didn't have anything for Don, but as he turned to leave, she stopped him. *By the way*, she said, *Baughman is working on a special assignment with Intel.* Hughes told him that because it was an Intel case, Baughman's daily logs would be short on details whenever he was working on it. The only detail she gave him was that the case had something to do with a recent incident that had gotten an officer in trouble at the Convention Center Area Command.

That incident was common knowledge in the Vice Section; everyone knew it involved a big-time pimp. Intel, however, was another story. Don knew it was secretive. It was something like a black hole within Metro: information went in, but never came out.

Don also didn't like that Intel seemed to prioritize cultivating informants over arresting bad guys. Don knew the history of law enforcement was littered with examples of cops who had screwed up managing informants. Through his experience, Don had come to believe that while informants could provide value in some limited situations, they were generally not worth the risks and challenges associated with using them. Typically, Don found, informants were criminals looking to exchange information for leniency in their own cases. They're going to manipulate the system to benefit themselves, not help the good guys.

Don thanked Hughes for the heads up about Baughman and went about his day.

Don was the oldest of four children, born in New London, Wisconsin, the son of a stoic Air Force lieutenant colonel and a stay-at-home mother who drank too much. He was a sensitive child, easy to cry, who loved sports and the outdoors. After years of working in Vice and seeing firsthand how life experiences shaped people, Don came to view his complicated relationship with his mother as the defining dynamic of his life.

In late 1978, Don's younger brother, Chris, was diagnosed with Neuroblastoma—a rare, pediatric cancer that develops in nerve tissue. He was given three months to live. In the wake of Chris's diagnosis, Don's mom began drinking more, and became obsessed with learning how her second-born son could suffer such a fate. She read as many books as she could on the subject. In one of those books, she read that cancer cells lie dormant within everyone and that all it takes is something in the environment to activate them.

Don's mom believed that terrible something was an incident that occurred about six months before Chris was diagnosed. Don's mom had left the four children in a running car when she stopped at a friend's house. Don's sister, who was only a toddler, grabbed the shifter and threw it into drive—sending the old, red Pontiac station wagon lurching forward and into a parked car. Don, himself only eleven at the time, panicked and tried reaching over the seat to put the car back into park. He wasn't quite able to get the shifter back to park, however, and accidentally put the car into reverse. As the station wagon rolled down the driveway, Chris, then nine, tried jumping out of the car, but got caught on the door and dragged. He needed more than one hundred stitches to sew up his shoulder. Don's mom blamed Don's inattention for the accident and, in the years that immediately followed, she occasionally reminded him of that when she had been drinking.

On July 10, 1981, Chris lost his battle with cancer. Don, who was only fourteen years old, and his family were devastated. Don's mom remained convinced the trauma of Chris's shoulder injury caused him to develop cancer.

Don's mom died of cancer herself in 1994, two years after he had joined Metro. He never knew if his mother really blamed him for Chris or if it was just a by-product of her alcoholism and her own sense of guilt for the accident. (He suspected it was the latter.) But even into adulthood, Don carried the guilt of his brother's death. He spent his life trying to make up for it.

When Don graduated from high school in 1985, he enlisted in the Marine Corps because he felt he had something to prove. He loved the Marines' creed of doing more with less and embraced the physical demands of the job. His slender, six-foot frame filled out and he became a helicopter mechanic, developing an aptitude for fixing (and building) things. In 1991, as his time with the Marines was winding down, he attended a law enforcement expo in Los Angeles, where he met a recruiter for Metro. He liked the recruiter's professionalism and squared-away nature, which reminded him of the Marines. He applied to the department and was accepted. In 1992, he moved to Las Vegas.

Don initially liked working Patrol, first as an officer, then as a sergeant. Sure, there were some frustrations—like when he and some other officers working out of the airport were sued by a woman for excessive use of force in 1996 and Metro settled for $24,999 (even though he said information disclosed during depositions undercut the plaintiff's case).[2] But for the most part Don enjoyed the work and felt like he was making a difference. But slowly, over the years, he grew tired of the public's scorn of people in uniform. One Christmas morning, he responded to an incident involving a gun. A woman at the scene was uncooperative. When he told her to listen so nobody would get shot, she responded, *Isn't it your job to get shot?*

Around the same time, Don's marriage of eight years fell apart. As he headed to divorce, he cast about for something to revitalize his life. Don had several friends who worked in the Vice Section. Whenever he'd bump into them, they'd suggested he should test for the unit. Don had always enjoyed their "war stories." The job sounded fun—something he wasn't having with his current assignment. You got to work undercover (so there was no cumbersome uniform to wear or strict grooming standards to follow). You were assigned a take-home vehicle to drive. You were fairly insulated from department politics. And you got to talk to girls about sex. Don was keen to learn how to work undercover.

After he was accepted to the section, he shadowed Vic Vigna, an experienced Vice sergeant, to learn the ropes. Vice was a different animal from Patrol. When Don started with Vice, all it mostly did was target prostitutes, which meant posing undercover as a sex buyer, either in a casino or on the street, and arresting working girls who took the bait. Vigna was considered something of a prostitution expert in the department at the time, so Don was eager to learn from him. But Don was uncomfortable with how he treated people, particularly prostitutes after they were arrested. That didn't seem right to Don.

Don didn't know a damn thing about prostitution when he entered Vice, other than what he saw in movies. Like some people, he thought prostitutes were just horny women who wanted to make easy money. But his eyes were opened quickly. Just a few days into his new job, Don participated in an undercover operation at the Motel 6 on Dean Martin Drive, just west of The Strip. Vice called the numbers in some online ads for prostitutes. Three Black women came to the hotel, each with a tattoo of a heart encircling the name Andre on their chest. That was Don's first exposure to branding. That same night, Vice also arrested a white woman who later agreed to plead guilty to prostitution—and requested that she serve jail time instead of paying a fine. Don understood she wanted to go to jail to get away from her pimp.

Over time, Don saw that Vice arrested the same women over and over and over again. He'd observe how their weight would change from one arrest to the next, along with the pattern of bruises on their bodies. It didn't take a rocket scientist to see that these women were dealing with some serious trauma behind the scenes and the source of that trauma was most likely a pimp.

It became clear to Don early on that Vice couldn't arrest its way out of this problem—the number of prostitutes in Las Vegas was just too overwhelming and their recidivism rate was astronomical. But Don did come to believe that arrests, if handled properly, could be beneficial.

Every arrest was an opportunity to make a connection, to build trust. Don made a habit of trying to strike up a conversation with every prostitute he arrested, asking her about how she fell into The Life. Too often, the women would tell him they were first "turned out" as children. Don saw that over a series of arrests, he could build a rapport with some prostitutes. Once trust was established, he discovered sometimes prostitutes would be willing to turn in their pimps or at least accept help to get out of prostitution.

Don expected the officers that worked for his team to treat every woman they arrested with respect. He didn't want them to compromise officer safety or let the women run over them; if given the chance, some of them would claw your face off. But he insisted that every prostitute who ended up in their custody be treated with dignity.

Don also realized that arrests and jail time served another critical purpose: they separated a prostitute from her pimp. Don read widely of books written by pimps and watched pimp documentaries (including the films *American Pimp* and *Pimps Up, Ho's Down* and the book *The Pimp Game: Instructional Guide* by Mickey Royal). He learned how they manipulated women by preying on their vulnerabilities and past traumas. A simple antidote to this brainwashing, Don discovered, was space. The longer a prostitute had a chance to be away from her pimp, the longer she didn't have him in her ear filling her head up with lies, the better chance she had to get some perspective and see that she was being played. Time away sometimes, but not always, broke the invisible chains that pimps had on their victims.

But in the early days, when Vice would arrest prostitutes, they'd be processed through the Clark County Detention Center in just a matter of hours. Then they'd be right back on the street again working for their pimps, this time with even more pressure to earn because now they had a fine to pay off, too. Don thought these "walkthroughs" were ridiculous. They didn't give prostitutes any meaningful time away from their traffickers. He began advocating within the section for policy changes.

But reform was slow. The first lieutenant Don worked for in Vice was an old-timer, just running out the clock until his retirement. His nickname was the Groundhog because he metaphorically stayed below ground most of the time, only peeking his head out occasionally to see what was going on. He had no interest in making waves in the department. (Other officers had dubbed the lieutenant the Groundhog before Don arrived in Vice. Don never thought the nickname was fair.) He let Don run his enforcement team however he wanted, but he was unwilling to engage in the battles that would be required to make widespread changes within the section, or to obtain additional resources. All he cared about was the number of prostitutes arrested. He believed large arrest numbers showed the section was working hard to address Las Vegas's prostitution problem.

Don's next lieutenant was more amenable to his ideas. Don got him to adjust Vice's schedule so the enforcement teams would work later at night when prostitution-related activity was at its peak. Many of the older Vice officers resented Don for suggesting this change; after years of serving on the force, they had no interest in working the Graveyard Shift. But Don knew if Vice worked later, the section would be more effective at addressing the issues prostitution was causing on The Strip. It would also provide the opportunity to encounter more victims and build a rapport with them.

Don also encouraged the new lieutenant to secure more resources to investigate cases involving juvenile sex trafficking victims and other Vice-related matters beyond enforcement. But that lieutenant only oversaw Vice for a year. When word came down that the section was getting yet another new boss, Don held his breath. Would it be someone who would take the issue seriously and fight for resources? Or would it be another Groundhog? Don was relieved when he learned the new lieutenant would be Karen Hughes. He had worked with her briefly in Patrol. She was smart, innovative, respected by Metro's brass, and had the cojones to stand up for what was right. She was the leader Don thought the section needed. He knew change was coming. But because Hughes had no experience in Vice, he'd have to help educate her on the subculture.

Early on in Hughes's tenure as the leader of Vice, she gave Don a wad of "imprest money," which his enforcement officers used to buy prostitutes drinks like any other john.

You guys are going to go out and party tonight? she asked.

That's not what we do here, Don replied. *We're not out here partying. When you have time, I'd like to explain to you what we do, because it's not what you think.*

That seemed to catch her attention.

Soon, Don had Hughes's ear and together they began remaking the Vice Section to be more compassionate and responsive to sex trafficking victims—including instilling a mindset throughout the unit that these girls and women, despite whatever appearances or attitudes they may have, are indeed victims. Don was pleased to see his new boss was open to his ideas. (It was under her that the jail walkthroughs ended.) But it went both ways. After she tried out two other sergeants on the Pandering Investigations Team, she approached Don about taking it over. Don resisted, feeling loyalty to the troops on his enforcement team. But Hughes could be persuasive. She got what she wanted.

About the only thing Hughes couldn't get Don to do was become more visible in the news media, talking about the plight of sex trafficking victims and what the section was doing to help them. Although Don had done his share of that, he was content to let Baughman stand in front of the cameras.

For months, Don heard nothing about Baughman's work with Intel. The only evidence he had that Baughman was doing something with the mysterious section came whenever Baughman would let him know that he was headed down to the first floor to meet with his Intel partner, Det. Warren Gray.[3] Then, in April 2010, Baughman submitted to Don an affidavit for the simultaneous searches of seven properties tied to Mally.

This was the first time Don had ever seen or heard of Jamal Rashid or Mally Mall. The affidavits laid out a criminal case against him for pandering. It was entirely circumstantial, based on Mally's connections to known prostitutes and his over-the-top lifestyle with no obvious source of income other than his escort service. Escort services are known fronts for prostitution in Las Vegas.[4]

Metro didn't have any victims ready to testify against Mally. But through hours of mind-numbing surveillance and a review of property and financial records, Baughman and Gray had found that Mally owned several expensive luxury cars and properties all across Las Vegas, including at a high rise called Turnberry Place east of The Strip.[5]

They also documented known prostitutes making cash drops to Mally's offices. To Don, the affidavits pointed to only one logical conclusion, that Mally was one of Las Vegas's biggest pimps. When he finished reading the affidavit, he thought, *Man, this is a really good case.*

CHAPTER 7

Bring the Noise

ON THE MORNING OF APRIL 28, 2010, AT LEAST SEVENTY METRO OFFI-cers coordinated seven simultaneous raids on properties tied to Mally.[1] Because Don's officer had written up the affidavit, he had to help plan it, even though the case was still technically Intel's. For the two weeks prior to the raid, Don spent almost all of his time rearranging officer schedules and enlisting cops from Narcotics, Patrol, and other sections to help in the raid. Even Animal Control had to be involved, because of the exotic animals Mally kept at his mansion. Don and Hughes and Baughman and Gray had to hold multiple briefings in the days leading up to the raid because there was no way they could get everyone who was going to be involved in the same room at the same time. It was a massive, complex undertaking with a lot of moving parts.

Mally had been under surveillance, so Metro believed he was going to show up at Turnberry Place after the raid was launched that morning. Baughman, Gray, and other Intel officers led the search at Turnberry; Don and Hughes headed up the operation at the mansion. Don and other officers blocked off the street while SWAT rolled up in an armored vehicle. *Occupants of 4311 East Oquendo Road,*[2] *this is the Las Vegas Metropolitan Police Department!* a SWAT officer announced over a loudspeaker. *We have a search warrant for your premises! Please come out with your hands up!* SWAT always gave occupants a long time to exit, so there was a lot of standing around. While they were waiting, neighbors started coming out of their houses to see what was going on. An old woman approached Don. *What's happening?* she asked. Don explained that they were executing a search warrant on the large mansion in the neighborhood. *Get that sand nigger out of here*, she said.

Several people were cleared from the property, including maids and landscapers and an Asian prostitute Don had previously helped get away from another pimp. Also taken into custody was a bodyguard, armed with a handgun. But that was just the beginning of the waiting. Next, SWAT had to clear the mansion—all 8,358 square feet of it—as well as the surrounding property to make sure no one was hiding in wait for the cops before the search could begin. Don knew when he was planning the operation that this would take a long time, and it did.

When SWAT finally gave the all-clear, Don and the others entered the mansion to find it in a state of chaos. The wolves behind the garage were barking like mad. The crystal-clear water of the aquarium became cloudy after SWAT cut the power. A technician would have to be called or else Metro would have a bunch of dead sea animals on its hands. (That's the last thing they needed.) Don saw a small monkey in a diaper, screaming in terror in what looked like a bird cage. Don felt sorry for the poor thing.

During the pre-raid briefings, they had stressed to everyone to keep an eye open for the exotic cat that was allowed to prowl the mansion. But once they got inside, the big cat was nowhere to be found.

Don and Hughes did a walkthrough of the mansion, which included four bedrooms and five bathrooms, and a game room with a pool table and arcade machines. They divvied up the rooms amongst the available officers, assigning Vice cops to the places where they expected the juiciest evidence to be found. Don and Hughes oversaw the operation, offering support and guidance where they could. Frequently, they called Baughman and Gray at Turnberry to ask if they wanted something seized for evidence.

The search was long and tedious given the size of the place. But a lot was found. In Mally's bedroom—where stripper poles adorned a stage at the foot of the bed—brown, bulletproof shutters covered the windows. Several guns were discovered, including a MAK-90, a 7.62-caliber, semi-automatic rifle, and lots of jewelry and pills.[3] Among Mally's personal things[4] they found an American Express "Black Card" and bottles of Valtrex, a prescription medication to treat genital herpes as well as shingles and cold sores.

The whole mansion gave off creepy vibes to Don. The house was filled with paintings of naked Black women and what he would later remember as "weird pimp shit," like porn DVDs and flamboyant decorations. At one point, when he was lost in thought, Don glanced up in the game room and suddenly saw the big cat standing on the edge of the pool table, looking at him. *Ah!* He shouted in surprise. *There it is!* He and some other officers chased it down a hallway and locked it in a room.

Around mid-afternoon, Baughman and Gray came to the mansion to see how the search was going. Don and Hughes gave them a tour of the property, showing them the evidence they had collected and asking what else they wanted seized.

We got good stuff, Don observed. *This is going to make a good case.*

Well, uh, actually, Baughman replied hesitantly, *we're not going to arrest him.*

Don felt his jaw drop. He looked at Hughes and saw her face twist in horror.

Intel thinks he'd be more valuable as a criminal informant, Baughman said.

Don could feel his temperature rising. Why had they gone through all of this if they were just going to make Mally a CI? No one had even suggested that that was a possibility. Don thought they had a strong case against Mally, especially after the search. And now they were just going to let him walk? Don wondered if this had been Intel's plan all along, that Vice was just being used as a pawn in someone's stupid game.

Did I hear that correctly? Don asked Hughes the moment Baughman and Gray walked away. *They're not going to arrest this asshole now?*

Yeah, Hughes replied, shaking her head, *I'm going to find out what's going on.* She walked over by herself and called Lt. David Logue,[5] the head of Intel, on her cell phone. Don watched as Hughes paced back and forth, gesturing animatedly. She was clearly angry.

When she hung up, Hughes told Don that Intel thought Mally would be more useful as an informant because of Las Vegas's exploding nightclub scene and the probability that more cops were involved in criminal activity within it. Logue wanted to see if Mally could help the department identify dirty cops. Hughes didn't like it, but she had no authority to overrule it. Despite Don planning the raids, it had been an Intel operation from the start, not Vice's. It was Logue's call to make. There was nothing Hughes could do.

What was the fucking point of that? Don wondered.

Part III

CHAPTER 8

Poppin' Bottles

PIMPING AND PROSTITUTION HAVE DEEP ROOTS IN POVERTY.[1] IN MEDI-
eval England, poor young women looking for jobs as servants were
duped into prostitution by "bawds," a word loosely equivalent to today's
pimps.[2] The actual word "pimp" first appeared in the English language
a short while later, around 1600. According to the lexicographer Jesse
Sheidlower, it was defined as "a person who arranges opportunities for
sexual intercourse with a prostitute."[3] In more recent times, poor Jewish
girls and women from Asia and North Africa became prostitutes in Israel
around the time of the Six-Day War in 1967.[4]

So, it's no surprise that when poor American women struggled to
earn equal wages during the 1800s, pimping and prostitution exploded
into what one study called "a gigantic social institution."[5] In a 1910 essay
on the topic, political activist and writer Emma Goldman portrayed
sexual exploitation as afflicting "not merely white women, but yellow and
black women as well." Fears that white women were being duped into
"white slavery" led reformers to push prostitution underground around
World War I.[6] With some exceptions, the pimp-prostitution subculture
largely remained on the margins of society until the second half of the
twentieth century, when a particular image of The Life advanced by the
writer Iceberg Slim and blaxploitation films began to capture the public's
imagination.

Born Robert Lee Maupin in Chicago in 1918, Slim worked as a
pimp from age eighteen to forty-two, then became a writer—one of the
bestselling African-American writers of all time. His memoir, *Pimp: The*

Story of My Life, portrayed pimps as anti-establishment heroes dripping with panache and style. Slim's books, including his novels like *Trick Baby: The Biography of a Con Man* and *Mama Black Widow*, were sold by the millions at urban newsstands, records stores, and head shops.

Today, Slim's writings are regarded by some as foundational to contemporary hip-hop culture[7] and they heavily influenced the blaxploitation era of cinema, when the release of films targeted to Black audiences— some made by independent Black filmmakers—surged. Among the most popular of these films was 1973's *The Mack*, starring Max Julien as John "Goldie" Mickens, a hustler fresh out of the joint who remakes himself into a powerful Oakland pimp. With its flamboyant coats, tricked-out rides, and memorable lines ("I'd have to lose all the brain cells in my head before I forget something as fine as you"), *The Mack* became a cultural touchstone in the world of hip-hop music, the art form that was born in the year of its release.[8]

With many name-brand hip-hop stars now in their 50s, it's easy to forget that the genre began as a youth movement. While many artists like to project a hardened, world-weary image, in truth a lot of hip-hop stars started out as little more than kids, many drawing on movies for their raps. As result, with some exceptions, hip-hop songs frequently depict pimps as glamorous characters like Goldie, canny and stylish, loaded with money, charisma, and girls. More often than not, pimping in hip hop is more of a metaphor for being cool or a super lover than it is for being a literal slave master. As LL Cool J once joked when listening to JAY-Z's smash hit "Big Pimpin" ("We doin' big pimpin,' we spendin' cheese"), "JAY-Z sounds like he is doing more tricking than pimping."[9]

Hip-hop's enormous popularity has just made the trappings of the pimp-prostitute subculture even more commonplace in American society. Rappers like Snoop Dogg[10] and Ice-T,[11] who embody the pimp persona on stage, have become not only bona fide Hollywood stars, but also pitchmen for breakfast cereal and beer. Pimping became so mainstream that when MTV premiered a new reality show in 2004 about customizing cars, hardly anyone blinked when it was called *Pimp My Ride*. Ditto a couple of years later, when "It's Hard Out Here for a Pimp" from the film *Hustle & Flow* won the Academy Award for Best Original Song in 2006.

But while many if not most hip-hop records soft-peddle pimping as living large or charming the ladies, as in Ludacris's "Pimpin' All Over the World," ("The women and the caviar / You know who we are / Cause we're pimpin' all over the world"), some rappers are brutally honest about The Game's realities. In the 2003 song "P.I.M.P.," 50 Cent describes recruiting a prostitute from a strip club ("Now, Shorty, she in the club, she dancin' for dollars"), then turning her out on the streets to search for johns:

> I ain't that nigga tryna holler to holla 'cause I want some head
> I'm that nigga tryna holler 'cause I want some bread
> I could care less how she perform when she in the bed
> Bitch, hit that track, catch a date, and come and pay the kid.

Still, the line between fantasy and reality is often blurry. In 2006, around the time she connected with Mally, Angela ran into the UGK rapper Pimp C at the Mondrian hotel in West Hollywood.[12] Pimp C approached her in the lobby, but Angela didn't want anything to do with him. *Bitch, I ain't a pimp*, he told her, then realized why she was trying to duck him, as recounted in Julia Beverly's 2015 book *Sweet Jones: Pimp C's Trill Life Story*. *I pimp the rap game*, he said, laughing. *I pimp the music*. From those humble beginnings, the pair struck up an unlikely, but genuine friendship, frequently speaking on the phone. Angela even appeared in the UGK music video for the song "The Game Belongs to Me" just a few months before she was arrested on the night of the De La Hoya-Mayweather fight. Pimp C, whose real name was Chad Butler, thoroughly embraced the pimp persona, wearing a mink coat in the hot Miami sun while shooting the music video for "Big Pimpin'." But until the day he died in December 2007 of an accidental drug overdose, Pimp C tried talking Angela out of prostitution. As Beverly writes in *Sweet Jones*, in which Angela is identified by the alias Jada, "The irony, of course, was that while Chad's alter ego was publicly a vocal proponent of 'the game,' [sic] he privately warned a woman he cared about of its dangers."[13]

Jamal Fayeq Rashid's infatuation with hip hop began in Northern California where he was born in July 1975.[14] As a young man, he was a follower of the Bay Area record producers Ant Banks and Rick Rock, who produced for a litany of big-name rappers, including Too Short, E-40, Snoop Dogg, Tupac, JAY-Z, Busta Rhymes, Mase, and Will Smith. He also claims to have been tight with the legendary Bay Area rapper Mac Dre, who was murdered in 2004, although stories about their friendship (or lack thereof) vary. Mally, however, says it was Mac Dre who originally dubbed him Mally Mall, presumably as a play off his real name, Jamal. "The name was given to me by Mac Dre," Mally told the online magazine *HipHopDX* in 2016.[15] "When we grew up, he was about seven or eight years older. It was Mac Dre, Mac Mall, we had E-40. As we know, the 'Macs' were popping. Remember Mac Mall, Mac Dre, Mac This, Mac That. I was mad because I wanted to be Mac Mall. But he was talented. I wasn't rapping back then. I was just producing and playing around. To make a long story short, now I'm glad I'm Mally Mall because the Macs are kind of dead—either literally dead or just burnt out. Nobody's tryna be a 'Mac' no more."

Mally grew up in a large white house on North West Lane, just outside the city limits of Lodi, California, an agricultural community north of Stockton, the largest metropolitan area in that part of the Central Valley. His mother abandoned him when he was six months old, which left him bitter, according to someone who knew him well.[16] His father, Fayeq Rashid, was a strict disciplinarian. Fayeq owned a local importing business called Rashid Imports. He left the parenting primarily to Mally's grandma, the only motherly figure in his life. Mally moved out when he was still a teenager.

As a young adult, Mally lived with a girlfriend in a home in Woodbridge, a small town just north of Lodi. Before he was old enough to buy alcohol, Mally started having encounters with law enforcement. On May 26, 1996, at the age of twenty, Mally was arrested on suspicion of statutory rape, although nothing came of that. Four months later, after he turned twenty-one, he was interviewed by the California State Fire Marshal's Office as part of an investigation into an arson at a car stereo installer in Lodi, where he worked, although he doesn't appear to have been arrested.[17] (Rumor has it Mally first met Mac Dre when he installed a stereo in the rapper's Lincoln Navigator sometime in the 1990s. But Mally says he met Dre when he was 14.)[18]

In late 1996, the Narcotics Unit of the Lodi Police Department received a tip from a citizen who said Mally was selling cloned phones.[19] Cloned phones use the stolen serial and identification numbers of legitimate cellular phones to make and receive free phone calls; the call charges are surreptitiously passed along to the legitimate users. The tipster, who said he obtained a cloned phone from Mally, told police that at one time Mally had about thirty phones for sale.

Searching California Department of Motor Vehicle records, Lodi police discovered that Mally once owned a 1985 BMW 325 with the vanity license plate "JAMALLS," but transferred ownership of the vehicle, plates and all, to his live-in girlfriend, a Latina a year younger than him. Police suspected the transfer was intended to conceal Mally's ownership of the car. Subsequent DMV searches found that Mally's girlfriend also owned a 1988 Cadillac, a 1992 Ford Explorer, and a 1995 Ford Mustang, all registered to the Woodbridge home. According to police, Mally's only legitimate sources of income at the time were working part-time for his father at flea markets and at the car stereo installer, FGA Trading.

Lodi police worked with a criminal informant who knew Mally by the alias "Jimmy." The informant provided detectives with a Motorola phone he said he obtained from Mally. Upon inspection, the phone was found to have an internal electronic serial number belonging to a GE model, making it a bona fide cloned phone. The informant also told detectives Mally was selling methamphetamine.

Lodi police directed the informant to contact Mally, asking to purchase two cloned phones and some meth. On June 4, 1997, Mally agreed to meet at the informant's residence. At 9:45 p.m. that night, Lodi police watching Mally's Woodbridge home saw him get into the 1988 Cadillac and drive to the informant's residence, where he was detained. Detectives found three ounces of meth on him, police reported. Police then searched Mally's home; a gym bag containing about twenty cloned phones was found in the Ford Explorer. In an interview, Mally's girlfriend told police that he had been cloning phones for about a year, and that he would bring home as many as fifty cell phones each week. A search the next day of safety deposit boxes Mally and his girlfriend had at a local Wells Fargo found $25,000 cash; an assortment of jewelry, including a woman's Rolex watch; and three floppy disks that included instructions on how to clone Motorola flip phones.

Detectives later spoke with one of Mally's partners in an alleged regional phone-cloning ring. According to police, the man said he met Mally in the summer of 1996, when he was getting a stereo system installed. He said Mally offered to clone his phone. The man declined but began working with Mally to sell cloned phones. The man told detectives that Mally modified phones in his bedroom in Woodbridge by using a "black box" electronic device, which allowed him to program the phones' internal, electronic serial numbers. The man also said that Mally had paid $6,000 for an Electronic Serial Number reader, which they used to intercept cellular phone data while sitting in Mally's Cadillac near Arden Fair mall in Sacramento. The man claimed that between September 1996 and May 1997 Mally had more than six hundred cloned phones.

Mally faced state prison, something he wanted to avoid. So, he cut a deal[20] to become a criminal informant himself. On March 23, 1998, Mally was sentenced to five years' probation,[21] then began feeding information to Lodi Det. Dale Eubanks, his handler. "He liked playing secret agent," Eubanks remembers. "It became kind of thrilling to him, that was my impression." Mally was chatty with the detective, calling late at night with tips and describing to the cop his dreams of owning a Las Vegas nightclub. Mally snitched on one of his partners in the cloned phone ring, Eubanks said, then started telling Eubanks about methamphetamine operations in New Jersey and Texas. His information was good, and increasingly fell outside of the police department's jurisdiction. By the time Mally told Eubanks that women connected to the Palestine Liberation Organization were leaving the San Francisco airport with hundreds of thousands of dollars strapped to their bodies—a claim Eubanks says was accurate—the detective passed him off to the FBI to see if the feds wanted to use him as an informant as well. Eubanks never found out what they did with him.

Despite his new associates in law enforcement, however, Mally apparently remained involved in the drug trade. He was busted with the ingredients to make PCP on May 5, 1999, convicted of another felony, and given a suspended sentence with more probation. But a few years later, in October 2003, Mally got that charge reduced to a misdemeanor.[22] By then, he had been arrested three more times in Las Vegas, on charges or suspicion of domestic violence, for failing to register as an ex-felon, and on suspicion of being an ex-felon in possession of a firearm as well as possession of a controlled substance and marijuana. The cases in all three arrests were dropped.

Also, while he was still on probation for the cloned-phone case, a woman filed a restraining order against Mally, alleging that he had subjected her to verbal, mental, and emotional abuse. In the October 6, 1999, filing,[23] the eighteen-year-old woman wrote that she had moved to Sacramento to get away from Mally, but he had followed her and her roommate to figure out where they lived. "He has to know where I am at at [sic] all time or he goes crazy," she said in the filing. One day, the woman wrote, Mally waited outside their apartment, but fled after she called the police and an officer arrived on the scene. Then, when she and her roommate tried to leave, Mally followed them to a party. "(H)e ran up to the car and punched the car window, yelling at me to get out of the car and go w/ him," the woman wrote. "I said no because he was acting crazy." An officer of the San Joaquin County Superior Court issued a temporary restraining order against Mally until the matter could be heard on October 26, 1999. But no one showed up to court that day and the case was dropped.

Mally moved to Las Vegas in 2001[24] apparently as word spread of his snitching in northern California and he started fearing for his safety. A year later, a random conversation with a local business owner inspired him to enter the escort business. The businessman, who owned a strip mall near the Sapphire strip club, told Mally he had three escort services operating out of his building. Owning an escort service struck a chord with Mally and he dived headfirst into the new venture. A woman he was dating at the time provided most of the seed capital to purchase office space, phone lines, and advertising, and Mally supplied the labor.

Every night, he'd prowl Las Vegas, handing out business cards advertising his new service to club owners and limo drivers, promising them a 20 to 30 percent kickback if they'd refer clients to him. Mally loved to schmooze, and he charmed legions of people—mainly taxicab and limo drivers—to spread the word about his service, dubbed VIP. Mally also was aggressive in recruiting women to sign on with the service, boldly approaching pretty women wherever and whenever he encountered them. Some of these women were smitten with Mally and a few asked him to pocket all of their earnings if, in exchange, he'd take care of them.[25] Once Mally heard that, he began aggressively asking women, *Do you want to be on our team?*

So began Mally's network of Priority Girls. Every woman who agreed to give Mally all of their earnings was set up with a place to live—initially in the same house with him and his girlfriend—and guaranteed the best clients. Those who didn't got the leftovers.

Based largely on Mally's charm and numerous connections across the city, the service started generating surprisingly high income for a new venture. But the business took a quantum leap when Mally discovered the power of online advertising almost a year after its founding. Until then, Mally had depended mainly on referrals from drivers and advertising in the Yellow Pages. But he was always searching for other forums to promote the service. That's how he stumbled onto Eros, the online escort directory. Mally bought some advertisements on the site, just to give it a try, and immediately saw business explode. Mally quickly became one of Eros's biggest advertisers and even lured a couple of employees away from the website to come work for him.

After only a year in business, Mally's VIP escort service had become the hottest in town, employing nearly three dozen of the "prettiest" escorts in Sin City, according to someone familiar with the operation. By then, a handful of the women gave him everything they made from selling sex—there was no pretense that anyone working for the service was just accompanying men to parties or special events or whatever. Presumably, Mally knew he had found a golden goose, and he was aggressive in expanding his operations. By August 2005, Mally's sex trafficking empire had grown so profitable he owned two 2000 Jaguars, a 2001 Mercedes-Benz, a 2002 Ferrari, a 2003 Land Rover, a 2004 Lincoln, a 2004 Dodge pickup, a 2004 Rolls-Royce, and a 2005 Bentley. In September 2005, he purchased the mansion for $2.6 million.

That's when Mally's real break into hip hop began.

With money earned by his "hos," Mally transformed the mansion into a party pad that would attract big musicians. In addition to the game room and theater, he outfitted the home with a recording studio, which at the time was hard to find in Las Vegas. Back then, about the only other place rappers could record in Sin City was at a studio at the Palms.

Mally also collaborated with Jason "Poo Bear" Boyd,[26] the R&B songwriter and record producer behind such hits as 112's "Dance with Me" and "Peaches and Cream" and Usher's "Caught Up." Poo Bear had a first-rate reputation in the music business; because of his resume and hits, young rappers wanted to work with him. Poo Bear eventually came to Las Vegas to work with Mally.

Mally carefully cultivated his image, surrounding himself with exotic animals and worrying over every aspect of his appearance. Almost exclusively, he wore designer clothes, with their logos easily visible, and gravitated to anything flashy—cars with exotic leather seats, diamond jewelry, anything to garner attention, which he loved. (Photographs of Mally online often show him in shades and hoodies, tank tops, or other shirts that show off intricate, colorful tattoos on his arms and neck.)

Mally made connections in the music business through his relationship with Shawn "Tubby" Holiday, the Interscope executive Angela says she saw getting a blowjob in the living room of the Los Angeles condo. Holiday was a rising star in hip-hop, having started out as a member of Bad Boy Records' famed street team,[27] which used guerrilla marketing tactics in urban areas to promote records and artists. His success in the business landed him an A&R gig at Interscope, which was associated with major hip hop artists like Dr. Dre, Eminem, and 50 Cent. (A&R stands for "artists and repertoire." A&R divisions are responsible for finding record labels new talent.) Today, Tubby admits he helped make introductions for Mally early in his music career. (He says the introductions were not part of any quid pro quo agreement; he says he paid for rent at the apartment as Mally's roommate.)

In this way, Mally began to establish himself as a music producer, although he didn't possess any great musical ability like Poo Bear. Instead, his greatest contribution was bringing people together, putting rappers and producers and songwriters all in the same room, sometimes by paying them to be there. Mally seemed to take great pride in calling himself a music producer, but to at least some it was a front,[28] much like his use of Bay Area slang (i.e. "Yadadamean," "hyphy," "hella," "beezy"). Mally was from the Central Valley, not the Bay, and to some he was a fake, not a genuine producer.

Over time, Mally's calculated efforts yielded results. In 2006, he landed a producing credit on the rap group Bone Thugs-N-Harmony's sixth studio album, *Thug Stories*, for the song "Do It Again." The following year, he picked up another Bone Thugs producing credit for "So Good, So Right," on the album *Strength & Loyalty*. By the 2000s, Bone Thugs' popularity had dropped from its high in the mid-90s when it released "1st of tha Month" and "Tha Crossroads." But these were Mally's first credits with a major, nationally known act. At the mansion and in his cars, he played "So Good, So Right," incessantly, so much so his escorts would practically roll their eyes.

Then Aubrey Graham came to Las Vegas for his twenty-fifth birthday.[29]

It was October 2011 and Graham, better known as the rapper Drake, was putting the finishing touches[30] on his second studio album, *Take Care*. Just two years earlier, Drake, a mixed race, Canadian, Jewish, former teen actor, had released a breakthrough mixtape—*So Far Gone*—which showcased his distinct style of mixing rap with singing. His debut album, *Thank Me Later*, came out a year later with Lil Wayne's Young Money Entertainment, and was both a commercial[31] and critical hit,[32] establishing Drake as the next big star in hip hop. Now Drake seemed determined to prove his bona fides and was working on an ambitious sophomore album that incorporated slow tempos and synth tracks. By October, the songs on *Take Care* were finished, but Drake didn't want to stop recording.[33]

One day, he called the Toronto producer T-Minus and asked him for a simple, up-tempo beat that would hit in the club.[34] T-Minus jumped on his computer and in about thirty minutes worked up a simple pattern of distorted 808 bass, claps, and snare. He sent the file to Drake, who was about to go to Las Vegas to celebrate his birthday.[35] In Vegas, Drake hooked up with a local musician named DJ Franzen,[36] who was also friends with Mally. Needing to record a hook for Rick Ross, Drake headed to Mally's home studio, where the rapper cued up the new T-Minus beat, as Franny later recounted in a 2018 interview with *DJBooth*.[37]

Whoa? What the fu—? Franny asked when he heard the beat's stark, dramatic opening, dum, dum, dum, dum-dum-dum. *What is this, bro?*

You like it? Drake asked excitedly.

This is like some Bay Area shit, bro, replied Franny, who is from the Bay. *You got to use that right now.*

On the first take, Drake spit a rollicking verse, shouting out his party mates, friends, Mac Dre, and the album's label (Young Money Cash Money Billionaires or YMCMB):[38]

Rest in peace, Mac Dre, I'ma do it for the Bay
Okay, getting paid, we'll holler whenever that stop
My team good, we don't really need a mascot
Tell Tune, "Light one, pass it like a relay"
YMCMB, you niggas more YMCA
Me, Franny, and Mally Mall at the crib-o
Shout goes out to Niko, J and Chubbs, shouts to Gibbo.

Drake also recorded a catchy chorus about living life to the fullest, dropping a line that would soon popularize a catchphrase: "You only live once, that's the motto, nigga, YOLO." Drake circulated the track to Lil Wayne, who recorded his own verse for the song, which was titled "The Motto." A few days later, on October 31, 2011, it premiered on the Los Angeles hip-hop station Power 106;[39] Drake released it on his OVO (October's Very Own) blog a day later.[40] "The Motto" became a smash hit, selling over 3 million copies[41] and peaking atop both Billboard's Hot R&B/Hip-Hop Songs[42] and Hot Rap Songs charts[43] and ranking 20 on the Billboard Hot 100 Songs year-end chart (for 2012).[44] "The

Motto" joined a growing roster of mainstream Drake hits that included "Best I Ever Had" and "Forever" (the latter also featuring Kanye West, Lil Wayne, and Eminem). Officially a digital iTunes Store bonus track for *Take Care*, "The Motto" was nominated for Best Rap Song at the 2013 Grammy Awards.[45]

For Mally, the high-profile mention gave his music career a major jolt. "As soon as Drake gave us a shout out," Mally said years later, "it's like almost people want to do anything to relate to Drake. So, like, you work with Mally Mall? Drake work with him. So I work with Mally Mall, too. The phone started ringing, the studio started getting booked."[46] For example, the pop star Justin Bieber called, asking if he could throw a surprise party at Mally's mansion.[47] Mally and Bieber quickly became friends, recording songs in the mansion's studio and playing with the house animals. Bieber particularly liked Mally's monkey, apparently a capuchin named Lil Bubs.[48] To some who know him well, Mally's collaboration with Bieber seemed to serve as a model for his career going forward: working with impressionable, young artists who were just naive enough to be drawn in by his charms and exotic persona.

Mally ended up snagging writing and producing credits on Bieber's 2013 album, *Journals*, for the songs "PYD," "Hold Tight," "Recovery," "Bad Day," and the bonus track "Alone." He and Bieber got matching roman numeral tattoos ("I IX VII V"),[49] signifying 1975, the year Mally and Bieber's mom were born. Bieber posted a picture of the two of them, showing off their new tattoos (Bieber's just below his collarbone, Mally's on his right bicep), on his Instagram feed in January 2013. Two months later, for Bieber's nineteenth birthday, Mally gave him a monkey of his own, a white-faced capuchin that Bieber picked up in Los Angeles.[50] That night, Bieber and his new monkey, named OG Mally, boarded a private jet to Munich, Germany, where Bieber was scheduled to perform a sold-out concert. Upon landing, German authorities took the monkey into custody when they claimed to have discovered that Bieber and crew did not have the proper documentation to bring a live animal into the country. The saga of OG Mally became tabloid fodder for weeks as Bieber tried to take back his new pet.[51] Eventually, the monkey was transferred to a German zoo.[52]

For Mally, it was great publicity. That same year, Mally received writing and producing credits on a Tyga song, "Molly," from the rapper's third studio album, *Hotel California*. The track, about the drug Ecstasy, featured verses by the Pittsburg rapper Wiz Khalifa and Mally himself, who said no more than fifty-eight repetitive words on the entire song:

Put it in my drink, p-put it in my drink
Put it in my drink, you already know
Put it in my drink, p-put it in my drink
Put it in my drink, you already know
She had me smokin,' had me smokin'
Sm-sm-smokin' on my reefer
She had me smokin,' had me smokin'
Sm-sm-smokin' on my reefer.

"Molly" was a modest success, reaching No. 66 on the Billboard Hot 100.[53] But the song seemed to help redefine Mally as a producer-rapper, making him at least appear to be a name-brand hitmaker, a musician who could appear on the songs he produced and in music videos. That put him in the rarefied air of a mega producer like DJ Khaled, who regularly appears on the tracks he produces and is a big celebrity in his own right, even though no one would confuse him with a skilled lyricist.[54]

Mally quickly took advantage of his newfound celebrity, landing a role on the 2014 VH1[55] reality series *Love & Hip Hop: Hollywood*, as strip club heiress and entrepreneur Nikki Mudarris's on-again, off-again boyfriend.[56] The gig amounted to a bit part, but it seemed be everything Mally had said he wanted. In the eyes of at least some VH1 viewers, he was a legit hip-hop star. By then, he had writing, producing and/or vocal credits to more than fifteen songs, including tracks by Lil Twist, French Montana, and Kurupt.[57]

In less than a decade, Mally built himself into a national hip-hop brand, largely on the backs of women like Angela.

CHAPTER 9

Mouths to Feed

CHRISTOPHER BAUGHMAN'S THIRST FOR ATTENTION SEEMED TO GROW as he continued in his starring role with Vice.[1] As the section built a national reputation for helping sex trafficking victims, television crews from NBC, MSNBC, and the quintessential police reality TV show *Cops* started coming around, wanting to do segments and ride-alongs. Don Hoier found their attention to be distracting and annoying. But Baughman seemed to enjoy it, eagerly participating in the shoots. He appeared on at least one show with Chris Hansen, a TV journalist perhaps best known for starring in *Dateline NBC*'s *To Catch a Predator*.

In August 2011, a small, independent publisher, Behler Publications, published a book written by Baughman, *Off The Street*, in which he portrayed himself as the leader of the Pandering Investigations Team, heroically saving sex trafficking victims.[2] It was full of ridiculous, self-congratulatory, purple prose:

> In me comes a reckoning, the wrath of justice, and the pain and torment of those I am charged with serving. Tempered from equal parts love and hate, compassion and vengefulness, I am forged by the intensity of this city into a sharpened tool, hammered into my present shape by God, and still glowing from His heat. My light allows some to see in this darkness for the very first time. Thankfully, my city has a plan, and knows just where to point me.

In the preface, Baughman set up the book as a retelling of one of his early pimp investigations, with cameos from his friends in Vice, including one of his partners, Det. Albert Beas,[3] who is described as a "Mexican whose ego is only matched by his attitude." But instead, the book read like an outlandish, self-promotional ego trip, with Baughman cast as some kind of avenging angel. It was a bizarre book and mocked by locals who took the time to read it.

While some in Vice didn't care for Baughman and the attention he was receiving, Don didn't have a problem with him. Baughman was just too good a cop. Within three months in the summer and fall of 2011, Baughman helped get two major pimps indicted—Raymond Sharpe and Ocean Fleming. Baughman helped take down Sharpe after one of the prostitutes who worked for him, Alisha Grundy,[4] ran out of his house in southwest Las Vegas wearing only a thong and began pounding on the neighbors' doors for help.[5] Neighbors saw the 5'11", 175-pound Sharpe drag Grundy back into his house by her hair. Baughman interviewed Grundy later that night and learned that Sharpe had recruited Grundy as a teenager after she was suspended from high school. Grundy told Baughman that Sharpe pulled up to her in a Mercedes-Benz while she was walking back to her house in Portland, Oregon. He said he was a record producer from Los Angeles. Grundy ran away with Sharpe, who took her to Fresno, California, where he immediately demanded that she begin prostituting for him. Grundy told Baughman that she worked for Sharpe for more than a decade and had a son with him. On the day she went running for help, Grundy told Baughman that Sharpe confronted her for talking with another Black man and pistol whipped her for being out of pocket.[6]

Baughman got Fleming—the pimp Angela left Mally for briefly— through a similar series of events. Baughman had been gathering evidence on Fleming, collecting victim statements, and tying him to known prostitutes, when one day, one of the women who worked for Fleming, nineteen-year-old April Millard,[7] ran out of the house she shared with Fleming and approached a woman backing out of her driveway in a gated community in southwest Las Vegas.[8] Millard begged the woman to drive her to the community's gate. But when she got into the woman's car,

Fleming roared up in a red Buick SUV, blocking them in the driveway. He jumped out of his vehicle, grabbed a rock, and threatened to smash the woman's windshield if she didn't unlock the door. The event was captured in a call Millard made to 911. Millard testified in Fleming's 2012 trial that he dragged her out by her hair (like he did Angela) and drove her back to his place. There, she said, he dragged her upstairs— again, by her hair—and beat her with her purse, which had perfume bottles in it. Then he forced her to strip naked and pistol-whipped her across the forehead and shoved the barrel of the gun in her mouth, she said. Then he whipped her with a Gucci belt, giving her welts on her back. At the time, Millard was pregnant with Fleming's child. The September 2011 incident supercharged Baughman's investigation, leading to Fleming's indictment less than a month later.

At the time, no one could have known how significant Fleming's case would be to Baughman. Or to Mally.

Fleming[9] and Sharpe were both convicted of the charges that resulted from these events, and both were sentenced to life in prison.[10] Baughman worked on the cases with a deputy district attorney named Elizabeth Mercer.[11] Don couldn't argue with Baughman's results. He was taking bad guys off the streets. Don respected the hell out of that.

By 2013, Baughman seemed to feel he had outgrown Vice. He wanted a bigger platform—and more attention. So, after more than a decade at Metro, he announced he was resigning to co-star in a reality television show on MSNBC called *Slave Hunter: Freeing Victims of Human Trafficking.* Seemingly based loosely on Chris Hansen's show, *Slave Hunter* would star Baughman and self-described human rights activist Aaron Cohen[12] as they tried to help trafficked women get out of prostitution in New York City. Don had not been shy about giving Baughman his opinion on these plans. Don had seen Cohen, the co-author of *Slave Hunter: One Man's Global Quest to Free Victims of Human Trafficking,* speak at an area church. The guy had talked in circles about human trafficking and the cosmos and black holes. He and Baughman had laughed at him. But Baughman's attitude suddenly changed when Cohen introduced himself to Baughman in the church's parking lot and said, *I've heard a lot about you.* Don couldn't understand why Baughman would want to work with Cohen.

More importantly, Don knew that Baughman was leaving about five years before he was eligible to retire with a pension at age fifty. Don had seen cops do that before and they always regretted it. Don told Baughman he was making a huge mistake, that virtually everyone he had ever known who left the department before locking in their pension eventually tried to get their job back. Baughman said, *So what? If I need to get my job back, I will.* But Don reminded him that if he waited too long to re-apply, he'd have to go through the police academy again and start over at the bottom. Don doubted he'd want to do that.

But Baughman was undeterred. He said his family supported his decision. So in September 2013, after using vacation time to shoot *Slave Hunter*, Baughman officially resigned from the force. At a little going-away party at the office, Don got up and gave a speech about what a good detective Baughman was and how he put his heart into his work. When it came time for Baughman to speak, he said he initially had thought Don was a poor choice to lead PIT, but he eventually grew to see him as a good boss. Don was surprised and confused. He had known Baughman since he graduated from the academy in the late 1990s. When Baughman had been an investigator for the Gang Section, working out of the same anonymous building as Vice, Don and Baughman had often chatted in the parking lot before and after their shifts. After Baughman joined Vice, he'd come over to Don's house every year for a fantasy football draft. Don had assumed they always shared a mutual respect. But apparently not. Don later wondered if Baughman may have been concerned that when he was named head of PIT, he would start stealing the glory.

Later, Det. Al Beas, one of the PIT detectives named in Baughman's book, held an after-hours party for Baughman in the front yard of a house he rented off Blue Diamond Road, about fifteen minutes southwest of The Strip. Don went but he was still stunned by what Baughman had said. Baughman arrived that night holding hands with deputy district attorney Liz Mercer. Baughman, a father of two, was recently divorced.[13] As far as Don knew, nobody in Vice leadership had any idea he and Mercer were an item. *When did that start?* Karen Hughes asked Don.

Less than a month after Baughman's retirement party, Don stopped by the downtown office of Chief Deputy District Attorney Marc Schifalacqua[14] to drop off some files for discovery for a case involving a pimp named Alvin Mitchell. Schifalacqua had bad news for Don. The district attorney's office had determined it couldn't take another pimp, Arman Izadi, to trial.[15] Izadi had been sitting in county jail for months, awaiting trial on numerous felony counts, including pandering, first-degree kidnapping, extortion, robbery, coercion, and domestic violence involving strangulation.

Why? Don asked as calmly as he could.

Izadi's case had bothered Don almost as long as Mally's. After the raid on Mally's mansion in 2010, Intel had asked to borrow Baughman again on another case, this one involving Izadi, an American of reportedly partial Persian descent[16] who promoted Las Vegas nightclubs while connecting wealthy partygoers with high-end prostitutes. Working together, Vice and Intel had caught Izadi in an undercover sting in which an officer posed as an Arab sheik looking for women, which Izadi was happy to provide. But as with Mally, Intel decided not to arrest him and instead used him as an informant to gather intelligence on the Las Vegas nightclub scene. Since that time, Vice continued getting vague tips about Izadi's activities, until around Christmas 2012, when, in short succession, three alleged victims told Vice he was their pimp.

Don said, *I don't care if he's an informant. We're should investigate this.*[17] A new case was assigned to Baughman, who again began gathering evidence on Izadi's operations. Meanwhile, Don told Det. Warren Gray, Baughman's old Intel partner and the officer responsible for managing Izadi as an informant, about the new investigation. Under Metro policy, Intel was supposed to stop using anyone as an informant the moment he or she became the target of a criminal investigation by another section. Don assumed Gray would follow policy. Over the next few months, Baughman dug into Izadi again. He interviewed witnesses and reviewed his financial records. Vice also put surveillance on Izadi. By the spring of 2013, the section had enough evidence to search Izadi's penthouse condo.

Don met with Gray again, asking when he thought Izadi would be home. He wanted to arrest Izadi when they raided his place. Gray told Don he knew Izadi was throwing himself a birthday party at the penthouse on April 23, 2013. Gray knew that because Izadi had, of all things, *invited him* to the party. (Don's ears perked up when he heard that. *Christ*, Don thought, *pimps are even trying to manipulate their handlers.* Of course Gray didn't go.) On the morning of April 24,[18] Don and the Vice Section raided Izadi's condo, finding it strewn with trash, balloons, and empty alcohol bottles; a huge "Happy Birthday" banner hung from the wall. When Izadi realized it was Metro raiding his place, he started yelling, *You can't do this! I'm a CI! I work for you! I'm helping you guys out!*

It was clear to Don that Izadi thought his status as an informant gave him a get out of jail free card. He was happy to see that son of a bitch go down.

But Schifalacqua told Don in his office that day that Izadi's defense attorney had recently given him reams of text messages between Izadi and Gray. Schifalacqua said the text messages conclusively showed that Gray had continued to utilize Izadi as an informant—even while Vice had been investigating him. (Schifalacqua also reviewed numerous text messages between Gray and Izadi from Metro's download of Izadi's cell phone, which was impounded when the department served its search warrant.) Schifalacqua said if the case went to trial, Izadi would likely argue that the police knew what he was doing and had encouraged it. If that happened, Izadi would very likely walk.

Instead, Schifalacqua told Don he was going to try negotiating a plea deal and hope that Izadi took it.

Schifalacqua told Don that after he was confronted with the text messages, he had asked Gray why Intel continued using Izadi as an informant. Gray insisted that Izadi wasn't an official informant—he was just a "source." But Schifalacqua told Don the text messages strongly suggested that wasn't the case.

Don left Schifalacqua's office fuming. Either Gray had never officially signed up Izadi as an informant or he didn't stop using him when Vice launched the new investigation. It didn't matter: Both were violations of policy. *I'm never working with Intel again*, Don thought.

Then Don had another thought: *I wonder if the Mally case will bite us, too.*

Slave Hunter was slated for a December 2013 premiere on MSNBC, around the same time Baughman published his second book, *Off The Street: Redemption*, clearly timed for promotional reasons.[19] Clips of *Slave Hunter*[20] showed a lot of dark hotel rooms and cityscapes over sparse, haunting soundtracks. The jowly, curly-haired Cohen was the show's main star and narrator. The setup was that he, Baughman, and others were acting as a team of high-tech, prostitute rescuers. Some nonprofit organizations and anti-trafficking advocates conduct freelance operations like this, particularly in foreign places like Bangkok or South America. But they're always risky and done without legal authority. *Slave Hunter* proposed to do the same thing, only in the most populated city in the United States and in front of a full camera crew.

Their capers would begin with Cohen and Baughman studying "hundreds of ads online" for prostitutes in New York City, looking for "key indicators" that a woman was being trafficked. Any signs they might see in an ad would be hazy and unreliable at best. They might see a photo of a white prostitute, but the text is written in blunt, urban slang, suggesting that her pimp made the ad. But even if the *Slave Hunter* crew chose randomly, they were likely to find women under pimp control simply because most prostitutes are being trafficked.[21] Cohen's voiceover made it sound like their process was targeted or even pseudoscientific. It wasn't. When they found a prostitute that they wanted to contact, Cohen would pose undercover as a sex buyer and call to arrange a meeting. Then, with Baughman watching on hidden camera, Cohen would slyly interview the woman in a hotel room, maybe over a room service meal, according to clips available online. The gritty, undercover footage, complete with blurred-out faces of the prostitutes, would be interspersed with interviews with Baughman and Cohen, commenting on what they had seen. In those interview cutaways, Baughman wore fashionable, black, horned-rim glasses while Cohen sported dark, military-looking shirts.

The show, which MSNBC touted as "groundbreaking,"[22] promised to give viewers an unvarnished look at the world of prostitution. In one extended clip, Cohen holds hands with a prostitute and—after she describes how difficult it was to get away from her pimp—reunites her with her mother. In another clip, Cohen describes taking a call from a prostitute named April, who was left on the streets after someone had seen her pimp strangle her. With her pimp in custody, April had called Cohen for help. But ominously Cohen tells the camera that April has been in contact with her pimp's associates. "That's a really dangerous thing," Cohen intones. In the next scene, Cohen picks up a call from April's cell phone, only to discover it is her pimp, who growls, "This is my motherfucking phone." Cohen puts the call on speakerphone and holds it up for the camera, while the pimp rants. "Where you at, motherfucker? Where you at?"

MSNBC promoted *Slave Hunter* as "captivating" and portrayed Baughman and Cohen as modern-day abolitionists.[23] Human rights groups, like the New York Anti-Trafficking Network, the Sex Worker Outreach Project–Las Vegas, and the Walter Leitner International Human Rights Clinic, however, seemed appalled. On December 9, 2013, two dozen of these groups wrote Deb Finan, MSNBC's vice president of production and programming,[24] demanding that the network offer shows that accurately reflected sex work and didn't threaten the safety of vulnerable women. The letter read in part:

> Surreptitiously filmed "interventions" in the lives of possible trafficking victims are ineffective and potentially dangerous. For example, in the preview for the program, Mr. Cohen poses as a client to make a date with a sex worker he believes to be trafficked, encourages her to leave an abusive relationship and gives her a ride to her mother's house. This intervention failed to identify why this person originally left her home, why she encountered and stayed with the alleged abuser, and failed to follow a safety plan or provide adequate support that would allow her to avoid future abuse. Because of Mr. Cohen's failings, he may have escalated the danger.

MSNBC canceled *Slave Hunter*.[25] Baughman was out of work.

About a year after Baughman's going-away party, an application packet appeared on Don's desk in the late summer of 2014. Baughman was applying to get his job back and had listed Don as a reference. *I knew it*, Don thought. He filled out the packet and sent it to Personnel.

Weeks later, Don got a call from a background investigator. *Do you know Chris to hang out with pimps?* the investigator asked.

He wouldn't hang out with pimps, Don said. *He hates them.*

That's not what we're hearing, the investigator replied.

What is he talking about? Don wondered. *You could knock me over with a feather if that's true,* he said.

Don told Karen Hughes about the conversation. *That's odd,* she said. Neither of them knew what to make of it.

On September 15, 2014, the music and reality television network VH1 premiered the third installment of its popular *Love & Hip Hop* franchise: *Love & Hip Hop: Hollywood.* Like its predecessors set in New York and Atlanta, *Love & Hip Hop: Hollywood* promised to follow the personal and professional lives of hip-hop performers, managers, and record producers, this time in Tinseltown. The cast included the R&B artist Ray J, known for his sex tape with Kim Kardashian; the rapper Soulja Boy; and the strip club heiress Nikki Mudarris. The show's second episode, broadcast the following week, introduced Mally as Mudarris's cheating boyfriend.[26]

Just before dawn on September 29, 2014, the same day VH1 was scheduled to air episode three, federal agents raided Mally's mansion and the office of his escort service. These raids were much bigger news than they'd been in 2010. Within hours, TMZ posted a breaking news story: "'Love and Hip Hop' Star Mally Mall—FBI Raids Vegas House in Criminal Investigation."[27] Mally reportedly was in Los Angeles at the time, filming the VH1 series. He tweeted to his fans, "Thank you all for your concern. Currently I'm not sure what's going on but, [sic] stay positive, truth will reveal. All faith in God. Inshallah" followed by the prayer hands emoji. His message was retweeted more than 35 times and received more than 60 likes. "@mallymall been praying all morning u will be just fine #Kingdom stay blessed [sic]," replied @JustJazz702.

Don was getting dressed for his afternoon shift when he caught a news story about the raid. He practically floated to the office. *I'm glad somebody finally got that asshole,* he told Karen Hughes. But Hughes was in no mood to celebrate. *Why didn't the FBI give us a heads up?* she wondered aloud. *That's a good question*, Don thought. Why hadn't they said anything?

About two days later, they got their answer. Joe Dickey,[28] the supervisor of the FBI's public corruption unit in Las Vegas, called Hughes to tell her that Baughman would be contacting her. Don didn't witness what happened next, but Hughes filled him in a short time later. A remorseful Baughman contacted Hughes and told her that he had fallen on hard times after *Slave Hunter* was canceled. He struggled to pay his child support. He thought Mally had changed.

Baughman said he had accepted a $5,000 loan from Mally.

Don was furious. *How could Baughman possibly have convinced himself that Mally had changed?* he wondered. That was the lamest excuse he'd ever heard—especially coming from somebody who should've known better.

Baughman's confession sent shockwaves through Metro. His haughtiness had made him unpopular with some in Vice, so several detectives were happy to see him step on his crank. But Vice leadership was worried about the bigger picture. Baughman's involvement with Mally could jeopardize all the cases he had built against other pimps. Any competent defense attorney could use this to demand a new trial. Worse yet, Vice's credibility in the eyes of the public would be destroyed when this became public.

For days, Don and Hughes talked over the situation, trying to predict what might happen and how the section should respond. They met with a deputy chief of police, who asked Hughes to put together a timeline of events involving Mally.[29] They also met with the new lieutenant in charge of Intel, Brian Evans,[30] who revealed, according to Don, that sometime before the FBI raid, Mally had allegedly told Warren Gray that he had given money to Baughman. But Evans told a slightly different story than the one Baughman had told Hughes. Evans claimed that Mally said he gave money to Baughman *while he was still a cop*, not after he had left the force.

Don didn't know what to believe. He couldn't understand how Baughman would ever be so foolish to take money from a pimp. Yet he had admitted to doing just that. So, did that mean Baughman could have accepted Mally's money while he was still with the department? Don couldn't outright dismiss it. But he also thought it was possible that Mally had twisted the facts when he talked to Intel. Pimps are schemers, manipulators. They play a long game. A good lie always has a kernel of truth.

Don did Mally's calculus in his head. A loan to an ex-cop might give the pimp leverage sometime in the future, either with Intel or someone else. Don hoped that's what had happened with the FBI. (The alternative was frightening.) Don thought that when the feds started sniffing around, Mally served up Baughman to take the heat off him.

If that was the case, Don thought, Mally could have served up Baughman to Intel, too. Informants are only useful as long as they're providing information. By 2014, Mally had been an informant for years. It's hard to keep spinning out stories, especially if you're only spinning out stories to benefit yourself, which is exactly what Don thought Mally had been doing. Don wondered if Mally had run out of things to say, so he gave Intel Baughman—but altered the story just a little. After all, Intel was looking for dirty cops. It would have found a story about an active cop taking pimp money interesting, even if it had happened years ago. A story about an ex-cop? Not so juicy.

Whatever the case, there was nothing Don or the Vice Section could do about it now. It appeared the FBI was in the beginning stages of a public corruption investigation. If Mally had indeed given money to Baughman while he was still with Metro, the FBI would address it. If he had given the money after he had left, there was no case. There's nothing illegal about one private citizen loaning another money.

Not surprisingly, Metro didn't rehire Baughman, who largely disappeared from public view. That was fine with Don. He was so angry he thought if he ever saw Baughman again he'd punch him in the fucking mouth.

CHAPTER 10

It's Like That

DON HOIER RETIRED FROM METRO IN MARCH 2015, A COUPLE OF months before Hughes, who had always planned to leave the force on her thirty-year anniversary.[1] Don didn't want to break in a new lieutenant at Vice and his dad had recently suffered a couple of mild strokes; he figured now was as good a time as any to retire. But Don probably could have been convinced to stay a little while longer if not for the tumultuous campaign for a new Clark County Sheriff.

In the 2014 race for sheriff, it came down to Assistant Sheriff Joe Lombardo[2] and a well-liked, retired Metro captain named Larry Burns. Burns had the overwhelming support of the rank-and-file Metro officers: 96 percent of the Las Vegas Police Protective Association, Metro's biggest union, voted to back Burns.[3] Lombardo, however, got the endorsement of the Metro brass, including the outgoing sheriff, Doug Gillespie, and much of the casinos' support. Chris Collins, executive director of the Las Vegas Police Protective Association, offered this description of the two candidates to the *Las Vegas Sun*: "Larry is a friendly, touchy guy who will quickly bring morale back to the department, and Joe is a little more of a harder guy who is kind of in the model of the sheriffs we've had."[4] Lombardo defeated Burns by 2 percentage points, 51 to 49.[5]

At age forty-seven, Don was burned out after years of fourteen-hour days at Vice and he didn't want to deal with the stress of a transition to a new sheriff. Plus, he wanted to be available to help his dad if his health declined further. Don figured he'd spend the next year fixing up his house at a leisurely pace, then sell it and move to South Dakota, where he owned some land.

But things didn't work out quite like he had planned. One big hiccup: he started dating Dr. Shera Bradley, a psychologist who ran a program for juvenile sex trafficking survivors.[6] Don and Bradley had known each other for years; she once did a ride-along with Don and had observed him teach an education course for convicted johns. Don always thought she was pretty, but whenever they'd bump into each other they were always in relationships with other people. Besides, Don didn't like the idea of getting involved with someone he worked with. However, after his retirement, Don and Bradley stayed in touch via text. Over time, they became flirtatious. He invited her to an Alice in Chains concert at the Palms Casino Resort in July 2015 and they soon became inseparable. Bradley hated cold weather, so South Dakota was off the table.

Then, in December 2015, Don faced another curveball: At age forty-eight, he was diagnosed with Lymphoma. His family's predisposition to cancer—which had taken the lives of his maternal grandparents, his brother, and his mom—had reared its ugly head again.

Before Don retired from Metro, he testified as an expert witness on sex trafficking a few times for the Clark County District Attorney's office. He was happy to do it, but he saw a flaw in the DA's system of using working Vice cops as expert witnesses. Ocean Fleming—Angela's ex-pimp—had tried to appeal his conviction in part by arguing that Chris Baughman had prejudiced him while testifying as an expert witness on his case—a case in which Baughman *also* served as a detective.[7] The appeal ultimately failed, but Don figured the DA's office was opening up its cases to unnecessary risks by using active cops as expert witnesses. Before he retired, he floated the idea of serving as an expert witness on sex trafficking cases after he left the force. The DA's office jumped at the offer.

In March 2016, while Don was undergoing outpatient chemo treatments (which exhausted him), the DA's office asked him to testify in a trial of a pimp named Robert Sharpe III. The nephew of Raymond Sharpe, one of the pimps Baughman had busted a few years earlier,

Robert Sharpe III faced more than a dozen felony counts, including sex trafficking and assault with a deadly weapon, for coercing an eighteen-year-old into prostitution and then beating her when she wanted to leave The Life.[8] Before he was called to testify on day seven of the trial, Don waited outside the courtroom and struck up a conversation with one of his old detectives on the Pandering Investigations Team, who was also set to testify in the case.[9]

After catching up, Don asked the detective how work was going. The detective told Don that a young FBI agent named Kevin White[10] had started investigating Baughman and Mally. Don wasn't surprised; he figured the Baughman-Mally connection would be investigated by someone at some point, and that he might even be questioned about it. (Heck, he was practically *waiting* for someone to ask him about it.) But he also knew an investigation into Baughman and Mally would put the entire Vice Section under the microscope. That wouldn't be good—but there was more. The detective told him that White had been talking with sex trafficking victims involved in active Vice cases. His questioning, implying corruption in Vice, was now making victims hesitant to cooperate with the section. The detective had also heard White had been caught in a lie while interviewing another Vice detective. White's investigation had become so contentious that Metro barred the FBI from visiting Vice detectives at their office. The detective told Don that White would probably want to interview him.

A couple of days later, Don came home from a chemo session to find a message from White on his answering machine. *This is Special Agent Kevin White of the FBI*, White said. *I'm wondering if you might be willing to talk to me about Chris Baughman.* Don called him back and said he'd do it, but also told the agent that he was in the middle of chemo treatments; Don offered to meet with White in a week or two, when his latest treatment cycle concluded. White instead offered to meet with Don when he was scheduled to be entirely done with chemo, in June 2016.

Don planned to just talk to the agent whenever the time came; he didn't feel like he needed an attorney because he didn't have anything to hide. But his girlfriend, Bradley, told him that was a bad idea, saying he of all people should know how things could go sideways in a law enforcement interview. She convinced him to find an attorney, just in case. George Kelesis, a Las Vegas lawyer since 1981, agreed to represent Don pro bono.[11] Kelesis told Don to refer White's next call to him. *I'll say you're being treated for cancer, and they don't need to talk to you,* Kelesis said.

In June, toward the end of his cancer treatments, tests revealed Don's white blood cell count had dropped to zero. (That came as a surprise to Don. Other than being tired, some weight loss, and catching a lot of colds, he tolerated treatment relatively well, especially compared to others he'd see at the clinic.) He was sent to the hospital for several days, where he was pumped full of antibiotics and his blood was cultured numerous times to ensure he didn't have an infection. Don was worried he and Bradley would have to cancel a special trip to Hawaii the next month. But his numbers improved, and he was allowed to do his last round of chemo. Almost immediately afterward, White asked for an interview again and told Kelesis he'd just subpoena Don if he didn't agree to talk.

Don told Kelesis to set up an interview as soon as possible, before their trip to Hawaii.

On the appointed day of his interview, the always casual Don dressed up in suit pants and a button-down shirt and headed to Kelesis's office, located in a converted house. When Don strode into the conference room, he was shocked at the number of people there. White was accompanied by Cristina Silva,[12] then an assistant United States attorney for the District of Nevada, as well as several US attorneys from Washington, DC. Don had heard that when local FBI agents had a hard time getting support for their cases from the US Attorney's office in Nevada, they'd sometimes ask attorneys in Washington for help.[13] Don wondered if there were so many DC attorneys present because the Nevada office had concerns about White's case.[14]

Silva began the interview by making it clear that Don was not the subject of White's investigation. She also added cryptically, *You're going to have a lot of questions we can't answer, but you're a smart guy. You'll figure out what's going on.*

White led the interview for the most part. He said that since he had started looking into Baughman, his investigation had *spiderwebbed* and now he was scrutinizing other people in Vice as well. To Don, that sounded like he was being overloaded with a lot of potentially spurious claims.

At one point, White asked, *Can you tell me what the department's policy is for CIs?*

Honestly, I'd have to look it up, Don replied. *While I know CIs serve a purpose, we really don't use them in Vice.*

White began to ask a follow-up question when Silva cut in: *Why don't you use* CIs?

Because our CIs would be pimps and prostitutes, Don said. *Prostitutes are either victims or suspects. Pimps are always suspects, and they're master manipulators. You can't trust anything they tell you. They're only going to feed you information to benefit themselves, like dirt on their competition. And the only way they're going to have access to information that would be of any interest to law enforcement would be if they were still pimping.*

Don figured based on White's questions that Mally was the agent's primary source of information. He thought Silva had asked that question specifically to undercut Mally's credibility and to drive home that point to White. Don believed that Silva's brusque manner bolstered his suspicion that the Nevada office had doubts about White's investigation.

At another point in the interview, White said that Baughman had taken his daughter to Mally's house to meet Justin Bieber. That was news to Don; he had never heard anything like that before and, when Don had been on the force, he had made it a point to stay up on Vice gossip. Don thought if that had happened, someone in the section would have said something. But the only thing Don had ever heard was that Baughman had once taken his daughter to a Bieber concert and that they had met the superstar after the show.

Well, wasn't that suspicious to you? White asked.

No, Don replied. *This is Vegas. It's built on networking and favors. Lots of cops know people who can hook you up with a celebrity.*

Through one of his own connections, Don had once got to hang out backstage with the rock group Air Supply. Stuff like that happened all the time to people at Metro. Don wondered if this was another example of Mally taking a kernel of truth and twisting it to suit his purposes.

White started talking about the different forms police corruption can take. Corruption could involve a cop taking money, setting up an innocent man for a crime—even sleeping with a witness. *Absolutely*, Don agreed. White presented a printout of text messages between Baughman and a sex trafficking victim and directed Don's attention to those highlighted in yellow. *Are these appropriate?* White asked. Don studied the messages, which documented Baughman's efforts to convince a prostitute, Alisha Grundy, to testify against her pimp, Raymond Sharpe. Don saw that the texts appeared flirty. In one, Baughman asked Grundy, "What's up beautiful. [sic]"[15] Don didn't think speaking with a sex trafficking victim like that was appropriate at all. But that was hardly what Don would consider "smoking penis" evidence that Baughman was fucking her either. Don told White he would never talk to a sex trafficking victim that way. But he added that a lot of prostitutes suffer from poor self-esteem and often need encouragement to cooperate with authorities.

These texts are just the tip of the iceberg, White replied.

At another point in the interview, White revealed that as part of his investigation he had interviewed Ocean Fleming in prison—and had told the pimp about his suspicions that Baughman and others in Vice were corrupt and secretly working with Mally. Don was silently stunned. *Why would he share unproven allegations with a convicted pimp?* he wondered. *Didn't he know what liars those guys are?*[16]

White also asked Don about Baughman's divorce—suggesting to Don that the agent didn't know exactly when Baughman may have taken the loan from Mally—as well as a bunch of questions about Vice officers who weren't involved in the Mally investigation and about Vice sergeants who didn't supervise Baughman. When it was all over, Don chatted privately with his lawyer in his office on the second floor of the converted house. They agreed that White's questions had seemed to be all over the place, like he didn't have anything solid. To both of them, it seemed that White was searching for evidence to support some wild accusations, that he didn't have a case at all. Don suspected those wild accusations were coming from pimps and their associates.

A short while later in Hawaii, where Don proposed to Bradley on the one-year anniversary of their first date, Don found himself rolling the Mally case over and over in his mind. It seemed to Don that Mally had played Intel, the FBI, everyone, by exploiting his relationships and his status as an informant. *What was even the point of using Mally as an informant?* Don wondered. Intel had wanted him to get information on dirty cops and other criminals, but Don wasn't aware of any cases built on information he had provided. As far as Don could tell, the only thing Mally the informant had accomplished was keeping Mally the pimp out of prison.

In conversations with his new fiancé, Don started referring to Mally as a modern-day James Joseph "Whitey" Bulger. Bulger was a Boston mob boss from the 1970s into the 1990s who avoided criminal prosecution for years because he was an informant for the FBI.[17] In law enforcement circles, Bulger's story is frequently cited as a cautionary tale about the dangers of employing informants.

CHAPTER 11

Exclusive

FIVE MONTHS AFTER HIS INTERVIEW WITH THE FBI, IN NOVEMBER 2016, Don received a link to a news story by KLAS-TV Channel 8, the CBS affiliate in Las Vegas.[1] George Knapp, the station's chief investigative reporter, was reporting on "an unexpected turn" in an FBI investigation into sex trafficking in Las Vegas—the 2014 raid on Mally's mansion.[2] Don almost laughed. Knapp was a prominent, long-time media figure in Las Vegas—a member of the Nevada Broadcasters Association Hall of Fame with more than twenty regional Emmys[3]—but Don considered him bombastic and prone to embracing conspiracy theories.

Knapp wrote and co-directed a documentary called *UFOs: The Best Evidence* in 1994 and six years later provided information for a TV movie called *UFOs: Then and Now?* In 2005, he co-wrote a book, *Hunt for the Skinwalker: Science Confronts the Unexplained at a Remote Ranch in Utah*, about an investigation into paranormal activities on a cattle ranch in Uintah County, Utah. In addition to his duties at KLAS-TV, Knapp regularly hosts a late-night syndicated radio program that reports on paranormal activities. An episode he hosted in late October 2016 featured an interview with a UFO researcher and author who claimed that alien abductions are more similar to demonic possession than extraterrestrial events, and an interview with an author who said that the smell of sulfur is associated with haunted locations, UFOs, and other paranormal events.

Two weeks later, on November 11, 2016, Knapp reported on KLAS-TV that a "possible focus" of the FBI's raid was a search for "any evidence of a business relationship" between Mally and Christopher

Baughman, who was described as one of Las Vegas's most prominent police officers. Citing unnamed "police sources," Knapp reported that Baughman had "admitted to having romantic relationships with women who had worked as prostitutes, including some of the victims who had come to him for protection from pimps." Knapp reported that "Multiple law enforcement sources have told the I-Team that one of their biggest concerns is what might happen when convicted pimps learn that Detective Baughman allegedly slept with victims who became witnesses."

Knapp also reported that the FBI's raid on Mally's mansion was initiated by the bureau's public corruption squad, not its sex trafficking team, suggesting that the feds' interest had always been Vice, not Mally himself.

But perhaps the most damning revelation was Knapp's disclosure that unnamed Vice officers had become "concerned about Baughman when he revealed he had taken his teenage daughter to Mally Mall's home so she could meet Justin Bieber." Knapp reported that Baughman's daughter knew Mally so well that she called him "Uncle J" (apparently a reference to Mally's first name, Jamal).

Don was incredulous after he had watched the segment a couple of times online. The first and only time Don had ever heard about Baughman taking his daughter to Mally's house to meet Bieber was in his interview with Kevin White. Don felt certain this allegation—that Vice officers in particular were concerned about Baughman's relationship with Mally while Baughman was on the force—was untrue. Don wasn't aware of anyone in Vice ever talking about Baughman taking his daughter to Mally's house so much that she called him Uncle J.

But here was Knapp reporting the same allegations as White, almost word for word. Don figured Knapp's unnamed source could only be White.

His thought became conviction a short while later when Don received a forwarded text message from a private investigator who was friends with White. *This is my case*, White had texted the investigator, along with a link to Knapp's story. In Don's experience, most cops hated it when the press writes about an active case. The publicity can endanger the investigation.

That is, unless the cop wanted the story to come out.

It was hard to interpret the tone of the text, but Don would have expected White to have said something more if he were mad about Knapp's story. To Don, it looked like White had cooperated with it. The way Don saw it, White hit a wall trying to prove his theories and had leaked the story to Knapp to try to shake the trees for more leads.

Part IV

CHAPTER 12

Trying to Come Up

WHO IS THIS?[1] I WONDERED WHEN I SAW THE CONNECTION REQUEST ON LinkedIn. By late 2016, I was spending a lot of time on the professional networking site, looking for jobs. Thirteen years after college, my journalism career had stagnated. For about a decade, I had worked for California newspapers, primarily as a political and investigative reporter. I had done a lot of stories I was proud of, stories that I thought had helped people. But while my peers were racking up national awards and landing bigger and better jobs, I was bored and going nowhere.

Three years earlier, I had quit my job as the Sacramento bureau chief for the *Orange County Register* and taken a mid-career fellowship at the University of California, Berkeley's journalism school, where I spent more than a year investigating child injuries and deaths in private foster care. I believed that story needed to be told and was grateful for the time and resources to do it. But I also had hoped that the fellowship would open some more doors for me. It hadn't. After my foster care story ran in *Mother Jones* magazine,[2] I ended up working from my home in Sacramento for a tiny news organization, writing about workplace safety and consumer protection. The gig was OK, but I was frustrated that our stories had little readership and that I was making about $10,000 less a year than I had at the *Register*.

At the same time, my wife hated her job at an insurance company, and we'd just had our first and only child, a daughter, whom we were forced to put into daycare. We both hated that. So, at the ripe old age of thirty-six, I trolled LinkedIn in my free time, searching for something that might change our fortunes.

I clicked on the LinkedIn request and saw that it was from the new investigative editor at the *Las Vegas Review-Journal*.[3] *Ugh, not them*, I thought. Like many journalists, I closely followed industry news and everything coming out of the *Review-Journal* lately had sounded awful. The *Review-Journal* was the dominant news source for southern Nevada, but some locals had long considered it a mouthpiece for the casino industry. Its cross-town rival, the *Las Vegas Sun*, was more liberal and perceived as more of a watchdog, but its finances were shaky. In 1989, the *Sun* entered into a joint operating agreement with the *Review-Journal* to keep itself afloat. Under the agreement, the *Review-Journal* handled the administration of the *Sun*, including printing and advertising; the *Sun* was responsible for its own news gathering. But that didn't significantly change the *Sun*'s fortunes. In 2005, the agreement was renegotiated, making the *Sun* an insert in the *Review-Journal*,[4] further solidifying the *R-J* as the largest and most important news operation in Nevada.

In December 2015, Sheldon Adelson, the billionaire casino magnate and major Republican donor, tried unsuccessfully to hide[5] that he and his family had purchased the *Review-Journal*. Using a Delaware shell company, they had bought the paper for $140 million. For nearly a week, even reporters working for the paper weren't sure who owned it. When the newspaper's journalists finally figured it out, bravely publishing a front-page exposé on their own owner,[6] a firestorm descended on Adelson and the *Review-Journal*. Across the country, media critics wondered how the Las Vegas community could ever trust the *Review-Journal* after Adelson tried to conceal his ownership.[7] "Mr. Adelson's purchase of the Review-Journal, carefully hidden until gutsy reporters at the paper rooted it out earlier this month, is deeply troubling," said Todd O'Boyle, then director of Common Cause's Media and Democracy Reform Initiative, in a press release after the *Review-Journal* unmasked its own owner.[8] "Mr. Adelson is perhaps the most deep-pocketed political donor in the country; he is expected to spend tens of millions of dollars—and maybe more—to secure the Republican presidential nomination and then the presidency itself for his preferred candidate. His purchase of the Review-Journal, the most important newspaper in a critical primary state, potentially gives him another critical tool toward accomplishing that goal." Every week, it seemed, I read reports of journalists leaving the newspaper in protest and disgust.[9]

I also had my own reasons to fear Adelson. When I was in Berkeley, the head of my fellowship program, the legendary investigative reporter Lowell Bergman, had been working on a documentary about gambling in Macau for the PBS show *Frontline*. Adelson figured prominently in the film. (Adelson, as chairman, CEO, and the majority shareholder of the casino operator Las Vegas Sands, was perhaps best known for owning the Venetian and Palazzo casinos in Las Vegas; however, his casinos in the Chinese party city were the primary source of his revenue.) While I was finishing up my *Mother Jones* piece, Bergman had asked me to help fact check the film. The documentary crew did some reporting on John L. Smith, a prominent Nevada journalist Adelson had sued. In 2005, Smith wrote a book called *Sharks in the Desert*, with one chapter devoted to Adelson's rise in the casino business and his early investments in the vending machine industry.[10] Smith's book explored organized crime's influence on the casino business but didn't link Adelson to it. Still, Adelson must have believed the book sullied his reputation. He sued Smith for libel. Smith said Adelson offered to drop the suit if the reporter admitted that he meant to hurt the casino owner. As an inducement, Adelson offered to give Smith $200,000 to cover his daughter's medical expenses—at the time, she was being treated for brain cancer. Smith rejected the offer and instead filed for bankruptcy. Eventually, Adelson dropped the suit. Later, Smith quit the *Review-Journal* after the new editor installed under Adelson barred him from writing about Adelson or Steve Wynn, another prominent casino owner with properties in Las Vegas and Macau.

The incident was scary—but the film never saw the light of day. *Frontline* canned the documentary. The show's executives claimed the film wasn't good enough; Bergman's team contended they were really afraid of litigation from Adelson and Wynn.[11]

I considered ignoring the LinkedIn request. Why would I want anything to do with that trainwreck? But then I thought, *Eh, what would it hurt?* I clicked "Accept" and went about my day. About a week later, I heard from the editor, who said she wanted to talk with me about an opening on the paper's new investigative team. Nervously, I agreed to hear her pitch. We spoke on the morning of November 9, 2016, the day we woke up to Donald Trump as our new president.

On that surreal day, as I sat at my hand-me-down desk in front of my wife's old laptop computer, the editor told me she had gotten my name from a famous investigative reporter we both knew. That caught my attention. *If she's friends with him, she couldn't be too bad*, I thought. She laid out her vision for the team and the role she thought I could play. She wanted to build a team of reporters with different skill sets and interests, with me playing the role of the narrative writer focused on long-term, people-centric stories, while others pursued shorter, government-accountability pieces. She also assured me that Adelson would have no influence over the team. She invited me to come to Las Vegas for a job interview. I wasn't sold, but I wasn't going to turn down a free trip to Vegas either. With a fussy infant at home, I figured I'd at least get a good night's sleep—in Vegas of all places.

A few weeks later, I flew to Vegas, where I was put up in a suite at the Venetian. A few minutes before dinner with the editor, I texted my wife, *Why am I even here?* But the investigative editor came prepared. Over a long dinner at the Venetian's Grand Lux Café, she charmed me with her knowledge of my work and her plans for tackling groundbreaking, high-impact journalism. She suggested that if I joined the newspaper, I might be interested in investigating sex trafficking. The idea resonated with me. Part of the reason why I had left my political reporting job in Sacramento was so that I could pursue more stories about marginalized people, people who had been hurt and needed help. In a roundabout way, I wanted to be more like my dad, who worked for decades as a psychologist, helping people sort out their problems. Sex trafficking victims seemed like people I might be able to help.

The following evening, after similarly positive discussions with other editors at the paper, I found myself on the flight home seriously considering taking the job if they offered. And they did, along with the largest salary I'd been presented in journalism. While our daughter napped, my wife and I researched the cost of living in Las Vegas. It was cheaper than Sacramento. With what the *Review-Journal* was offering to pay me, my wife could stay at home with our daughter and we could afford to buy our first house.

I was still queasy about Adelson—several journalists I consulted with told me working for him would be risky—but it also was clear: This was a good financial move for my family, certainly the best I could hope for at the moment. I took the job.

By the spring of 2017, my family and I had started to settle in. Las Vegas was a bit of a culture shock—Slot machines at the grocery stores?—but we treated it like an adventure. We purchased a house in the northwest corner of the city, which afforded my wife and daughter access to numerous nearby parks. At the paper, my colleagues seemed nice.

A few weeks after I arrived, the *Review-Journal*'s top editor swung by the investigative team's row of cubicles. He asked our team to come up with a big story for early April 2017, when the *Review-Journal* was planning to roll out a redesign of the newspaper. He wanted a big one to go with the redesign.[12]

The senior member of the I-team, a reporter who had worked in Las Vegas for decades, suggested that we investigate spending by the Las Vegas Convention and Visitors Authority, a public agency that runs the Las Vegas Convention Center and works to bring big conferences to town. My colleague said the authority's spending on meals and entertainment had been questioned in the past.[13] Its spending practices were something we could investigate in a few weeks, which was essential if we were going to make the April deadline. We requested the authority's spending reports and entered them into a spreadsheet.

The story ran on the first Sunday of April 2017,[14] when the newspaper unveiled its slick new look, complete with a sketch of The Strip's skyline below the *Review-Journal* nameplate.[15] Our piece documented how the convention authority had spent millions of taxpayer dollars on liquor, expensive meals, and first-class flights. The response was mixed: Some readers thought it was a hard-hitting exposé and others thought that was just how the convention business worked. But it did generate several tips, including word that the agency's chief financial officer had questioned these expenses.[16]

I drove to the CFO's house, knocked on her door, and asked if she wanted to talk. Her husband answered and told me to leave. About a day later, the authority's president and CEO sent a letter to several casino executives,[17] complaining that I was harassing one of his employees.[18]

At any other newspaper I had worked for, such a letter would be no big deal. But Adelson was both the paper's owner and a casino owner.[19]

While the paper publicly defended my reporting tactics in an article responding to the authority's letter,[20] the *Review-Journal's* top editor pulled me aside and told me that he had spoken to Adelson, who wanted to know why I had visited the CFO's home. Adelson apparently had told the editor he wouldn't want a reporter to knock on his door. The editor laughed. *I told him you're so rich a reporter could never get to your door!* he said.[21]

That made me uncomfortable. Knocking on doors is a basic reporting tactic. I approached the CFO at home on the assumption that if she really had been upset, she probably wouldn't want to talk about it at work. At best, Adelson's apparent comment suggested that he didn't understand the fundamentals of news gathering. At worst, it meant he didn't respect journalism. I would have hoped the editor would have done something to communicate that to our owner.

On Sunday, October 1, 2017, about eight months after moving to Las Vegas, my wife and I spent the day at an outlet mall and a children's museum. We were trying desperately to wear out our eighteen-month-old daughter, who'd wake up each morning by 5 a.m. raring to go. By the time evening came around, she was, thankfully, exhausted—and so were we. I turned in early, before 10 p.m.

Not long afterward, a high roller named Stephen Paddock opened fire with a rifle from his suite at Mandalay Bay Resort and Casino on The Strip, killing sixty concertgoers and injuring hundreds more at a country music festival across the street. It was the largest mass shooting in modern US history and huge, international news.

That night, the *Review-Journal* was able to get in a story on Monday's front page about the shooting,[22] but it didn't come close to capturing the gravity of the massacre. Understandably, the true toll of the shooting would have to be captured in real time on the newspaper's website and later in its Tuesday edition.

No one from the newspaper called me that night,[23] while scores of people around the globe watched live reports on television and on social media about the carnage on The Strip. I learned of the shooting the following morning after I woke up and checked the headlines. I later heard stories about other *R-J* reporters who learned the news on their own and hurried to the scene.[24]

When I woke up and learned the news, I rushed to throw on some clothes. As I was getting ready, the investigative editor called me and told me to head directly to the newsroom, where I would be working with another reporter, tallying the dead. When I arrived at the newspaper's low-slung, red-brick building a short while later, I was surprised to find the parking lot relatively empty. Inside the newsroom, rows of cubicles were vacant, though a handful of mid-level editors were standing or sitting in the center of the main room. I asked them what needed to be done. No one had anything. I started trying to figure out how the coroner might handle the influx of bodies.[25]

About a half hour later, the other reporter I was assigned to work with arrived. We tried for a while to figure out where the coroner might set up his operations and how quickly the dead would be identified, but we couldn't get anywhere. We decided she should drive around and try to figure out what was happening, and I'd stay back at the newsroom and take feeds from her. Not long after she left, however, we realized the coroner wouldn't be releasing detailed information that day, so my reporting partner went to help elsewhere.

At around the same time, the *Review-Journal*'s top editors gathered in a conference room. After what seemed like hours, they came out. I and several other reporters were tasked with tracking down the families of victims.[26] This effort obviously involved contacting scores of people who were just learning that their family members had been killed or injured. Our group didn't have a leader, however—no one was coordinating the effort. I was worried the *Review-Journal* might accidentally anger some families by calling them twice if nobody was keeping track of who was being contacted. I took the lead and developed a Google spreadsheet to track which reporters were making calls on which victims.[27]

For the rest of the week, I was assigned to work with another reporter on a big story for the Sunday paper, but nobody had any idea what it would be about. After a few false starts, we wrote a long feature story about a family that got separated at the concert venue and reunited at their hotel.[28]

After that, the entire newsroom worked long hours for the rest of October. But coverage plans seemed to be made up on the fly every morning, with editors ping-ponging me from one random assignment to another. For example, I was tasked with monitoring donations to GoFundMe campaigns that had been opened in the wake of the shooting.[29] Meanwhile, the *New York Times*, the *Washington Post*, and other national outlets, who were all relying on reporters who had parachuted into Las Vegas, were telling gripping tales about survivors or recreating the shooting from video evidence.[30]

At home, my wife followed the story. She read the *Los Angeles Times*.

By the time October 2017 wrapped up, I had accepted that this wasn't the job I had hoped it would be. But, on the home front, things were great. My wife and I had purchased a three-bedroom house we liked. My salary allowed us to live off one income, which we never could have done in northern California. Our daughter thrived with her mother's attention. They spent their days at the park or the library, playing and reading. My wife, who makes friends easily, soon had a packed schedule of playdates and a phone book full of mom friends. Sure, I was discouraged by the newspaper's leadership, but otherwise the move to Las Vegas had been everything we had hoped for. My family was happy.

And whatever misgivings I might have had about the *Review-Journal*, I still had hope that I could find professional satisfaction through my research into sex trafficking. When I arrived at the paper, I began reading widely on the topic—government reports, academic studies, past news stories. From the beginning, I noticed two things. One, Las Vegas was frequently cited as a hub for sex trafficking, but it was rarely mentioned as a national leader in addressing the problem. Two, I found the news industry's depictions of sex trafficking victims and survivors to be two-dimensional and out of sync with the experts' analysis of them.

News stories, I saw, generally portrayed sex trafficking victims as characters in a Liam Neeson movie: generic women plucked off the streets and forced into the sex trade. Academic and government research, on the other hand, painted a far more nuanced picture. Experts reported that sex trafficking victims often experienced severe trauma long before they were ever sold to sex buyers.

I read about and later interviewed former prostitutes who were sexually abused as children, who lost their brother to homicide or their father to suicide, who bounced around in foster care placements or grew up in unstable, toxic, abusive families,[31] all before they ever thought about turning tricks. These were women anyone with an ounce of humanity would feel for. Yet, they'd throw on a tough and unappealing exterior, maybe pick up an attitude. Then they weren't perceived as sympathetic, which I thought was wrong.

As I learned more and more, I began to think of sex trafficking victims as some of the most marginalized people in the United States.

To begin my research locally, I filed a series of basic records requests with the Las Vegas police department, asking for soliciting arrest reports and closed sex trafficking investigative files. For a while, Metro sent me on a wild goose chase, claiming—incorrectly—that the district attorney's office maintained the arrest records. Then the department said it would be difficult to search by criminal categories, a claim I thought was ridiculous. After a couple of months of back and forth, it was clear the department was not interested in helping me. If I wanted records, I was in for a long fight.

Slowly, I began to develop sources. I reached out to local churches and Christian organizations, like the International Church of Las Vegas, Casa de Luz, and F.R.E.E. International, where the pastors worked with sex trafficking victims. I connected with national and international organizations, like Shared Hope International, the Human Trafficking Legal Center, and the Polaris Project,[32] the operator of the National

Human Trafficking Hotline. I spoke with therapists and the directors of women's charities, who specialized in helping sex trafficking survivors. I interviewed lawyers, anti-trafficking advocates, academics, and law enforcement personnel. And, eventually, tentatively, I started talking with the survivors themselves.

It was not easy. Almost everyone I tried to interview initially wanted nothing to do with me, especially when they heard I worked for the *Review-Journal*. But, as I showed them I had done my homework and wanted to explore the issue in all its shades of gray, some people—however reticently—started to open up. I was used to working with hesitant sources after my reporting on foster care. But this was a whole different animal. At least the folks involved with foster care typically had *something* they wanted to talk about, maybe anger over their children being taken away or exasperation with an unresponsive agency. People involved with sex trafficking, by contrast, had very little they *wanted* to talk about. I needed to build trust with my sources slowly and deliberately. This wasn't going to be a project I could finish quickly, I realized.

In the meantime, I decided to comb the local courts for cases against pimps and other traffickers. Luckily, there were dozens of files to review, with many including detailed police reports or witness statements. I spent weeks, on and off, reading the files, collecting stories about pimps and working girls, and learning about the tactics the Las Vegas police used to catch them both. Unfortunately, most of the cases didn't go to trial, which is where the best information was usually revealed. Over time, I began to get a sense of the pattern. The pimps and their defense lawyers would delay, delay, delay as long as they could, to see if the prosecutors could produce a victim. If they did, the pimp often would cop a plea.

Unlike a murder or rape case, which might turn on ballistic or DNA evidence, sex trafficking cases rely a lot on witnesses. ("No face, no case," as the Clark County prosecutors who handle sex trafficking cases used to say.) If the state could secure a credible victim to testify, pimps knew they were going down. But, as I had discovered, few people wanted to talk about this stuff.

The few cases that did go to trial were like gold mines. I spent hours poring over those files. One day, while reading through the trial transcripts of convicted pimp Robert Sharpe III, who was sentenced to life in prison, I came upon the testimony of a sex trafficking expert, a former Las Vegas Vice cop who had been called to testify by the district attorney. The transcript was enthralling. The witness spoke candidly, describing police strategies and the mindsets of pimps and prostitutes. Halfway through, I knew whoever this speaker was, I had to interview him. He could be the guru source investigative reporters are always looking for, the expert whose encyclopedic knowledge of a topic might shave months or even years off your research. I went to the front of the transcript to find out his name. It was Donald Hoier.

CHAPTER 13

Business

GEORGE KNAPP WAS JUST GETTING STARTED.[1] FOR ABOUT A YEAR AND a half,[2] he and the KLAS-TV I-Team steadily dribbled out stories about the FBI's investigation into Mally, Baughman, and alleged corruption in the Vice Section.

Knapp reported allegations made in court that Deputy District Attorney Liz Mercer—who married Baughman in the summer of 2016—"coached witnesses into giving exaggerated testimony" against pimps as part of "an ongoing criminal conspiracy" in which Baughman colluded with Mally to take down Mally's competitors in the Las Vegas sex trade. Knapp also reported that Arman Izadi's lawyers thought the charges against Izadi were dropped because of Baughman, a notion refuted by Don's conversation with Chief Deputy District Attorney Marc Schifalacqua, who was stymied by Izadi's work as a criminal informant. One segment featured interviews with Izadi and his lawyers who complained that he had been blackballed from the Las Vegas nightclub scene over a bunch of trumped-up charges. Knapp's stories portrayed him as a successful but harmless nightclub promoter who simply got swept up in Baughman and Mally's alleged corruption. "Izadi's life is ruined," Knapp said. To his credit, Knapp reported that "Izadi reluctantly entered a no contest plea to a single count of pandering," but he added that since the FBI was now looking into Baughman, "Izadi is talking to his lawyers about trying to change that deal."[3] (Izadi's deal was never renegotiated.)

Most of Knapp's stories focused on Ocean Fleming, Mally's ex-bodyguard, who Angela worked for briefly and who FBI agent Kevin

White spoke with as part of his investigation. In February 2017,[4] Fleming sought a new trial, claiming that he had been unfairly convicted because of Baughman's alleged misdeeds, among other things. Knapp reported that in court filings one of Fleming's attorneys, Janiece Marshall,[5] alleged Vice detectives working "under" Baughman regularly had sex with prostitutes who later became witnesses against defendants like Fleming. However, Baughman, a detective himself, never supervised anyone at Metro.

Knapp closely followed Fleming's motions and the police department's efforts to block Fleming's team from deposing Baughman and other current and former Vice officers. The department argued that Fleming's efforts essentially amounted to a fishing expedition.

The Clark County District Attorney's office had to recuse itself from the case because Mercer was implicated in the proceedings. Oddly, Adam Gill, who at that time was a defense attorney who sometimes represented pimps, was appointed special prosecutor.[6]

The courtroom drama stretched for months, as Fleming and the police department squabbled over the appeal. Eventually, Baughman was deposed, but he invoked his Fifth Amendment right more than four dozen times in less than an hour and a half. Baughman declined to answer pertinent inquiries into whether he ever received money from Mally or took his daughter to Mally's mansion. But he also refused to say if he had heard that the sheriff had told a TV station that the FBI was investigating the Vice Section or whether it was Baughman's policy as a Vice detective to interview anyone who may have witnessed a crime.

Baughman also avoided answering several questions about Mercer, invoking his Fifth Amendment right and his right not to testify against his spouse. This fueled speculation that Baughman and Mercer got married just to avoid having to testify against each other.

Fleming's attorneys made a transcript of the deposition public by including it in a court filing. Baughman's testimony was perceived by many as damning. But the transcript also made clear that his attorney had advised him not to answer any questions that might pertain to Fleming's case. (He was, after all, apparently still under an FBI investigation.)

Then Fleming's defense team dropped a bomb. It produced an affidavit from a prostitute who had testified against Fleming in 2012 as well as an affidavit from a former driver and bodyguard for Mally. The prostitute, Jessica Gruda,[7] said that Baughman scared her with photographs of injured women allegedly beaten up by Fleming and that Mercer coached her into testifying that Fleming had strangled her, which she now said didn't happen. Gruda also said that she had a sexual relationship with Baughman's partner on the Vice squad, Det. Al Beas, who had hosted Baughman's going-away party. Gruda said Beas gave her $400 and rented a car for her during their relationship. (Affidavits of a second prostitute who testified against Fleming, April Millard, were also produced at different times during Ocean's appeal. She said in a 2018 affidavit that she was similarly coached and coerced like Gruda. She also reported that she was working for and having sex with Mally when she testified against Fleming in August 2012.[8] In fact, Millard said that Mally stashed her on the East Coast after Fleming was arrested in the fall of 2011 and then then ordered her to return to Vegas to testify against him the following year.)

The most sensational affidavit, however, was the bodyguard's. Don Ramos said he worked for Mally from 2005 to 2016. Beginning in 2010, he said that Mally started meeting with Metro police officers, including Baughman, and giving them money. Ramos said the amounts varied, but he remembered one monthly payment of $10,000. Ramos also said that Mally provided information to the police about Fleming, and that Mally told him he helped Baughman land his book deals. Most startling was his claim that not only did Baughman take his teenage daughter to Mally's mansion multiple times, but that while she was hanging out in Mally's recording studio, Baughman would leave to have sex with prostitutes in the main house.[9]

Clark County District Court Judge Michael Villani[10] scheduled an evidentiary hearing for May 2018, when Fleming's defense team would get the chance to question what Knapp called "a parade of key witnesses" about the alleged corruption in Vice. Among those scheduled to testify were Don and Las Vegas Justice of the Peace Melanie Andress-Tobiasson. Judge Andress-Tobiasson's inclusion was eyebrow-raising and posed a potential conflict of interest. In April 2018, KLAS-TV broadcast an interview with the judge in which she complained that Vice cops failed to investigate tips she had given them about a store she alleged was connected to prostitution, and in particular a felon named Shane Valentine who had had contact with her teenage daughter.[11] Valentine was a person of interest in an unsolved October 2016 double murder and, according to Judge Andress-Tobiasson, also allegedly an associate of Mally.[12] Gill, the special prosecutor representing the state in Fleming's case, had previously represented Valentine as a defense attorney.[13]

When Don saw that the judge was with him on the list of witnesses set to testify, he thought the entire case had turned into a circus. *How can Gill prosecute this case if one of the witnesses is going to testify about one of his ex-clients?* Don wondered. *This is like something out of a movie, it's so ridiculous.* But in a meeting with Metro's legal counsel, Don learned the department was gung-ho to move forward with the hearing. Metro's private attorneys felt Fleming couldn't make a case, that the witnesses behind the blockbuster affidavits wouldn't show. At the same meeting, Don also was told, definitively, that Baughman took the $5,000 from Mally after he had left Metro, not while he was still a cop. Baughman had jeopardized scores of criminal cases by taking that loan, but he had committed no crime.

Don braced for a bizarre, scorched-earth hearing. But at the eleventh hour, Gill, the special prosecutor, offered Fleming a deal to drop twenty of the twenty-three charges for which he was convicted in 2012—if, in exchange, the pimp dropped his appeal. The deal, which Fleming accepted, ensured that Fleming would get out of prison much earlier and that his defense team would stop asking questions.[14]

Understandably, this fueled rampant speculation that the police were trying to conceal widespread corruption within Vice—even though the deal was negotiated by Gill, the special prosecutor, not Metro or the DA. Still, no one in authority, not Gill, the DA, or Sheriff Lombardo, offered any public explanation—and Mally's status as a criminal informant remained a secret. Las Vegas residents were left in the dark and confused about what had really happened.

About the only thing that was clear was that Fleming, one of the most violent pimps the Vice Section had ever busted, would soon be back on the streets.

I tried tracking down Don after I read that transcript from the Robert Sharpe III case, but I had no luck. Then, about a month after the state offered to drop Fleming's charges, I attended a court hearing and bumped into Don's wife, Dr. Shera Bradley. I told Bradley that I wanted to talk to Don and passed along my phone number. To my surprise, Don texted me a short while later and we met at Starbucks.

Don and I hit it off immediately. I liked his humility and his quiet confidence, which reminded me of my dad. He liked my earnestness and honesty. We talked a lot about football, both college and professional. As a Nebraska native, I'm a fan of the University of Nebraska's college football team (even though I didn't attend the school). As a Wisconsin native, Don is a huge Green Bay Packers fan. His home office is wallpapered with the framed jerseys of several Packer greats, including running back Ahman Green's. Green not only starred at Nebraska in college, but he also attended my high school in Omaha. Don and I had a lot to talk about.

We started having lunch weekly at his house on the southwest side of town. During our hours-long conversations, I'd pick his brain on police tactics for investigating pimps and prostitutes while he showed me his latest LEGO creations or home improvement projects. Invariably, Don would digress into stories about Mally and Fleming. It was clear from his tone they were a sore subject. Don's voice would harden as he'd wonder aloud why a snitch like Mally was taken seriously by anybody. He also told me, repeatedly, that he thought Knapp's stories were bogus and that the reporter was going to end up with egg on his face for broadcasting Fleming's claims.

I found Don's tales about Mally and Fleming fascinating—particularly that Mally was secretly a police informant—but I was hesitant to dive into a story that KLAS-TV had dominated for months. I couldn't imagine my editors would respond well if I pitched that. (As I understood it, they wanted me to pursue original ideas, not follow anyone else's reporting.) Besides, Don wasn't going to go on the record because the case was still ongoing. So instead, I concentrated on asking Don about police procedures and record-keeping practices, and about the realities of the pimp game.

With Don's help, I began fleshing out several major investigative stories about sex trafficking for the *Review-Journal*. Each story addressed a different angle of sex trafficking in Nevada, while also humanizing victims and survivors through what I hoped would be a nuanced retelling of their personal stories.

One of the stories we talked about would look at Clark County's practice of locking up minors arrested for prostitution-related offenses in juvenile jail, even though state law defined any minor engaged in prostitution as a sex trafficking victim by default.[15] Long before I met Don, I had started researching this topic by regularly attending a special Wednesday court dedicated to these cases. Every week, teen sex trafficking victims were held in juvie while other minors charged with seemingly more serious crimes, like auto burglary, never saw the inside of a cell. Adding insult to injury, these state-defined victims, like all juvenile detainees, were shackled when they were transported outside of juvenile hall.

It seemed pretty black and white to me: this practice was wrong. Barbaric even. But Don saw the issue in a million shades of gray. He explained that locking up so-called child prostitutes was literally the only surefire, legal way the county had to keep them away from their manipulative pimps. He didn't *like* that the girls were being housed with other detainees, he didn't *like* that they were being shackled, he didn't *like* that they were being charged with crimes. But given a choice between that or seeing them under the control of an abusive trafficker? Seeing a girl as young as fourteen or fifteen stay in the clutches of The Game for even a day longer? He much preferred the former, especially given that his experience had shown him that the longer a trafficking victim was isolated from her trafficker, the more likely she would start to see through his brainwashing. He and I had long discussions about policy changes the county could make to avoid stigmatizing the girls while still breaking the invisible chains of their pimps.

Another story we discussed at length was the potential for illegal sex trafficking in Nevada's legal brothels. I spoke with some ex-brothel workers who described some pretty exploitive working conditions, and I learned oversight of at least some of the facilities in the rural counties was weak and unsophisticated—that is, unprepared to manage the nuanced issues inherent to regulating sex work. Don told me about encounters he had had with brothel workers hanging around The Strip with paying clients. That seemed to him to be a violation of Nevada law, which says legal sex work is restricted to a brothel's premises. Don told me in his experience sex workers are all "wallowing in the same mud hole," whether they're working in a brothel or a strip club or on the streets or in a casino. Exploitation and coercion can happen anywhere in the sex trade, he believed, regardless of legality. He gave me some ideas for trying to root out brothel workers who were under pimp control.

But perhaps the story we talked about the most was Metro's enforcement of prostitution laws on The Strip. After many months of fighting with the police department over my initial records requests, I was pleasantly surprised when the paper filed a lawsuit on my behalf. After the suit was filed in late May 2018,[16] Metro slowly began trickling out soliciting arrest reports to me. The reports were typically only a few pages, but they included some critical information: the name and gender of the arrestee as well as the location and details of the arrest. I realized that if I could aggregate the information, I could create a picture of who Metro was arresting for prostitution and where. But some of the reports were filled in by hand, while others were typed out. There was no good way I could figure out how to automate the data collection.

So, for several weeks I entered the information, by hand, into a massive Excel spreadsheet. I logged thousands of soliciting arrests in all of Clark County, from 2015 and 2016. When I ran the numbers, I was shocked: hundreds and hundreds of prostitutes were arrested on The Strip, but only dozens of johns.[17] I was stunned by the huge discrepancy. If Metro wanted to stop illegal prostitution, wouldn't it want to target buyers and sellers equally?

When I asked Don why Metro was arresting prostitutes far more than johns, he didn't blink. *Vice detectives believed there was an unwritten rule against arresting johns in Strip casinos*, he said, although they never were explicitly discouraged.

What? Why?

The casinos don't want their customers getting arrested. It's bad for business.

Don told me a story about arresting johns at a prominent casino and taking them to the security office as he would a prostitute. He said he was later confronted by the casino's security director, who threatened to deny resources for future Vice operations (such as hotel rooms for undercover stings) if that happened again.

Don was so frustrated by what he viewed as a taboo against arresting johns that his boss at Vice once encouraged him to ask an undersheriff in an open meeting in 2006 about the department's willingness to arrest them on The Strip.[18] The undersheriff danced around the question without ever really telling Don if the department supported such arrests.[19]

I couldn't imagine this had ever been explicitly spelled out in a document, or that anyone in Metro's executive offices would ever admit it. *How can I prove this?*, I asked Don.

Don thought it might be hard to prove, but not impossible. He suggested I talk to Bill Young, who served as Las Vegas Metro Sheriff from January 2003 to January 2007 and then became vice president of security for the Station Casinos, a company that operates a chain of ubiquitous off-Strip casinos in Vegas. He also served as a lieutenant over Vice in the 1990s. Don knew Young to be a straight shooter. *Bill might talk about it*, Don said.

I interviewed Young a couple of times, in late December 2018 and in mid-January 2019, at the Red Rock Resort, the crown jewel of the Station Casinos holdings, crystal-encrusted property in northwest Las Vegas. Young was forever chatty. He talked glowingly about his bosses, the Fertitta family,[20] the majority owners of Station Casinos, and about his former protégé, the then–Clark County Sheriff, Joe Lombardo.

I was apprehensive to ask him about the discrepancy of john arrests on The Strip, but he didn't seem bothered whenever I brought it up. Young said that the casinos didn't explicitly instruct cops not to arrest johns, but he admitted that the casinos hated it when they did and that arresting johns hurt the Vegas economy and its reputation with tourists. (Sin City's motto, of course, is "What happens in Vegas stays in Vegas." If police started arresting johns on The Strip, it'd be more like, "What happens in Vegas can land you in jail and get you divorced." That's not as snappy as a sales pitch.) Young said he wouldn't recommend any "hard-core, heavy-duty policing" of The Strip and that when he ran the Vice squad and when he was sheriff, he didn't let officers actively arrest tourists soliciting prostitutes.

"All you're doing is humiliating them," he said.[21]

CHAPTER 14

Broken Glass

AROUND THE END OF 2018, THE INVESTIGATIVE EDITOR TOLD ME THE top editors of the *Review-Journal* felt my research into sex trafficking was taking too long.[1]

By then, I had witnessed dozens of court hearings; conducted untold hours of interviews with survivors, government officials, anti-trafficking advocates, and other sources; amassed tens of thousands of pages of court records, police reports, studies, and other documents; and analyzed seemingly endless rows of data. I had a lot of good material, both quantitative and qualitative. But there were still some critical components missing from each of the stories I was pursuing.

For the story about soliciting arrests on The Strip, we were still waiting on loads of records from Metro. Getting anything out of the department was like pulling teeth. In an August 2018 hearing about our lawsuit, Clark County District Court Judge Joe Hardy Jr. said that it was "clear that Metro has not complied or even come close to compliance" with the state's public records laws, adding that the department's recalcitrant response to my records requests "boggles the mind."[2] To anyone paying attention, this should have hardly come as a surprise. In the wake of the October 1, 2017, mass shooting at Mandalay Bay, national news organizations, including the Associated Press, *New York Times*, the *Washington Post*, and the *Los Angeles Times*, sued Metro for failing to fulfill records requests. At the rate Metro was dripping out soliciting arrest reports to me, it would be a long while before I had three years of data—and I wasn't even sure that would be enough to really pin down the department's pattern of ignoring johns.

As for my inquiry into alleged illegal sex trafficking through Nevada's brothels, I had made a major breakthrough when I connected with T. J. Moore, the former madam of both the Love Ranch South and Alien Cathouse brothels near Pahrump, Nevada, about an hour west of Las Vegas.[3] The brothels Moore worked at were owned by Dennis Hof, who became famous through the HBO reality TV show *Cathouse,* about the Moonlite Bunny Ranch in Carson City in northern Nevada. For a time, Moore oversaw Hof's operations in southern Nevada; she was one of the people who found NBA star Lamar Odom when he overdosed on drugs at the Love Ranch South in October 2015 and in the days afterward she had done a lot of interviews with the news media. But Moore told me she became disgusted with the business after she saw how much Hof seemed to enjoy all the attention Odom's personal problems were bringing him and his brothels. She quit working for Hof[4] in December 2015 and told me she was willing to speak out about the "bad" things she had seen.

Moore told me she knew some women working in her brothels were being trafficked by pimps. She told me about a Las Vegas pimp who had two girls in the Love Ranch South; he would regularly come by the brothel to pick up their earnings. The only problem was there was no way to prove it unless women were willing to talk—and despite Moore's best efforts she couldn't find anyone to talk to me. So, while she tried to work her charm, I requested brothel work cards from the counties where brothels were legal and sent personal letters to every ex-brothel worker I could find, asking them if they'd be willing to talk to me about their experiences in the business. I hoped one of them would not only say yes but admit to being trafficked.

The most frustrating story, however, was the one on juvenile sex trafficking victims. From attending so many juvenile court hearings, I knew how the system worked in Clark County, and I had conducted many hours of in-depth interviews with not only several underage trafficking victims but also their parents about the way they were treated by the criminal justice system. I had collected some great anecdotes about the conditions the girls lived under in juvenile hall and about how they were treated by officers of Clark County Department of Juvenile Justice Services after they were put on probation. I could document in vivid detail how Clark County was failing them.

But there was one critical piece of information I still needed: data on how long girls charged with solicitation spent in juvie compared to all other juvenile offenders. I knew from attending all those hearings that this population typically spent a long time in juvenile hall, several days or weeks. A former public defender for the girls told me that girls charged with soliciting were easily among the detainees who spent the most time in juvie. But I couldn't prove that without obtaining the incarceration data from Juvenile Justice Services—and the department steadfastly refused to give it to me, saying "any information regarding juveniles is confidential and cannot be released," even information so heavily redacted you could never identify individual children.

For months, I talked with people in Clark County government, trying to pry loose the data, to no avail. Then I hit on a novel strategy for getting the information. The juvenile court judge who ran the special weekly calendar for sexually exploited youth had tried for years to get the county to build a special housing facility just for underage trafficking victims, to keep the girls out of juvie and to show them that the county really didn't consider them to be criminals. But county leaders had repeatedly rejected his pleas for money for a separate facility. So, the judge was always looking to partner with academics to show how Clark County's system didn't have the resources necessary to treat these girls fairly. I knew a group of data journalists with a university. Working together, the judge and I made a plan where he'd inform Juvenile Justice Services that he was partnering with the university on a study of juvenile incarceration rates. The data journalists would work with me as a reporting partner; they'd analyze the incarceration data and provide results for me to use in the *Review-Journal*. The arrangement was complicated, but the judge thought it would work—eventually. Juvenile Justice Services, like Metro, was slow to respond to requests, and there was only so much pushing the judge could do. The data, after all, wasn't his.

The investigative editor knew all about these obstacles I was facing in my sex trafficking research, which I conducted while I did other stories.

Earlier in 2018, I published a big investigation into serious problems with the Nevada secretary of state's business registration system and similar problems in other states.[5] But the editors didn't seem to care. I offered to tackle another, smaller sex trafficking project, but the investigative editor told me that wasn't an option.

She didn't tell me to stop. She didn't give me any directions at all. So, I just hunkered down and kept reporting.

One day, the investigative editor asked me to analyze my big spreadsheet of soliciting arrests to account for where prostitutes were being arrested on the Las Vegas Strip. I learned this was a bad idea because Don told me that the exact location where a prostitute was arrested wasn't indicative of where she might actually have been working, at least on The Strip.[6] Undercover Vice officers might meet a prostitute at one casino or on Las Vegas Boulevard, but then walk with her to another Strip hotel where more Vice officers were based to arrest her. The data I had could only differentiate between soliciting arrests made on or off The Strip, or in other locations, like massage parlors or strip clubs. But I wasn't in much of a position to argue, so I ran the analysis.

Oh shit.

The data suggested that the top hotel location where prostitutes were being arrested was the Venetian—the casino owned by Las Vegas Sands and its chief executive Sheldon Adelson, the *Review-Journal's* owner. I wondered if this would create a conflict of interest for my editors.

But it seemed like I was skating on thin ice; I couldn't afford to ignore my supervisor's request. So, I turned in a memo with my findings, along with a detailed note about how prostitutes may be picked up at one hotel but arrested at another. Days went by and I heard nothing more about it, other than an offhanded comment from the new managing editor, who remarked to me in a meeting that the worst place for prostitution on The Strip was owned by our employer.[7]

For Sunshine Week 2019—an annual, nationwide journalism initiative held in mid-March that promotes the importance of access to public records[8]—I was asked to write a story about the newspaper's lawsuit with

Metro over sex trafficking records. *Gladly*, I said, figuring it might take some heat off me.

The story was a simple regurgitation of what we had already reported about our ongoing legal struggle to obtain basic records from Metro. But it included fresh quotes from the *R-J*'s executive editor extoling not only the virtues of public records but also the importance of investigating the police's handling of sex trafficking cases.

"It's important for Nevadans to understand that in many other states, these kinds of records are available to anyone and everyone, no questions asked," the editor said in the story. "It should be the same in Nevada, but Metro takes the position that the public doesn't need to know how it enforces laws intended to combat a growing national problem with devastating consequences for young victims."[9]

Maybe they still support this project after all, I thought.[10]

Any goodwill that the Sunshine Week story might have engendered didn't last long, because a short while later the investigative editor demanded that I draft a story based on the research I already had in hand. *Do the juvenile one*, she told me. *OK*, I said. *I can draft something without the incarceration data.* But I still needed some direction from her on how we were going to handle the identification of underage victims.

When I had started my reporting, in early 2017, I had assumed victims and survivors (no matter their age) would know if they were safe revealing their identities to the public (if they wanted to, of course). But after I learned more about the prostitution subculture, I discovered that any prostitute who speaks out can sometimes become the target of violence from random pimps she doesn't even know. That made me leery about naming underage victims in particular, which I had always understood my editor wanted me to at least try to do.

I asked the investigative editor how the paper intended to address this potentially huge safety problem. *We're just going to have to figure it out ourselves*, she told me, implying she and I would discuss it without input from upper management.

But I never got the guidance I was looking for. I ultimately was left to figure it out on my own.

With another pit in my stomach, I spent several days putting together a draft of the juvenile story, relying on my in-depth interviews and observations from the hearings I had attended. It had a lot of holes, but I thought it showed a nuanced understanding of the issue and portrayed the unjust treatment juvenile sex trafficking victims face in Clark County's justice system.

On my own, I decided the responsible thing to do, for the time being at least, would be to leave all underage sex trafficking victims unnamed in the story—even one who was trafficked while she was a minor but was now, at the time of my drafting, 19 years old.

Without clear direction from any editor, I had not moved to make any final decisions with my sources on how they'd like to be named in print.[11] I figured I could always discuss it more with the editors later after they read my draft.

I turned in the long draft and again got radio silence. Not knowing what else to do, I went back to reporting. At one point, I heard back from one of the letters I had sent to an ex-brothel worker. She was willing to talk to me. We spoke for an hour on the phone on April 10, 2019. She was the brothel worker I had been desperately searching for. The woman, twenty-five, told me that she had been illegally trafficked through three legal brothels in Elko County, in northern Nevada, by her physically abusive husband who brainwashed her into making money to feed his drug addiction. When we hung up, I breathed a sigh of relief. *I got it*, I thought *The bosses will be pleased.*

I stood up from my desk and went to get some ice from the cafeteria. On the way, the top editor poked his head out of his office and motioned for me to come in. The editor of the *Review-Journal* rarely talked to me (at least substantively). One of the few times I had spoken with him since the turn of the new year had been just the previous week, when he congratulated me on my secretary of state's office investigation taking first place for business and financial reporting in the Best of the West journalism contest.[12] *That's a big one*, he had told me, obviously pleased.[13] So, I was unprepared when I sat down and he said, *I'm sorry to say, but today will be your last day at the Review-Journal.*

The editor said he had no faith that my sex trafficking research would ever be finished. He also expressed disappointment that I didn't name the juvenile victims in my draft. That was the only explanation I was given for why I was being fired.[14] I started to protest, but a human resources representative cut me short, saying, *The decision has already been made.*[15] The editor escorted me from the building.

Take care, he said as he ushered me out the door.[16]

Part V

CHAPTER 15

Traveling Light

AFTER SHE WAS ARRESTED ON THE NIGHT OF THE DE LA HOYA-MAY-weather fight in 2007, Angela was held at the Clark County Detention Center (CCDC) on a fugitive warrant out of Texas.[1] She was wanted because she had failed to abide by the terms of her probation, which stemmed from her drug-dealing conviction. By then, of course, Angela had cycled through CCDC before. But her stay this time was unlike any of her previous experiences. For the first time, she was taken upstairs, where the cellblocks and common rooms were reserved for longer-term inmates. There Angela frittered away her long, changeless days, hanging out with three incarcerated prostitutes, seasoned escorts who were totally reliant on their pimps. Angela was struck by how beautiful each of the women were, yet they seemed incapable of feeling love. Angela felt sorry for them.

At CCDC, Angela faced a choice on whether to challenge her extradition to the Lone Star State. Had she chosen to fight it, she could have been held in the jail for ninety days. But instead, she waived her right to an extradition hearing, which gave the state of Texas only twenty-five days to pick her up.[2] Angela imagined that her extradition would be a low priority for Texas, and it seemed she was right. When twenty-five days had passed and nobody from the state of Texas had arrived to pick her up, the Las Vegas Metropolitan Police Department was forced to let her go in late spring 2007.

By the time she was released, Angela had grown disillusioned with Mally. Where was his dream team of lawyers? But she wasn't anywhere near ready to leave The Life or his network. She was addicted to the money. (Or at least *earning* lots of money. Even if she couldn't keep the cash she raked in, it was a rush to know she could make so much.[3]) She couldn't imagine any other way to live.

When she got out, Mally spoke with her on the phone and said Las Vegas was "too hot" for her now, that there was no way she could continue working there. Angela couldn't disagree; she doubted she'd ever be able to beat a fugitive warrant hold again. (She felt Texas's failure to pick her up was a lucky break.) Taking the tone of a wise father telling his daughter that she needed to change schools because she was getting into too much trouble, Mally told Angela that she would have to take her services on the road to avoid the Las Vegas police. Angela couldn't deny the logic, but she also knew people were telling Mally that she was out of pocket, a loose cannon. He probably was worried that she would choose up with another pimp and he'd lose a source of revenue. Sending her on the road seemed like Mally's way of keeping his hooks into her. It was another manipulation that Angela acquiesced to.

So began her introduction to Mally's national operations, which required Angela to bounce from city to city, servicing non–Las Vegas clients who connected with the escort service through its host of websites. Angela knew Mally maintained some kind of presence on the web— remember, she initially connected with his network when she found the online ad for Dallas Top 10. After she started working for him in Vegas, she'd sometimes ask clients how they found her, and they'd often point to a website. But once she started working for his "roadshow," Angela saw just how expansive Mally's online operations truly were.

Mally had a lot of websites, with names like CityOfPink.com, where he'd advertise his "hos" to johns across the nation. He also spent tens of thousands of dollars further advertising his service on sites such as Backpage and Eros in major cities in the United States. Mally had a particularly close relationship with Eros, an online guide of escorts across the country. Mally told Angela he spent so much money advertising with Eros that the company once bought him a flat-screen TV as thanks.

Mally sent Angela all over the country—New York, New Jersey, Chicago, Boston, Washington, DC. Initially, he put her up in fancy hotels.

Later, he purchased apartments for his flock of traveling prostitutes to use in Chicago and Boston. When she was on the road, Angela never stopped working. She'd log sixteen hours a day. And she was constantly on the move, flying from one city to another. Sometimes, Angela, Mally, and his lieutenants would sketch out a travel schedule for her, but it was always subject to change. Demand dictated where she would go and when. Between Mally's long list of websites and the numerous ads he regularly posted across the country, he and his lieutenants could see, in near-real time, where the demand for sex was highest in the country and move his "hos" accordingly. It was grueling—and the working conditions were often cruel.

Once, when Angela was working in Chicago, she got a bacterial infection that made it painful for her to have intercourse. She begged her primary handler Tia, the woman who initially recruited her into Mally's network, to let her see a doctor. Tia made her wait a week—and the whole time she waited Tia insisted Angela keep sleeping with clients. On another trip to Chicago, Angela had to beg Tia for a jacket; it was cold and all she had was a sweater. During that trip, Angela was staying at a swanky hotel. But she didn't have the basic clothing necessary for the season. People looked at her like she was nuts. No one thought to ask if something was wrong or if she needed help. It was one of the countless instances in Angela's life when the people around her missed a warning sign of sex trafficking—in this case, a young woman checking into a nice hotel without the proper clothing. Angela ultimately got a coat, but only after Mally's crew thought she had earned it.

While she was traveling, Angela talked to Mally every two to three days and texted him daily. Her biggest responsibility, however, was making her daily drops into the escort service's bank accounts. When she worked in Vegas, drops were easy. She just handed her earnings over after a date or encounter with a client. But she couldn't do that when she was on the road. For an average pimp, this would be a serious problem, both from a logistics and reliability perspective. With multiple women working far away from him, how could Mally ensure that they turned over their money? As usual, Mally found an elegant solution: he assigned each of his traveling escorts a number.

Angela's number was seven initially, then later fifty-two. Whenever she would deposit her daily earnings into Mally's Wells Fargo or Bank of America accounts, she was instructed to deposit the total amount she earned that day plus 7 (or 52) cents. So, if she made $2,500 one day, she would deposit $2,500.07 (or $2,500.52).[4] In this way, Mally quickly could scan his deposits and see whether each of his traveling "hos" had made their daily drops. It was a clever and inexpensive solution to what otherwise could have been an obstacle to running prostitutes all over the country. Mally's scheme relied heavily on the power of his manipulations, on the strength of the invisible chains he used to make Angela and the other traveling women do as they were told, even when they were hundreds of miles away. It was a testament to his control over the women that he made the system work.

Angela lived on the road in this way for about five months, until October 23, 2007, when Tia sent her out on a call in Chicago and the john turned out to be an undercover cop.[5] The officer arranged the date through an ad on Eros-Chicago.com, which showed a photograph of a naked woman available in the downtown area who "loved meeting generous men for an hour or the night." The officer called the number in the ad and a woman on the phone said he could receive full service for $500 at an apartment about twenty minutes south of Wrigley Field. At about 3:30 p.m., Angela buzzed the cop up to the fourth floor, where she greeted him in a short dress and promised, "We're going to have fun here." The cop told Angela, who identified herself as "Makenna," that he was expecting to meet a blonde woman. Angela played it off and again reiterated that they were "going to have a lot of fun here." The cop handed her $500—then called for backup. Chicago Police found the apartment devoid of food or clothes. Angela told them her "agency" took care of the place and had a cleaning service; she was staying at the nearby Westin hotel. Angela told the cops she was surprised to be arrested by an undercover officer, saying her agency was supposed to screen customers. "What type of questions were used in the screening process," she asked them, "because evidently the screening process failed."

Angela told them everything about her fugitive warrant from Texas, figuring if she tried to bullshit them the outcome would just be worse.

The cops took her to a Subway and bought her a sandwich; they felt sorry for her. But inside Angela felt relief. The night before she was arrested, she had prayed to God for help for the first time in a long, long while. The arrest felt like an answer to her prayers.

At the Cook County jail, Angela called her mom, who got Mally onto a three-way call. Angela said Mally could have paid $10,000 to get her out right then, but he said he was too hot with the feds and that she'd have to wait for his help until she got transferred to Texas. He assured her his dream team of lawyers would soon be activated.

Later, Angela was extradited to Texas in the "ho clothes" she was wearing when she was arrested. On the plane, the cops escorting her let her order a Bloody Mary, because they knew she'd be going to prison for a while.

Angela spent about a year in custody, most of it at a state prison in Gatesville, Texas, about two hours north of Austin. There, she worked at a ranch, tending to crops and hogs. Angela found the environment peaceful, a welcome respite from her life as a prostitute. But still she tried to stay in contact with Mally and his crew. Mally kept telling Angela's mom that he was going to send her $7,000, but it never came. Neither did his dream team of lawyers.

One day, Angela wrote Mally a letter from prison. She didn't ask him for anything. She was just lonely and wanted to connect with a friend. Her letter was returned unopened.

CHAPTER 16

Bad Dreams

ANGELA WAS PAROLED FROM THE TEXAS PRISON SYSTEM IN NOVEMBER 2008.[1] When she got out, Tia contacted her and apologized for sending her on a call with an undercover cop. Tia asked her to return as a Priority Girl. Angela was desperate for money with the holidays coming up, and unsure of what to do next, so she agreed and hopped on a plane headed east.

For the next several weeks, she resumed her old roadshow routine, bouncing from city to city, serving clients. One day she caught an apparent rerun of a Diane Sawyer special, "20/20 Prostitution in America: Working Girls Speak."[2] That was the first time that she had ever heard the term "sex trafficking." For years, she'd get high with her prostitute friends and tell them they were all being sold a load of bullshit. Her friends thought she was joking, but she had been serious; she really did think they had been brainwashed or something by their pimps. Sawyer's program not only confirmed her suspicions, it also finally gave her the words to describe what she had experienced her entire adult life. *That's me*, she thought, when the program talked about sex trafficking victims.

The show inspired Angela to try to seek help. She learned of Christopher Baughman and tracked down his number in Las Vegas to report Mally, but she says he never called her back. She also tried contacting the Polaris Project (now known as just Polaris), one of the nation's leading anti-trafficking nonprofits. But she never heard back from them either. Experts often cite a statistic that says it can take sex trafficking victims as many as seven tries before they successfully leave The Game. Those calls might have qualified as Angela's first attempts.

Angela kept traveling for Mally late into December 2008. She wanted to go back to Houston for Christmas, but once again he kept using his heritage as a Muslim as an excuse for her to keep working. At the last minute he relented, and Angela flew home from Boston on Christmas Eve.

By then, Angela was fed up with life as a Priority Girl. She decided she was done with it and, for a while at least, ignored calls from people in Mally's network.

But she wasn't out of The Life. Not yet. Her relationship with prostitution and Mally would continue for many more years to come.

In the summer of 2009, Angela moved with a friend to New York City. Since the beginning of that year, she had been working at a strip club in Texas and dabbling in prostitution, trying to get her shit together. She dated a couple of guys, but she came to realize they were losers, that she had poor choice in men. Everywhere she turned she seemed to bump into pimps. She thought a change of scenery would help.

In New York, she danced at a Sapphire strip club and worked as a renegade, landing dates through a variety of escort services, including Mally's. Tia always seemed to be metaphorically lurking around, checking up on her. Angela was bitter over how Mally had failed to come through with his dream team of lawyers. But his escort service was always good for a referral. So, out of necessity, she kept working with his crew, especially when she was short on money.

For a long while, Angela just sort of drifted. She became aware that Mally's mansion was raided in 2010, but she was under the impression that it wasn't that big a deal. She followed Ocean Fleming's trial from afar.

Angela occasionally traveled to Las Vegas and even stayed in touch with Mally directly, visiting him several times. At one point, she tried to get herself cast on a reality TV show, *The Real Mistresses of Atlanta*, which never got off the ground. Mally let her film her casting video from his mansion—it would make a memorable backdrop. While she was there, Mally peppered Angela with questions about Fleming and other prominent Las Vegas pimps like Big Will and Big Mike. His questions were not subtle. *Do you know their addresses?* he'd ask. Angela thought it was weird.[3]

Over the winter of 2013–2014, Angela grew fed up with New York's cold weather and decided to move back to Las Vegas. She figured she'd be safe moving back there because she was no longer interested in being around pimps. But once she returned to her old haunts, she got sucked right back into The Life. She danced at the Sapphire Las Vegas, making $800 on a bad night and $7,000 on a good one, and also continued working as an escort. She got herself a big party pad at Veer Towers, a twin, thirty-seven-story residential complex on The Strip, where a lot of her girlfriends would stay with her. Vegas was still as toxic as ever, but things generally were OK for Angela.

That is, until the FBI raided Mally's mansion in September 2014. Maybe because she was in town for this raid, it seemed like a huge deal to Angela. She figured everyone she knew was going to get arrested. Rumors were flying around like crazy on the street. It was like a bomb had gone off in her world and it was only a matter of time until they were all locked up. The whole thing freaked Angela out. But it wasn't enough to drive her out of The Life.

In fact, Angela found herself fading away from stripping and back more heavily into prostitution. She tried to remain a renegade, but most of the girls working for escort services had pimps and they were always recruiting. She talked to a pimp and decided to give him a try. He had her move from Veer Towers into a mansion in Summerlin, a Las Vegas planned community. But her stint with the guy was short-lived. They parted ways after some of his other girls jumped her near the Hard Rock Hotel and Casino and she had to get staples in her head.

That's when an acquaintance introduced her to Tyree Wright,[4] the pimp who would change her life. In July 2015, Wright picked up Angela in his black Maserati with red interior and took her to a martini bar where they talked about their experiences in The Game.[5] Wright had a similar story to Angela. His dad was Kenny "Motherfucking" Red,[6] a violent, stone-cold "gorilla" pimp, who spent much of Wright's youth "cross-country pimping," driving his "hos" out of state in search of johns.

As Angela understood it, Red didn't show much interest in his son until he became good at football. Wright came off to Angela as a real "daddy's boy," desperate for his father's approval.

He told Angela, who was now thirty-one, that she had played The Game all wrong, that she had been working as a prostitute long enough that she should be poised to retire. He said if Angela stuck with him, they both could be on their way out of The Life in just a short while. Despite all her experiences with pimps and their empty promises, Angela bought it. She figured she'd give it another try.

For the next year and half, Angela worked for Wright, on and off. He started her off with a nightly quota of $1,500, then bumped her up to $2,500 when he saw she could earn. He was violent and aggressive with her. He yelled at her like a football coach and once beat up another girl in front of her at a Greens and Proteins restaurant. He also beat Angela, hitting her in the ribs, shoving her, kicking her to the floor, choking her, busting her lip open with a slap from the back of his hand. She'd work for him for a while, get upset at his behavior and leave, then come back.

At the end of December 2016, Wright called Angela and asked her for some money. His pimp father was reserving a table at Drai's for New Year's Eve and Wright wanted her to contribute to the cost of the reservation and come along. Angela "caught a date," gave Wright a few thousand bucks, and, reluctantly, went with him to the nightclub. But at the club, two new prostitutes working for Wright got into a fight over the pimp. So Wright made his party leave. At the valet stand, Wright got into Angela's face and started yelling. A Metro officer separated them and threatened to arrest Wright. To protect her pimp, Angela told the officer he was drunk and dealing with a family issue. Her plea worked; the cop let Wright go. But if Wright felt grateful, his behavior suggested otherwise. On the car ride home, he choked Angela so hard that she was pounding on the window for air.

That's when she had enough. She cut off communication with Wright, blocking his number and blocking his friends on social media. She moved her stuff into a friend's townhouse and tried to lay low.

On the morning of January 13, 2017 (a Friday), Angela ordered a Lyft to go to the Venetian. As she was getting ready to leave, she heard a knock on the door. She looked out and saw someone she understood to be Wright's cousin holding a bouquet of flowers. *Hi*, she said, opening the door. *I'm on my way out.* Suddenly, Wright charged around the corner, fast and low, holding a nightstick. Wright pushed Angela back into the townhouse, where the pimp proceeded to savagely beat Angela. Angela suffered a fractured skull;[7] her right arm and left hand were broken. A metal rod had to be inserted into the ring finger of her left hand. (Her finger is permanently deformed; she'll never be able to fully extend it.) Her body was black and blue, grotesquely bruised for weeks and she required facial reconstruction surgery. Angela said Wright robbed her of all her cash and left her bleeding, nearly dead, in the townhouse.[8] The Lyft driver she had called drove her to the hospital.

Wright didn't send anyone to the hospital to check on Angela, but she was visited by Don's old colleague on the Pandering Investigations Team, the one who told him about Kevin White's investigation. *Which one of Kenny Red's sons did this to you?* the detective asked Angela. The detective told Angela her beating was one of the worst the detective had ever seen. The detective was also surprised that Angela had managed to stay off of Vice's radar for so long.

Angela had never cooperated with the cops before, and after her arrests with Vic Vigna, she didn't exactly trust Las Vegas Vice. But she had prostitute friends with her when the detective came to visit, and they all agreed that the detective seemed like a good person.

On January 31, Angela testified before a grand jury for more than an hour, describing her relationship with Wright and how he beat her. Wright was indicted the following day on nine felony counts, including sex trafficking, living from the earnings of a prostitute, first-degree kidnapping, robbery, battery, and attempted murder.

The experience was the shakeup Angela needed. As she recovered from her injuries, she also set about remaking her life away from The Game. She got connected to advocates and counselors who held her hand and guided her through the laborious steps of rebuilding her life, brick by brick. Her recovery was as psychological as it was practical. She had to learn how to manage her own schedule, think for herself, cope with the panic that would rise in the back of her throat when she encountered something that triggered one of her traumatic memories from her life as a prostitute. She was like a patient recovering from a coma; she had to re-learn some of the most basic skills for living in American society. Her months-long recovery journey took her to several locales, including places in Texas and New York, and it involved loads of counseling, heartfelt conversations, and prayer. It took nearly dying for Angela to swear off prostitution for good. But with the help of a lot of patient people—particularly the folks at the New York organization Safe Horizon and a group of nuns she lived with for a period—she did it.

Prosecuting Wright was just as hard. Not long after he was indicted, the detective working with Angela called her upset. Angela said the detective told her Vice was being reorganized (apparently in the wake of the Mally scandal) and, while that happened, the detective was barred from working on Wright's case. Wright, however, was pushing for a speedy trial. The detective feared upheaval in Vice would cause the authorities to bungle the case. The detective promised to make it right, work on off hours to ensure that Wright didn't walk. But the detective was worried, and suggested that Angela file an internal affairs report complaining that the detective was being blocked from working on her case.

Angela filed the IA report, then called everyone in authority she could think of. *If Metro doesn't have the resources to do this case, then maybe you should handle it!* Angela told anyone who would listen. Somehow, Angela eventually got connected with someone at a domestic violence office within Nevada state government. The woman on the phone was appalled at what Angela told her. She promised to speak with a Metro captain.

The following week, the detective told Angela whomever she spoke with had raised so much hell that not only was the detective being allowed to work on the case again, but everyone on Vice was instructed to help, to ensure that it was finished in time. Wright pleaded guilty to three felonies—sex trafficking, second-degree kidnapping, and battery with a deadly weapon resulting in substantial bodily harm—and was given an aggregated sentence of nine to 29 years in state prison.

Angela got justice, but it felt like it could have slipped through her fingers with the apparent Mally-inspired reorganization. Mally could have ruined her life again.

All of the Lights

DESPITE ALL THE RUMORS SWIRLING AROUND HIM IN THE WAKE OF THE 2014 FBI raid, Mally maintained a relatively high profile, both in the hip-hop community, where he continued to work on records, and in the local news.[1] In May 2016, a fire broke out at his mansion, killing his female exotic cat Nyla and causing damages in excess of $1.6 million.[2] TMZ reported that Mally was "pissed" when Clark County's official Twitter account tweeted a picture of his dead exotic cat accompanied by "laughing so hard you cry" emojis.[3] The gossip site said the county deleted the tweet within minutes and apologized for using the "wrong emojis," apparently intending to use "crying" emojis instead. "Still, we're told Mally's furious and says it's totally insensitive and an invasion of his privacy," TMZ reported.

Just weeks before the fire, Mally began leasing a 7,312-square-foot, hilltop mansion in southern California for $15,000 a month. After the fire rendered his Las Vegas home "uninhabitable," according to a subsequent lawsuit, Mally relocated to this mansion in Encino, California, about forty minutes west of Los Angeles. About three years later, in April 2019, the Los Angeles Police Department and the California Department of Fish and Wildlife raided that mansion, as part of an investigation into human trafficking and the trafficking of exotic animals.[4] George Knapp reported on KLAS-TV that the raid "could be the tip of more significant legal troubles" for Mally,[5] but once again he wasn't arrested.[6] By then, his catalog of music had expanded to more than fifty-five released or leaked songs.

On October 21, 2019, the US Attorney's Office in Nevada published a press release[7] reporting that Mally had pleaded guilty to one count of using an interstate facility in aid of unlawful activity. The statement said that Mally had admitted to operating an unlawful prostitution business disguised as a legal escort service for more than twelve years. The eighteen-page plea agreement, filed that day in federal court, said that he had "persuaded, induced, enticed, and caused numerous women to engage in prostitution" and documented the interstate travel of seven of his victims.[8] Under the terms of the deal, Mally faced one to thirty-three months in prison, to be decided by a judge at a future sentencing hearing.

KLAS-TV apparently asked the US Attorney's office about claims that Mally was working with corrupt officers in Metro's Vice Section.[9] The US Attorney's office sent the station an additional statement:

> In the course of investigating Mr. Rashid, the U.S. Attorney's Office in partnership with the FBI did examine and develop information regarding allegations of related wrongdoing that generally have been the subject of media coverage. Following an extensive inquiry we concluded that there was not sufficient evidence to support any additional charges relating to Mr. Rashid, his associates or others, and therefore closed the investigation.

Don had suspected all along that there was nothing to the corruption allegations against Baughman and other Vice officers. Now that the investigation had ended with no charges, he appeared to have been right. And yet, because of those allegations, Ocean Fleming, Angela's violent ex-pimp, was scheduled to be released from prison at the beginning of 2020[10] and Vice's reputation had been dragged through the mud.

Don decided he couldn't remain quiet any longer.

By the time Mally pleaded guilty, I had been reduced to a quivering mass of nerves. After I was fired, I found a work-from-home job as an assistant to a businessman, beginning a long cycle of unsatisfying gigs, ranging from ghostwriting to hawking sponsorships to an online bartending school. The pay was a steep cut from what I had been making at the *Review-Journal.* I reached out to colleagues, but most were of no help. (That wasn't surprising; job prospects in journalism are grim these days.)

Every month, my wife and I worried if we'd be able to pay our mortgage. My wife looked into going back to work, and we talked about the possibility of having to move in with my parents in Nebraska. All the while, we tried to put on a happy face for our daughter, who had turned three years old shortly before I was fired.

The stress of our new reality exacerbated a long-simmering problem I'd had with anxiety. I didn't sleep well and I worried about my family's future. I also felt guilty for failing to finish my sex trafficking research. In the months after I was fired, I remember occasionally hearing from sources, including at least one working girl. They were just checking in or wanting to tell me something. But it felt like I was letting them down, or somehow failing sex trafficking victims in general, when I'd reveal I was no longer with the newspaper. It hurt whenever I was reminded that I hadn't finished the story.

I tried negotiating for the rights to take my research to another publication. I even inquired at one point about signing a severance agreement in exchange for it. The agreement, drafted by the paper when I was fired, included a nondisparagement clause, which would have prevented me from ever publicly discussing why I was fired.[11] But the newspaper steadfastly maintained the information I had uncovered was their property[12] and that it was not up for discussion.[13] So, I didn't sign anything with the paper, and I didn't know what to do. I was pretty sure the *R-J* couldn't stop me from pursuing research based on public records and interviews with sources I had developed. But given Sheldon Adelson's deep pockets and ability to bankrupt a journalist, an attorney I consulted with advised me to proceed with caution.

(The *Review-Journal* continued pursuing its lawsuit against Metro over my public records requests through April 2022—and even won a $150,000 settlement from the police department.[14] But it never published anything based on my research. In fact, the newspaper hasn't published any big investigations on sex trafficking since I was fired.[15])

Don and I remained in touch after I was canned. We texted occasionally about sports and got together a couple of times. He knew I was struggling and that I wanted to resurrect my research. The day after the US Attorney's office announced Mally's plea agreement, Don texted me. "I've been looking at the stories regarding the conclusion of the Jamal Rashid saga," he wrote. "Do you have any interest, at some point, in exploring the idea of collaborating on a book regarding this fiasco??"

I immediately grasped the implications of what he was suggesting. Mally's story wasn't one I had followed while I was at the *Review-Journal*, so the paper couldn't stand in my way if I wanted to write about it.[16] But the themes of his story were similar enough to what I was originally researching that I could still use it for my goal of humanizing sex trafficking victims.

Seeing that text, I felt a twinge of something I hadn't experienced in months: hope. But I also knew a book was a big commitment. And even if the paper couldn't stop me from pursuing this line of inquiry, I figured my former co-workers would still attack me the moment I published anything—to say nothing of the loads of criticism I would surely face from other corners.

Then I thought about a book I had read recently, *Man's Search for Meaning*, by the Austrian neurologist and Holocaust survivor Viktor Frankl. The book, about struggling to find meaning in one's pain, had given me some comfort in the days after my firing. I was reminded of a passage in the book where Frankl wrote that it doesn't matter what we expect from life, but rather what life expects from us:

> We needed to stop asking about the meaning of life, and instead to think of ourselves as those who were being questioned by life—daily and hourly. Our answer must consist, not in talk and meditation, but in right action and in right conduct. Life ultimately means taking the responsibility to find the right answer to its problems and to fulfill the tasks which it constantly sets for each individual.

I decided that Don's text was life's way of calling me to take up my sex trafficking research again, to use Mally's story as a vehicle to finish what I had started and hopefully help the world see trafficking victims and survivors in a more sympathetic light. I told Don I was interested in trying to write a book, with him serving as one of the main sources. In my spare moments when I wasn't trying to make money, I began researching Mally's case. After a little research, I realized that I knew an anti-trafficking lawyer in Reno who represented a woman who said she was trafficked by Mally.[17] That woman was Angela.

Angela and I spoke for the first time over the phone in November 2019. I explained to her that I was thinking about writing a book about Mally. She readily agreed to help. She told me she was planning to speak out against Mally at his sentencing hearing.

Soon, Angela and I fell into the same pattern Don and I had months before. We started talking weekly, at 11 a.m. on Wednesdays, when she'd tell me about her life and how she became a cog in Mally's giant sex machine.

In the months that followed, while I eked out a living, I also steeped myself in the twists and turns of Mally's saga. I began roughing out an outline of Don and Angela's narratives and where they intersected. I could see the makings of a compelling story—but, at the moment, it was a story without an ending. We needed to see what Mally's sentence would be: one month, thirty-three months or somewhere in between.

Initially, his sentencing was scheduled for three months after his plea agreement, in January 2020. But in late November, it was delayed until March 2020—and by then, the COVID-19 pandemic had hit. For about eighteen months, Mally remained out on his own recognizance, while his sentencing hearing kept being delayed. In July 2020, for example, Mally's lawyers asked for a delay because he was admitted to UCLA Medical Center for COVID-19 treatment.

Angela fumed whenever I told her about the latest postponement. *He's milking this*, she'd tell me. *He just wants to keep partying.* Indeed, during the pandemic, he filmed not one but two reality TV shows: *Poker After Dark* on the PokerGO streaming service, where he competed against poker pros and other celebrities, and *Marriage Boot Camp's* fourth "Hip Hop Edition" on WE TV, in which hip-hop couples work through their relationship troubles. The court also delayed his sentencing hearing so he could apparently finish shooting *Marriage Boot Camp*. At least fifty songs Mally worked on would be released or leaked between the date of his plea agreement and his eventual sentencing.

Angela held fast to the hope that Mally would be punished for his crimes. In July 2020, she was asked to write a victim impact statement for his sentencing hearing. She shared with me what she submitted to the judge, Gloria M. Navarro,[18] a heartfelt, two-page letter about the lasting impacts of Mally's manipulations. "This crime is only a fraction of what Mr. Rashid has done to victimize, coerce, manipulate, and brainwash myself and many other women to work for his illegal nationwide sex trade operations," she wrote. She explained that she was "given no choice on the hours" she worked and "was not allowed" to turn down any sex buyers Mally's network assigned her.

"Once I was given an employee number . . . at one point I was #7," she wrote. "When I would provide sexual services to multiple men in exchange for money I would be instructed to deposit the amount +7 cents to identify me. I was stripped of everything I knew and loved and turned into a professional trained sex worker. I no longer knew myself. Soon I felt like I was a robot sex slave to this man and his company, no more than employee #7."

Angela described how she had to "earn" her winter coat in Chicago and how she had to "beg to see a gynecologist after sexually serving so many clients." She told the judge that she wanted her to understand that "manipulation and coercion is much more dangerous" when it's perpetrated by people with means, like Mally, who "was always painting a pretty picture" of "luxury living," as though he were the "Hugh Hefner" of pimps.

"Today I suffer from PTSD and have a hard time trusting people," Angela wrote. "I live my life day to day not knowing when my PTSD will take control of my day. When I am overwhelmed with memories it makes me have panic attacks." She said she suffers because, unlike a street prostitute who is sold for fifteen minutes at a time, Mally sold his girls to clients for one to eight or more hours. "I have the worst memories of feeling owned by the sex buyer and pressured by Mr. Rashid's business to sexually please these disgusting men," she wrote. "I can't even enjoy a common family vacation because hotel room [sic] and lavish amenities remind me of being stripped of my dignity and forced to compromise my morals."

She closed her letter with a simple request: "Please consider my existence and the many other women he exploited when sentencing him for this crime because every soul counts!"

In September 2020, with the date of Mally's sentencing hearing still in flux, his defense team submitted its arguments for why Mally should only serve one month in prison. Their sentencing memo said Mally was "deeply remorseful and fully accepts responsibility" for his crime and had stopped pimping in September 2014 (after the FBI's raid). "Since that time (a period of approximately 6 years), Mr. Rashid has focused on his talent in the music industry and has produced music with numerous Grammy award winning artists."

The package included reference letters from music manager Gordon Dillard;[19] Cash M. Jones, aka Wack 100,[20] the loquacious CEO of the record label 100 ENT; Mally's recording partner Jason "Poo Bear" Boyd; and Nima Nasseri, then a manager at Roc Nation, the entertainment agency founded by JAY-Z. "We look forward to a long and successful relationship with Mr. Rashid and can assure the Court that if the Court in its discretion were to grant him the privilege of house arrest as part of his sentence his business activity with us will go uninterrupted," Nasseri wrote, using the exact wording that appeared in Wack 100 and Poo Bear's letters. "Mr. Rashid has been a pleasure to work with making amazing international Hit records we have yet to work with anyone that has been able to complete the musical tasks Mr. Rashid has." (Roc Nation later moved to have this letter stricken from the record.[21]) In all, Mally's defense team collected more than a dozen letters and videos from people attesting to his musical talent and good character.

Mally's sentencing memo also dug for sympathy for the defendant, noting he "had a tough upbringing with his mother abandoning him when he was six months old. Mr. Rashid's father was very strict and imposed 'heavy handed' discipline. As a result, Mr. Rashid was primarily raised by his grandmother. Mr. Rashid moved out of the house when he was approximately 16 to 17 years old." It also reported that Mally has three children—one of whom he didn't even know about until three years ago. "(W)hen Mr. Rashid learned that he had an adult son, he immediately took steps to be a part of his life." As almost an afterthought, the memo mentioned as well that Mally was at risk of re-infection from COVID-19 if he were sent to prison. His defense team was throwing everything against the wall to see what would stick.

Eight months later, when it became clear that Mally would be sentenced on May 13, 2021, the prosecution filed its own sentencing memo, arguing for thirty-three months in prison. The memo said Mally "employed hundreds of women as escorts" over at least twelve years as part of what became an "extensive, nationwide business" that earned him "millions of dollars." The US Attorney's Office concluded from the FBI's investigation that he "enticed . . . numerous victims to engage in prostitution, including approximately 35 Priority Girls." The memo said the FBI interviewed about forty women who worked for Mally from 2000 to 2014 as well as about fifty-five other witnesses who knew about his activities. "The brazen nature of the defendant's criminal conduct is highlighted by the fact that he continued to operate his prostitution business after LVMPD executed searched warrants on his business and residences," the memo said. "Defendant obviously believed he was above the law and continued operate [*sic*] and grow his illegal enterprise."

Considering the harm he inflicted on numerous women, the memo argued that thirty-three months was "more than reasonable."

For sex trafficking victims, facing your trafficker in court and saying in effect, *You did this to me*, can be a cathartic experience. It can also, alternatively, be traumatizing. Angela had already been through something similar once before, when she testified before a grand jury against Tyree Wright,[22] the pimp who nearly beat her to death. She found that difficult, but at least she didn't have to do it in front of Wright himself.

At one point, when it looked as though Mally's hearing was going to be held in 2020, Angela had a panic attack. But she was committed to seeing it through. She wanted to ensure that at least one of Mally's victims spoke at his sentencing hearing.

In fact, leading up to Mally's sentencing, Angela talked to me about what she wanted to wear while she made her statement. Because it was during the pandemic, she thought about getting a mask made that said "#MeToo" or maybe "Real men don't sell women."

On May 11, just two days before his hearing, the US Attorney's Office told Angela that it wouldn't pay to fly her to Las Vegas. *You can watch it online*, she was told. Angela was crushed. We traded a flurry of texts over those two days, both of us speculating that Mally was set to get off with a slap on the wrist. Angela was most concerned about a friend of hers, who had also been trafficked by Mally. Angela thought if Mally escaped justice again, her friend would be devastated.

On the morning of May 13, I arrived extra early at the federal Lloyd D. George Courthouse in downtown Las Vegas.[23] The courtroom administrator had told me there would be limited seating due to COVID-19 and, given what had happened with Angela, I figured I couldn't afford to be late. But Mally's hearing began promptly just after its scheduled 10 a.m. start time. There were only a handful of people in the audience, including reporters for KLAS-TV and the *Review-Journal*.

This was my first chance to see Mally in person. He was a big man, solidly built, but not as physically imposing as I would have expected. He wore a grey shirt with a skinny black tie, tattoos peeking out from behind his ears. I had looked at a lot of photos and videos of Mally by then, but something seemed different about him. Then I realized that in almost all of his public appearances, Mally wore sunglasses, big, thick, dark sunglasses that gave him the appearance of a boss. He looked lost without his shades, his eyes cautiously tracing the courtroom. At one point he locked eyes with me and nodded. (He had no reason to know who I was.) I held his stare until he turned away.

About fifteen minutes into the hearing, which began with a bunch of perfunctory introductions and housekeeping matters, I got an exasperated text from Angela. She said the FBI had contacted her five minutes before the hearing and said she could make a statement against Mally via video conference. Angela wasn't prepared, so she declined. But she felt awful. She watched the hearing on her phone from Houston.

When it came time to argue for the length of his sentence, the prosecution went first. "I feel, you know, a lot of pressure to convey to the Court what these victims have gone through, and a lot of it still affects them till this day," said the prosecutor, Nicholas Dickinson.[24] "So it's great Mr. Rashid stayed out of trouble for—you know, since 2014, for the most part, and it's great he has support, and it's great, you know, he can make a living. But the Court—this is a serious offense, and the Court needs to send a message." Dickinson said the victims in this case aren't just victims because the sentencing guidelines say they're victims—"They're victims by any stretch of the imagination."

Dickinson briefly told the story of two victims—one, who at nineteen years old flew to Las Vegas and ended up in the clutches of a violent pimp before she was picked up by Mally in his Bentley, and the other who thought she would be modeling when she went to work for him. "A lot of them feel let down by the criminal justice system," Dickinson said. "A lot of them in 2010 thought they could get out when there was some activity by the state. That didn't come to fruition. Then the FBI does the search warrants, and while the business might have shut down, this has taken a long time."

I was glad to see the prosecution focus on the human impact of Mally's misdeeds, but I was surprised by Dickinson's flat, matter-of-fact tone. I wondered if his words were having any influence on the judge.

I was also deeply disappointed when Dickinson later said no victims would be speaking. "We thought we might have one," he said, "but [FBI Special] Agent [Megan] Beckett's been in contact, so no additional victims."[25]

Next came Mally's defense attorney, David Chesnoff, who over the years has represented a litany of celebrity clients. "I want the Court to reflect upon the fact that he has accepted responsibility," Chesnoff said. "He is contrite. He made a point of expressing himself to everyone involved—the Court, the government who worked hard on this case, and—and the women—and let them know that he is truly accepting the fact that he engaged in conduct that he shouldn't have."

He said Mally had rehabilitated himself. "I understand that he's going to be incarcerated, and I understand the Court's sincere concern for the victims and the—what the court believes to be—and no one would argue some horrific facts," Chesnoff said. "We're not going to quarrel. But I would ask you to, in some way, mitigate the time of incarceration so that it sends the message that the Court wants to send, but by the same token, gives him a reward for straightening himself out and sends a message to him that your own self-rehabilitation is being rewarded, and that's the way you need to continue for the rest of your life."

Chesnoff's argument was much more impassioned than Dickinson's. But based on some of the judge's comments during their speeches, it sounded like Gloria Navarro sided with the prosecution.[26] She said Mally's work with a charitable organization serving teens in crisis made her "skin crawl." She even mentioned at one point that she had read that Mally's victims had to beg for permission to see a gynecologist or to buy a winter coat, apparent references to Angela's victim impact statement. Still, I honestly didn't know how she'd rule. I found myself holding my breath when it finally was her turn to deliver the sentence.

"It looks like you have made very positive steps to move in the direction of becoming a compliant law-abiding person in the community and—and not the monster that you've been in the past," she began. But she said the message she wanted to send was that "crime doesn't pay," and his plea agreement made clear that he managed an interstate, prostitution network for years. "You can't just say 'I'll stop now that I'm caught,' say 'I'm sorry,' be good for a little while, and everyone will forgive and forget. So you're hereby committed to the Bureau of Prisons for a term of thirty-three months."

Mally stood stoically as his sentence was delivered. As far as I could tell, he didn't react in any way. Later, I learned from Angela that she wept when she watched the judge give him thirty-three months.

Navarro gave Mally ninety days to get his affairs in order before he'd be required to turn himself in to the US Marshals Service on August 13, 2021.[27] "It might not feel like you got a break today," Navarro told Mally, "but I think you really did, because it's not a sex trafficking offense, you know, you're not registering as a sex trafficker or sex offender, and you're not doing 10, 15 years. It's—it probably doesn't feel right now like a break, but I think you did get a break. And if you don't take advantage of that, you're going to go away forever."

"Thank you, Your Honor," Mally replied in a muted voice. "You won't see me here again."

When Navarro adjourned, I followed Mally out of the courtroom. *Do you want to make a statement?* I asked as he walked with one of his attorneys toward the elevator. Mally looked over his shoulder at me, his eyes soft. He shook his head and walked away.

CHAPTER 18

No Answer

"It had the potential to be a much bigger story," George Knapp said of the Mally Mall scandal.[1] "But it kind of fizzled at the end."

Just a few days shy of his seventieth birthday, the white-haired investigative reporter met me for lunch at Doña Maria Tamales, a modest Mexican restaurant popular with locals just north of The Strip on Las Vegas Boulevard.[2] Knapp was one of a long list of people I wanted to talk to about Mally—and Knapp was more than happy to talk. I had come prepared with more than fifty questions typed out, but I hardly got to ask any of them. He started rambling almost from the moment he sat down.

I wanted to interview Knapp because his reporting on Mally and Baughman had helped shape the public's perception of Metro's Vice Section, the main law enforcement unit dedicated to combating Las Vegas's overwhelming sex trafficking problem. His stories had cast the section as shockingly corrupt, and the stain on its reputation had stuck. Las Vegas sex trafficking advocates distrust Vice, even years after Knapp's last story on the case was broadcast.[3] I thought Knapp needed to answer for that, especially because his reporting looked one-sided now that the feds had closed their investigation without charging anyone on the police force.

But Knapp didn't see it that way.

He defended KLAS-TV's coverage. He said that Baughman was "a dirty cop" who only got away with it because the powers that be in Sin City wanted the whole thing covered up. Mally's client list included lots of celebrities and other powerful people, he said. The "power structure" in

Vegas wouldn't want that to get out. "It's Las Vegas," he said. "It circles the wagons."

That's why the case fizzled, Knapp believed—it was a conspiracy—not because there wasn't enough evidence to back up the claims his sources made. Both Knapp and I had heard a grand jury had been empaneled to consider charging Baughman and other alleged corrupt cops. I asked Knapp, *If Baughman was a dirty cop, why wasn't he indicted?* After all, the standard for indictment is so low that a former New York state judge once famously said a prosecutor could get a grand jury to "indict a ham sandwich."

"Good question!" Knapp thundered in response. "You tell me!"

Knapp, understandably, wouldn't identify all of his sources, but he said they were a mix of pimps, prostitutes, and cops, including the sheriff at the time, Joe Lombardo, who Knapp said was his initial source, confirming the FBI's interest in Baughman. He declined to say whether Kevin White was a source of his but did say he met with White in person at least once, and that White tried to get intel *from him* during their interactions, particularly later in Knapp's reporting. "It was clear he was pumping me for information," Knapp said.

Knapp admitted that some of his cop sources seemed to resent Baughman for his outlandish self-promotional tactics. (Knapp himself said he thought Baughman was a braggart or a "hotdog.") He also acknowledged that his sources in general had "multiple motives" and "shifting alliances," which made him worried if he was getting the story right. But he said that when you hear the same things from multiple people, "you're confident your reporting is accurate." Besides, he said, he quoted a lot from public court records; under the law, journalists usually can't be held liable for false information if they quote from court records.

I tried several times to ask him whether he had considered if his sources had an incentive to stretch the truth or outright lie—perhaps due to their resentment of Baughman, or the involvement of criminal informants—but he brushed me off time and again. He made it clear that his standard for evidence for interviews was hearing the same allegation from multiple people.

Knapp bristled whenever I suggested that his reporting was incorrect. I asked him, for example, why he reported that there were Vice detectives working "under" Baughman when Baughman was never a supervisor. He shot back that while Karen Hughes led the entire Vice Section, Baughman headed up the Pandering Investigations Team. I told him that wasn't true, PIT was led by a sergeant (Don Hoier). Knapp didn't miss a beat. Well, he said, Baughman "portrayed" himself as the leader of the team, so the reporter stood behind that characterization. Other officers followed Baughman, he said. Baughman was the ringleader.

What troubled me the most, however, was Knapp's descriptions of two of his main subjects, the pimps Arman Izadi[4] and Ocean Fleming,[5] neither of whom agreed to be interviewed for this book. After his case, Izadi began a second career as a minor YouTube star alongside influencers Jake and Logan Paul,[6] and as keeper of a gaudy Las Vegas attraction, the Graffiti Mansion, which constantly changes its exterior paintjob. Knapp acknowledged that Izadi was a pimp, but insisted he wasn't violent, just more of a "party manager." Police records disagree on that point. Under a Nevada Public Records Request, I obtained hundreds of pages of documents from Metro about Izadi. They described allegations of him trying to force a woman into prostitution and prevent her from leaving his sight; becoming violent with men and women in various incidents; and threatening a front desk employee at his condo building as well as security at a nightclub.[7]

Fleming, Knapp acknowledged, was certainly a violent pimp. But the reporter expressed sympathy for him, nonetheless, calling him a "victim" in the whole Mally Mall ordeal. "He was done wrong," Knapp said. "It was wrong what happened to him." Fleming was released from prison in January 2020—then re-arrested less than two months later for suspicion of domestic battery by strangulation and burglary, but the charges were dropped because he had an alibi.[8]

Don shook his head when I later told him Knapp's perspective on Izadi and Fleming.[9] *Pimps can even manipulate the media*, he sighed.

As I tried requesting interviews, I found over and over again that George Knapp was the exception. Few people wanted to talk to me about Mally.

I tried contacting dozens of people connected to Mally in the entertainment industry, representatives of big-name musicians and his reality TV shows, little-known studio techs and producers. Hardly anyone even responded, let alone was willing to comment. The networks behind two of Mally's reality TV shows, VH1 (*Love & Hip Hop: Hollywood*) and WE TV (*Marriage Boot Camp*'s "Hip Hop Edition") declined to talk about Mally; representatives of PokerGO, the streaming service behind Mally's other reality TV show (*Poker After Dark*) never responded to requests for comment. Also failing to respond: representatives of Poo Bear and Justin Bieber. Drake's representatives declined to comment.

Shawn "Tubby" Holiday, Mally's former record executive roommate in Los Angeles, spoke with me briefly, saying he had no idea Mally was involved in sex trafficking when they were roommates. In fact, he said he rarely saw Mally in Los Angeles. Holiday said he also owned a house in Atlanta at the same time and said Mally was often in Las Vegas when he was in Los Angeles. But he said when they did get together Mally never had any girls with him. "I thought he had real estate investments," he said, after describing Mally's Vegas mansion as like a luxury resort, with a pool, a saltwater fish tank, and exotic animals.

Holiday said he "doesn't condone" sex trafficking. "It was all a shock to me," he said when he first learned about Mally's criminal charge from reading about it online. Yet Holiday, who now represents artists through Full Stop Management,[10] also said in June 2023 that he had recently spoken with Mally on the phone and described Mally as a "good friend" for whom he is a "big supporter." I asked him how he could still be friends with a sex trafficker; he said, "That's the thing," he's never spoken to Mally about his criminal activities. When I asked him why he didn't confront Mally about his crimes when they spoke on their recent call, he said it was "none of my business," then said he didn't have any more time to talk with me and hurried off the phone.

Most of the people I contacted in the entertainment business—the anonymous professionals working behind the scenes in the music industry—just ignored my emails, texts, and voicemails. But one publicist took it upon herself to forward my inquiry to Mally's team. I knew something like that was a possibility when I started reaching out to the show biz people. But I didn't anticipate who from Mally's camp would call me.

In late August 2022, just hours after the publicist had forwarded my interview request, I received a call from an unfamiliar Las Vegas number. The woman on the phone identified herself as only "Nita" and said she was an associate of Mally's. *What do you want?* she asked with a hint of annoyance. I vaguely explained that I was a journalist interested in learning more about Mally's work in the music business, avoiding any discussion of his criminal activities. *I'll get back to you,* she replied curtly, and hung up after less than a minute on the phone.

I immediately Googled the number and saw that it was registered to Tarnita Woodard—Tia, Angela's old handler when she worked for Mally.

Nearly a month passed before I heard from Tia again. On September 20, she emailed, saying she had researched me and knew I was investigating Mally. Yet she was exceedingly complimentary, saying she thought I had an "impressive resume" and seemed like a man of "good character." It was obvious she was trying to butter me up. "I'm looking for a journalist who is willing to write an article on Jamal's road to redemption," she wrote. "Please let me know if this is something you have interest in as I'm exclusively offering this article to one respected journalist."

I had to proceed carefully. I wasn't quite ready to confront Tia with all I knew about her and Mally—I still had a few more interviews to do before that could happen. But I couldn't exactly ignore her either. I asked her what she had in mind. She suggested we get together for lunch.

Eventually, we agreed to meet at a restaurant called Lazy Dog in downtown Summerlin, the Las Vegas planned community. Out of an abundance of caution, I took extensive measures to prepare for our lunch. I didn't know if she just wanted to talk to me, or if she was setting me up to be followed home. So, I scoped out the restaurant before we met, planning where I'd park and how I'd walk to and from the building, so I could spot any possible tails or surveillance. I also planned to not wear my wedding ring just in case Tia and company didn't know about my family.

Tia and I met for lunch at noon on October 7, 2022. She arrived a few minutes after me, wearing a sleeveless brown sweater, black slacks, and what appeared to be a black pork pie hat adorned with a short, speckled feather. (Angela called if "a pimp hat" when I told her about it later.) Her nails were immaculate, a nude color with a single red stripe on one finger of each hand. Around her neck she wore a chain with what appeared to be a large diamond. Her makeup looked flawless.

She ordered a mimosa, and we began to talk. She said she wanted to meet with me in person to gauge my character, to see if I was someone that she and Mally could trust. She said the way I contacted people about Mally made her think that I was trying to write a negative story about him. But after she looked into me, she thought maybe I'd be willing to write a positive one. I just nodded along.

Tia said if you only read about Mally online you'd think he's a bad person. But she insisted he's really not. She said she was looking for someone who was going to get to know him and portray all the positive things he's doing in the community. She said if she and Mally decided I was someone they liked, they'd want me to sign an NDA before they'd talk to me.

What do you do for Mally? I asked, playing dumb. *Are you his publicist or a record executive?* Tia said she was Mally's "right hand," but clarified that she didn't work "for him." "I work *with* Jamal," she said. *Oh,* I said. *What's your day-to-day schedule like?* Tia said that was hard to say, because every day is different. But she said her work is focused on "women empowerment." *What do you mean?* I asked. She said she goes to conferences and mentors women. *Oh, like in a mentoring program?* I asked. No, she said. She just goes about her life and if she encounters women in need, she befriends them and becomes their mentor.

That sounded an awful lot like pimp recruiting to me.

At one point during our lunch, she asked me about my interests. I said I had a small sneaker collection—some Nike Dunks and Jordans. *What's your size?* she asked. She offered to hook me up with sneaker deals and other shoes Mally had. I said that wasn't necessary.

At another point in our conversation, she made a big show of telling our waitress, who was a single mom, how strong she was. She stood up and gave the waitress a hug.

We parted on good terms after about an hour, with me telling Tia I was in no rush with my research, which she seemed to like. As far as I could tell, nobody followed me after I left the restaurant. I thought that would be the last I'd hear from Tia for a while, but I was wrong. In the weeks after our lunch, Tia texted me periodically, apparently just to check in. She sent me Bible verses (Psalm 23:1–3, Genesis 2:2–3, Luke 1:79), wished me a "Happy Gratitude Day" on Thanksgiving and a happy New Year, and even at one point tried to hire me for some publicity work, which I politely declined. Her texts were always casual and peppy, with her referring to me as "bro" and "love." I eventually came to realize what Tia was trying to do to me.

When I first started talking with Angela, she told me about a case involving a Wisconsin john named Kirk Riddle. Riddle once was an employee of the Kohler plumbing product company. He partied hard with women from Mally's escort service in Las Vegas and as he spun out of control, he ended up embezzling money from Kohler in 2013.[11] Angela, who wasn't involved, encouraged me to look into the case because she said it illustrated how Mally and his crew egged clients on. She said escorts had been "running game" on him—that is, cozying up to him in order to manipulate him.

I think that's what Tia was trying to do to me—run game.

By March 2023, I was ready to confront Tia with what I knew about her. Initially, we were scheduled to meet again for lunch on April 7, but then she postponed it, saying she had to travel for three weeks, for "back to back [sic] charity events." Ultimately, we met again on April 28, at a vegan restaurant in southwest Las Vegas. She wasn't dolled up as before, just black pants and a black shirt, with an animal print headband. One of the first things I asked her when she sat down was about her travels. She said she didn't travel as planned, that she had nearly died from a bout of Lupus and had spent some time in the hospital. She later coughed several times, underscoring her apparently fragile health.

Our conversation started out pleasant, but turned contentious the moment I said I had asked to meet because I wanted to request an interview with her for a book I was writing about Mally and the investigation into his sex trafficking operations. Tia's face betrayed no emotion, but from that point on I got the distinct impression she was trying to manipulate me.

First, Tia accused me of being aggressive and spiteful in my tone. Then she said she and Mally already knew about my book (which was possible because I had spoken to a lot of people by then).[12] *We aren't concerned about a book,* she said. Then she said I should hold off writing anything because more information about the case was about to come out and I'd look silly if I published before then. I told her that's exactly why I'd like to speak with her and Mally, to get their side of the story.

You should look further into the federal agent involved, Tia said.

I've looked into him, I replied.

You should look further, she retorted.

Again, I reiterated that I wanted to hear her and Mally's version of events. She said she and Mally would expect to get paid if they participated. She said she wouldn't want to see Mally get exploited for profit. I told her I wasn't expecting to make any significant money from this book—and besides my research indicated she and Mally had exploited vulnerable women.

No one was exploited, she said firmly.

That's not what I've heard, I replied.

You're only hearing that from people who are no longer in the industry, she shot back. *I've done my own research.*

I said again I just wanted to hear their version of events. *Well,* she replied, *we'd want to read the book before we'd agree to participate.* She said they only wanted to work with someone who was interested in supporting Mally, not tearing him down.

No, I told her.

Why not? she asked. *We'll be able to read it when it comes out.*

I told her journalism ethics precluded me from allowing her or Mally to read a draft manuscript of the book before it's published. But I promised I'd share with her and Mally everything that would be reported in the book.

Well, she said, *then we have nothing to talk about.*

The Las Vegas Metropolitan Police Department, the FBI, the Clark County District Attorney's Office, and the US Attorney's Office all declined to comment for this book, as did several critical law enforcement officers involved in this narrative, including Chris Baughman[13] and Warren Gray[14] (although Baughman debated for several weeks whether he would sit for an interview).

Also declining to comment was the former sheriff who oversaw Metro at the height of the Mally Mall scandal, Joe Lombardo—who became the governor of Nevada in January 2023.

Don provided for me a phone number and an FBI e-mail address he had for Kevin White. The email I sent bounced back to me, suggesting White no longer worked for the bureau. (Knapp told me the last he'd heard White had been transferred to the bureau's office in Chicago.) I called the phone number a few times and in March 2023 a young-sounding man picked up. When I asked to speak to Kevin White, he hung up. I immediately called back, and it went to voicemail.[15] Subsequent calls to the number also went directly to voicemail. That's the closest I ever got to speaking with White.

I likewise faced an uphill battle obtaining public records from law enforcement agencies involved in the case. The FBI "categorically denied" releasing any records pertaining to the Mally investigation, citing "the personal privacy interests" of the people involved. On appeal, I tried arguing that the bureau should release records to provide transparency on a high-profile case that's made anti-trafficking advocates skeptical of Metro, but the US Department of Justice rejected all the points I laid out in a thirteen-page letter.[16]

My records request with Metro ultimately was more fruitful, but no less frustrating. While the department charged me more than $3,000 for records[17] and refused to give me certain documents because I didn't meet the narrow definition of a reporter under state law (because I was not affiliated with a media establishment), the department did cough up a stunning police report from December 2020[18]—more than a year after Mally had pleaded guilty to his federal charge but was still awaiting sentencing.

The report and accompanying witness statement and interview transcript are heavily redacted, obscuring most names and a lot of important details. But the general gist of the story is clear. On December 20, 2020, Metro officers responded to a woman at a Shell gas station on Las Vegas Boulevard. The woman said she had worked on and off for Mally beginning around 2009, according to officers. (Because of the redactions, the kind of work she did for Mally was unclear. But obviously "work" is often used as a synonym for prostitution.) The report also suggests she worked for Mally until 2017 or 2018, which would have been years after the point at which he later claimed to have stopped pimping (September 2014—the same month the FBI had raided his mansion).

Detectives interviewed the woman for almost three hours. The police report lists Mally as a "person of interest" in the case. The woman's name is redacted. In a note, Metro said it redacted her name because she was a "Victim of Sexual Offense."

The woman, who told police she started working for Mally when she was eighteen years old, relayed a story that, in the report, reads as though he once drugged her. Angela told me a remarkably similar story, about her suspicion that Mally once drugged a bottle of water he gave her.[19] The woman's interview transcript also indicated she traveled for Mally to New Jersey, Hawaii, and Texas; discussed with Mally how much money she made on a given night; that her possessions were kept in his name; and that he paid for her housing. At one point, a detective asked the woman if Mally was "still working." She said she didn't know if he "still has services going on right now."[20]

Because of the heavy redactions, it's hard to determine exactly what the woman did for Mally, but she makes statements highly suggesting that she worked as a prostitute. At one point, she said, "I told Jamal that I did not wanna do that." Then later said she "kept rolling with it" because she "didn't have much"—she apparently needed money. Taken altogether, the documents suggest that Metro may have had reason to investigate

Mally for sex trafficking[21] while he was awaiting sentencing on a federal charge and after he had allegedly stopped pimping.

Rumors and innuendo continued to follow Mally around. While researching this book, I heard several outrageous stories about him involving sex and violence and even a street gang. But with so many people unwilling to talk to me on the record, there's a lot in my notes I couldn't confirm for this book or didn't feel comfortable reporting.

Here's what I can tell you: Less than three months after Mally copped his plea deal with the feds, a fitness model named Quashay Davis sued him in January 2020, alleging sexual battery and assault.[22] In court records, she said that Mally initially contacted her over direct message on Instagram and later said he wanted to help promote her. In January 2019, she flew from the Dallas area to Los Angeles, where she was driven to Mally's Encino mansion. There, Davis alleged, Mally drugged her, choked her, and at one point told her, "You're my new bitch." She said she snuck away from the mansion while Mally was asleep and went to an urgent care center, where the treatment provider found her injuries were consistent with rape. Her complaint says the center contacted the Los Angeles Police Department, who transported her to a hospital for further care. TMZ reported that she filed a report with the LAPD and that this incident was a factor in the subsequent raid on his Encino mansion in April 2019.[23]

A representative of Mally's told TMZ that Davis's lawsuit was "a blatant attempt at extortion."[24] The lawsuit was removed from the court's active caseload when Mally filed for bankruptcy, first in January 2021, before he was sentenced, and a second time in September 2021, about a month after he turned himself in to the medium-security federal prison in Sheridan, Oregon.[25] There, he was prison mates with Demetrius "Big Meech" Flenory, a leader of the Black Mafia Family, an infamous drug cartel depicted in the television crime drama *BMF*, executive produced by 50 Cent.

After he was sentenced, Mally reportedly told a celebrity gossip blog called The Neighborhood Talk[26] that "an obsessed FBI agent" named Kevin White blackmailed him into pleading guilty. "I had to take a plea deal to keep from doing 5-10 years for something I didn't do," he said. Mally claimed that White coerced women to speak out against him in exchange for money. "Those girls, all they care about is money, not the verdict," he said. Mally also claimed that White tried to get him to snitch on others, but he refused. "I ain't no 6ix9ine," Mally said, referring to a rapper who became a government witness against a gang. "I'm going to do the time because I'll never snitch on nobody, but the things they're saying about me aren't true . . . now that I've been sentenced, I can finally tell my side."

It sounded noble. But he displayed little virtue when the latest season of *Marriage Boot Camp*'s "Hip Hop Edition" aired two months after he went into custody, in October 2021. On the show, he and the woman introduced as his girlfriend, TV personality dancer Tresure Price, displayed odd, contentious behavior; other cast members openly called out Mally for being inauthentic and unreasonably hard on Price, for being a "master manipulator." Then in one of the season's final episodes, Price dropped a bombshell while the cast sat around a table. "We made up a story about us being here and us being in a relationship to be here so both of us can help our careers," she said to the stunned looks of the other cast members. "We had agreed to come on this show because I would have liked to get more publicity for my career," she said. Looking at Mally, she said, "You wanted to get more publicity so you wouldn't have to go to jail." Mally and Price were kicked off the show.

As you might imagine, Mally and Price's[27] deception didn't go over well with the other castmates. ("Why are these motherfuckers playing us?" rapper Amber Laura asked.) But his hip-hop career continued. More than a dozen records Mally worked on were released or leaked after he was sentenced, and his name continued to appear in entertainment news blogs that mentioned his various projects. On March 16, 2023, Mally was transferred from the federal prison in Sheridan to "community confinement overseen by the Bureau of Prisons (BOP) Residential Reentry Management (RRM) Office located in Phoenix, Arizona," in preparation for his return to society. The bureau didn't tell me where Mally had been transferred. (The Bureau doesn't discuss the "confinement conditions" of any inmate as a matter of security, a public affairs official wrote.) But the bureau did say community confinement means either home confinement or a halfway house.[28] Angela had heard Mally was on home confinement and Don figured if he wasn't home already, he'd be getting it ready for his return. So, I periodically began driving by Mally's Las Vegas mansion,[29] just to see if I would witness any activity there. I never saw Mally or even lights on in the cream-colored house with a Spanish-style roof. But I did see a 1,028-square-foot, two-story addition under construction on the west side of the residence. The $35,000 addition was first permitted by the county in October 2020, after Mally had copped his plea deal, but before he filed for bankruptcy. His bankruptcy attorney, George Haines, declined to talk to me, referring questions to Mally.

In late March 2023, months before his scheduled release date of July 14,[30] Mally put out a press release proclaiming, "The Return of Jamal 'Mally Mall' Rashid: Wiser and Stronger Than Ever Before!"[31] The release said "During his time away, Jamal had the opportunity to reflect not only on his personal life, but on making an impact in our society," and mentioned that he worked out with Big Meech. "Jamal has been very busy since his return and has an upcoming single being released in May with Lil Baby and Bay Swag that is anticipated to go #1 on Billboard 100," the release said, continuing:

> In addition, Jamal is honored to collaborate on a big concert entitled "Justice for Women [International] in Collaboration with The Hip Hop Alliance[32] Presents: Concert Series for Global Justice!," which will be held on June 19, 2023, at the KIA Forum in Los Angeles. This All-Star lineup of celebrities continues to grow with big names such as Akon, Macy Gray, Desiigner, Tiffany Haddish and many more scheduled to attend to help raise awareness and resources for those impacted by human trafficking and the violence on women and children.

The press release concluded by saying Mally would be "working directly with Tarnita Woodard . . . to continue his mission of impacting lives and changing the world."

News of this concert caught my attention. I had been trying to figure out where I should try to confront Mally with questions about the allegations in this book. The concert, I thought, might be a good place to try to talk to him. But when I met with Tia the second time, she indicated he wouldn't be there.[33] So that was a dead end. (Besides, the concert apparently never happened.)

Beginning in at least mid-April, Mally began posting videos to his Instagram account of him working in the studio, strongly suggesting he was indeed back home.[34] With no other way to track him down, I figured I'd just have to knock on his door at some point. But then a funny thing happened after my second encounter with Tia: I messaged Mally's Instagram account requesting an interview and received a reply, in a group chat including Tia's Instagram account. Whoever was responding to me from Mally's account spoke of Mally in third person, suggesting it wasn't him, but I wasn't entirely sure if that was just an act. "We will set something up shortly after July 14," @mallymall wrote. "We would appreciate objectivity before you attempt to assassinate jamal's [sic] character. He will invite you into his home, his space so you can feel his soul, his energy & see him for who he really is. Reach back out on July 11th for a date. May the Lord keep you & your family safe and healthy! [sic]."[35]

Could it really be that easy? I wondered. Of course, it wasn't. A short while later, I received an email from one of Mally's attorneys on a Saturday evening, saying Mally *didn't* want to talk to me and that I should never try to contact him again. I immediately emailed the attorney and messaged @mallymall, asking for clarification. The attorney said if Mally wanted to talk to me that was his choice and he'd back off. Whoever was answering Mally's Instagram account reiterated that we would talk again on July 11—but then suggested I shouldn't talk to anyone else about Mally until I met with him sometime in July. I would never agree to such terms, I tried to start a dialog, without conceding anything. Whoever was responding to me seemed to get annoyed, writing, "It's Saturday 8pm. These are not professional hours. We are at dinner with family." Then Tia started berating me about how unprofessional I was being, by not respecting their boundaries. It was a weird accusation coming from people who had messaged me at odd hours.

We managed to end the conversation peacefully, but the whole interaction left me a bit bewildered. Don, however, was not surprised. "This is what pimps do to their victims: they confuse with chaos and their ever changing [sic] BS rules that apply to you but not to them," he wrote to me in a text. "Fuck that and fuck them." So, I continued with my research and waited to see how they'd react if word ever got back to them that I'd been asking more questions about Mally.

Over the next several weeks, I tried keeping up with what Mally and Tia were doing, mainly by checking their Instagram accounts daily. Tia didn't make it easy for me: she blocked me on the platform about two weeks after my last chat with her and Mally's account. But that wasn't hard to get around. I just borrowed my wife's phone to look at her posts.[36] During that time, Mally posted a lot of himself and others in the studio as well as posts showing off the interior of the mansion and the exterior of the recording studio, which sports an elaborate mural of hip-hop stars and athletes on its façade. In his selfies, Mally always seemed to be wearing sunglasses indoors. He also posted a couple of videos of someone delivering him crab legs, apparently while he was on home confinement. "Hooked a nigga up," Mally said in one of the videos as the crab deliverer unwraps a tray of legs. "Ooh, boy, I know you want some of this!"

Tia didn't post nearly as much. But through her account I learned that in May 2023 Justice for Women International and the Hip Hop Alliance were invited to Washington, DC, to meet with members of Congress. According to a post on Justice for Women International's account, the invitation came from Sen. Marsha Blackburn, R-Tennessee; Sen. Amy Klobuchar, D-Minnesota; and Sen. Robert Menendez, D-New Jersey. Tia and Jacqueline Yvette, the publicist who put out Mally's comeback press release, posted pictures of themselves posing in what appeared to be a room used by the US Senate Committee on Rules and Administration and with the Queen of the Democratic Republic of the Congo. Mally reposted one of the pictures too. Seeing those photos, I wondered if someday someone would get in trouble for bringing Tia to Congress.

It was also through Instagram that I learned Mally would be a featured guest on the pilot episode of what was portrayed as a new show premiering on NBC in mid-June. A little bit of digging, however, revealed the social media wasn't exactly true. The show was actually paid programming *airing* on NBC at 5 a.m. Las Vegas time. The schlocky infomercial, which vaguely promoted an array of products and services, featured poor audio, views of the mansion, and nearly a full minute of Mally just sitting in the studio bobbing his head to a song. If that wasn't weird enough, the next scene showed Mally and Tia sitting around a dinner table with a woman who described being sexually abused by her mom and stepdad. "My mom actually held me down while my stepdad did it," the woman said while Tia sat there stone faced and Mally rubbed his bald head. The subsequent episodes gave loads of screen time to Daphna Edwards Ziman, the head of Justice for Women International, and Jacqueline Yvette, the publicist behind Mally's press release.[37]

In early July, Mally posted videos celebrating his forty-eighth birthday, which was July 3. Among them was a series of videos showing him and friends racing go-karts at an indoor track in Las Vegas.

With Mally's release date rapidly approaching, I began planning for a potential interview, although I wasn't entirely convinced that he'd really grant me one. Still, I had to prepare as if he would. Both Angela and Don didn't think it would be a good idea for me to meet with Mally alone, so I began searching for a bodyguard to accompany me to an interview. I eventually found Dennis Brooks, an "executive protection" professional who was happy to take me on as a client.

On July 11, 2023, as requested by whoever had communicated with me through Mally's Instagram account, I sent a message asking to schedule an interview. There was no response. I messaged Mally's account every day for eleven days. No one ever responded. On July 21, Mally's account apparently blocked me—but only after the messenger showed my last message had been "Seen by Mally Mall."

With no other options, I contacted Brooks to make plans to try to knock on Mally's door—or at least buzz his gate. As luck would have it, Brooks wasn't available to accompany me to Mally's mansion until July 30, which fittingly is the annual World Day Against Trafficking in Persons. A source I had developed who was once very close to Mally but asked to remain anonymous for fear of retaliation from him told me that

Mally usually sleeps until about 3 p.m. So, Brooks and I planned to meet up at 3:45 p.m., then drive to his mansion.

Brooks didn't want Mally to get a look at his license plate, so we parked his Tesla a little ways away and walked up to the main gate, which was still decorated with two metal palm trees like when Angela had first visited seventeen years before. On the way, we could see the two-story addition was now complete. A light glowed outside the front door. Brooks pointed out two security cameras aimed at us as we approached a silver and black console outside the gate. Another camera looked out from above the console's keypad.

On the console, a tiny, dirt-encrusted screen directed visitors to enter a room number or dial four zeros. But no matter what buttons I pushed, the screen just kept saying the call failed. While I bent down in front of the console, fiddling with the keypad and trying to read the screen, Brooks eyed the house warily. I held up my business card in front of the console's little camera. When that didn't work, I turned toward the house and called out, "Hello! Hello! Hello!"

Brooks motioned to one of the mansion's front windows. "That blind was down for a second," Brooks told me, pointing to a plantation shutter. When we had first walked up, Brooks had noticed that shutter was partially cracked. But now it was closed. "They definitely know we're out here," Brooks said.

But whoever was inside wasn't talking. I left business cards on top of the console and in the mailbox and we walked away. The following morning, I received a call from someone who identified himself as Robert Anderson.[38] He said he was the property manager of Mally's mansion and had found one of the business cards I had left behind. He said he saw me outside the gate. But because I didn't have an appointment, he ignored me (as he does anyone who comes to the house unexpectedly, because Mally's a celebrity). He said Mally was not home when we stopped by, but he'd pass my information along to him.[39]

The whole experience left me frustrated. But Don, once again, wasn't surprised. Mally was just doing what he'd seen pimps do time and again: minimize their risk by sticking to what they can control. Mally was now a free man, off federal supervision, able to go anywhere he pleased and do whatever he wanted, without anyone looking over his shoulder. Why would he waste his time with me? Don figured Mally had decided a while ago he'd never do an interview, after he had seen I wasn't susceptible to his (or Tia's) charms.

Pimps don't want scrutiny. They don't want to have to defend their actions—to anyone. They want total control of a situation, or they want nothing to do with it at all. If the legal system and entertainment industry were going to let Mally off the hook, there was no way he was going to help me try to hold him accountable.

"A pimp is just a pimp," Don said, "and they're all just as cowardly."

Epilogue

ASIDE FROM HIS ONGOING BATTLE WITH CANCER (WHICH HE'LL LIKELY deal with for the rest of his life), Don's retirement from Metro has been happy and prosperous. He spends most of his days fixing up the house he has called home for the last eighteen years and helping to raise his wife's two elementary-school-age boys from a previous relationship. Don officially adopted them as his own in 2018. He takes them to and from hockey practices, attends their games, shuttles them to and from school, and cares for them when his wife is at work. He remains one of the Clark County District Attorney's preferred expert witnesses for sex trafficking and, when the opportunity arises, takes cases as a private investigator. There is no doubt that his time in law enforcement has served him well personally.

There are times, however, when Don feels like his career as a cop was a waste. He sometimes thinks all those years he spent trying to make the Vice Section more responsive and compassionate to sex trafficking victims amounted to nothing because Vice's reputation is now in tatters. Between George Knapp's reporting, Ocean Fleming's release, and those fruitless raids on Mally's mansion, Don believes hardly anyone trusts Vice in Las Vegas anymore. Even local anti-trafficking advocates who had worked closely with the section for years aren't sure what to make of it these days. Are Vice officers fucking prostitutes? Are they colluding with pimps? People don't know what to think, and the authorities sure as hell aren't offering any insights. When he starts thinking that way, Don tries to think of the victims he and his detectives were able to help over the years. *They know who we really are*, he tells himself.

Vice is the primary law enforcement entity charged with policing sex trafficking in arguably America's worst city for sex trafficking—and it has little credibility with the hundreds of prostitutes who flood The Strip every night. Meanwhile, Ocean Fleming, one of the most violent pimps Don had ever encountered, is a free man, as is Mally, who spent only two years under federal supervision and was released an astounding nine months earlier than what he was originally sentenced. If Don thinks about it too much, he'll just start screaming.

The way he sees it, sex trafficking victims in Las Vegas are worse off now than when he retired in 2015. And for what? So Christopher Baughman could chase fame? So the Intel Section could sign up informants? So FBI special agent Kevin White could try to make a name for himself? So George Knapp could break a big story? All of these people were in a position to help sex trafficking victims, but they all wanted something else more. If they had just cared about the victims and the justice they deserved, Don truly believes everything would be different.

"Law enforcement never seems to learn from its mistakes," Don said as he sat at his kitchen table one sunny summer morning. "The landscape of law enforcement is littered with CI capers that have gone awry. The FBI clearly hasn't learned from that because this is, in essence, the sex trafficking version of Whitey Bulger.

"Clearly victims are still not the priority," Don continued, shaking his head. "It's disgusting. They always tend to be an afterthought with anything that goes awry. And I suppose it's even easier with sex trafficking victims because society as a whole, I don't think, gives a significant shit about them. It's easy when you're uneducated and think they chose this life and that whatever happens to them is their fault.

"My hope would be that this story would serve as a cautionary tale to those in law enforcement, to make them more mindful that every little thing that they do matters in the bigger picture. Because this is like a hodgepodge of little bits that pimps were able to weave together to benefit themselves. None of this happens if cops do what they should have done to begin with, just arrest pimps. That clearly didn't happen in Izadi's case and in Rashid's case, and that just opened Pandora's Box.

"The bottom line is everything matters, even if you're a reporter. What you report matters."

Don said he's probably always going to be upset about this case. But he takes solace in knowing that this book is being published to set the record straight. Don thinks he'll get some closure from that.

"I'm going to feel a heck of lot better knowing the truth is out there, or at least as close as we could get it," he said. "People are going to choose to believe what they want to believe."

The events depicted in this book—and my later efforts to turn those events into a book—have changed me in ways big and small. On the smaller end of the spectrum, I find I second guess my choice in music a lot these days. Since my senior year of high school, in 1998–1999, I've been a fan of hip hop. I loved the swagger and confidence of Snoop Dogg and 50 Cent, the beats of Dr. Dre, the rhymes of Tupac and Biggie. But after I learned how much pimp culture is reflected in rap, I've had to ask myself if it's appropriate to listen to certain songs or artists anymore. Does rapping along to E-40 and Keak da Sneak's song "Tell Me When to Go," signal my approval of sex trafficking? (At the end of verse two, Keak chirps, "I drink white, with a snow bunny." "Snow bunny" is pimp slang for a white prostitute.)

I stuck with this research through so many ups and downs because I feel sex trafficking survivors and victims deserve more respect and compassion in American society. Does listening to hip hop that glorifies the pimp game perpetuate their marginalization? I worry that it does. But then I think about Angela's friendship with the late Pimp C and his efforts to get her out of prostitution and I wonder if I'm overthinking it. I don't have a good answer for which songs and artists are appropriate and which ones aren't. But I do find myself changing the station now whenever I catch pimp slang on the radio.

More personally, I feel terribly conflicted about my chosen profession and about American media in general. When I became serious about writing this book, I got advice from a lot of people about how to proceed and many suggested it would be easier to sell a book if I published a story in a newspaper or magazine first. So, I pitched this story to several publications and none of them wanted it. A magazine editor of one online news organization known for its hard-hitting investigative reporting about the FBI told me she wasn't interested unless Mally was a campaign contributor or connected to public figures other than celebrities. A magazine editor wanted a story about pimping's influence on hip hop. I struck out when I applied for writing grants and a journalism fellowship to support this project.[1]

That just strengthened my resolve to see the book published. Originally, when I first started looking into sex trafficking, I found the topic interesting because sex trafficking victims seemed similar to foster children—that is, they are a marginalized and underrepresented population that policymakers clearly don't think a lot about. But as I continued on this journey, I came to feel like I could relate to them. Trafficking victims I interviewed talked about feeling misunderstood or left out. I definitely know how that feels. Some women told me about their struggles with post-traumatic stress disorder, which sounded a lot like my own difficulties with anxiety.

I've asked myself many times over the last few years, why is this of all stories the one I'm willing to put it all on the line for? I think it's because, in a strange way, sex trafficking victims are my people, despite all the obvious differences between them and a middle-aged, suburban dad like me.

By the way, at the time of this writing, all the *Review-Journal* editors specifically referenced in this book remain in high-paying, leadership roles in journalism, either at the *R-J* or at the newspaper in Dallas, while the *R-J*'s reputation has only improved in recent years. In January 2021, Sheldon Adelson died,[2] removing perhaps the biggest reason for criticizing the *Review-Journal*. (The paper remains in the hands of Adelson's family members, who apparently share his ideology, but aren't nearly the lightning rods he was.)[3]

In September 2022, one of my ex-colleagues on the *R-J*'s investigative team, Jeff German, was fatally stabbed, allegedly by a local elected official who, as the subject of one German's investigations, had received unflattering coverage in the paper.[4] Investigative Reporters and Editors Inc.,[5] an association of investigative journalists, gave the *R-J* a "special citation" in 2023 for its efforts to stop law enforcement from searching the late reporter's personal devices, which could have revealed confidential sources.[6] Three of German's *R-J* colleagues also delivered the keynote address at the organization's 2023 annual conference, in Orlando, Florida. After years of denigration, the *R-J* now seems to hold some genuine esteem in the news business.

And now here I am, speaking out against it.

I have no idea what's next for me. But I feel at peace knowing I tried to comfort some of the most afflicted people in America.

If you're looking for hope in this story, look to Angela, who in six years has remade her life from top to bottom, proving that there is a future after sex trafficking. If you ran into her on the street today and didn't know a thing about her, you'd probably think she was just another harried thirty-something-year-old mom, struggling to entertain a willful preschooler. Which is just the way she likes it.

In her years since leaving prostitution, Angela has steadily demanded more for herself and from the people in her life. She got married after she left The Game and changed her name to Angela Williams. She and her husband had a daughter, but they're now separated. Angela says they weren't a good fit. Earlier in her life, she might have put up with that. But not anymore.

Today, she lives in Houston, where she spends her days playing with and caring for her daughter, who shares her mom's stubborn spirit. She's held some "square" (i.e., noncriminal) jobs, including working as a housekeeper at Houston's VA hospital. Angela describes her life as boring and normal, her wardrobe as Erykah Badu on a Target budget. She says she now hardly wears makeup and intentionally tries *not* to look provocative.

This isn't a fairy tale, however. Angela still struggles. She often runs late and is admittedly flakey and sometimes pays her bills after they're due. When she's under stress or having a bad day, she can lash out, sometimes sharply. But she's learned how to calm herself and generally gives off the impression of being more often happy than not. She still hates all of her traffickers, and she probably always will—especially Mally, who she believes sold her the biggest lies of all. Today, she considers all of her encounters with clients to have been the equivalent of rape—countless rapes over more than a decade. She's tried to black out their memory, which can be traumatizing. Overall, Angela describes herself as bitter, but unlike Don and me, it doesn't seem to show as much. Her positive energy is infectious.

Besides motherhood, which understandably consumes an enormous part of her life, Angela has devoted herself to helping not only other sex trafficking victims, but also people in need in general. She says her hero is Mother Teresa, and in the time I've known her, she always seems to be doing something to help her community, whether it be volunteering to feed the homeless or helping to spread the word about a prostitute who has gone missing. Angela is strong in her Christianity and isn't bashful about crediting Jesus with her transformation.

Angela also has been brave and put herself and her story out in the public numerous times, besides this book. In September 2021, she became the lead plaintiff in a public-interest lawsuit filed against the then-governor of Nevada Steve Sisolak, and other defendants, including Mally.[7] The suit alleges that the Silver State created the conditions for Angela's sex trafficking in Las Vegas by permitting legal prostitution at brothels in its rural counties and *de facto* legal prostitution through escort agencies and strip clubs elsewhere. The suit is ongoing—at the time of this writing it's not expected to be resolved for at least another half a year, at the earliest—but Angela has already won a victory against one of the defendants, Mally, whom she sued for declaratory and injunctive relief. Mally was served with the suit but failed to answer. On April 28, 2022, the court's clerk filed an entry of default against Mally and his business entities, making it likely the court will issue a default judgment against Mally and grant Angela a formal, legal win over her former trafficker.

Also in 2021, Angela starred in the documentary *Surviving Sex Trafficking*, which chronicled her and other survivors' efforts to recover from the horrors they experienced in The Life. The film includes some shocking footage of Angela's body after she was beaten by her last trafficker, Tyree Wright, and rebroadcasts a tearful interview she did after her near-fatal beating.[8] In late March 2022, I attended *Surviving Sex Trafficking*'s Los Angeles premiere at the Landmark Theatre, sitting with Angela's cousins and mom.[9] After the showing, Angela and other survivors featured in the film answered some questions. "I feel liberated through this film," Angela told the crowd. "I'm priceless. I can't be sold." She and the other women received a standing ovation. Her mom cried.

Despite her growing public persona, Angela has no interest in becoming what is known in the anti-trafficking community as a "survivor leader." She's disturbed by trafficking survivors who name organizations after themselves and who seem intent on garnering attention. Angela thinks that's ridiculous. She wants to help end trafficking, but she wants to live a quiet, anonymous life. Angela has always struck me as genuinely humble, and even though she is candid about her experiences in trafficking, she also can be private. She asked that certain, specific, sensitive details about her life not be shared in this book, and I was happy to oblige. Angela is much more than a woman who was trafficked, more than just a symbol, and deserves the same respect afforded any member of our society.

There's no doubt that trafficking has shaped the person Angela is today, but it doesn't define her or her future. No longer a slave to The Game or any pimp, Angela is free to chart her own course in life and she does so with a faith that her best days are still ahead of her.

Policy Discussion

As with a lot of public policy issues these days, many Americans believe the fix to domestic sex trafficking is simple. After all, people think, sex is a natural, human behavior. How hard could it be to police something instinctual? But that's the wrong way to look at the issue. It inappropriately conflates consensual sex with sex that is forced or coerced, which are not the same things. Not even close. Just because sex is wired into our DNA doesn't mean that we all intuitively understand sex trafficking.

The issue needs to be approached with sensitivity and tremendous care, not assumptions and arrogance.

There are several schools of thought when it comes to reform. As mentioned in the Introduction, many on the Left favor decriminalization, in which all criminal penalties are removed for both the buying and selling of sex. Another similar proposal is the legalization of commercial sex, much like what's allowed in Nevada's rural brothels: sex work under limited and regulated conditions. Both of these proposals seek to destigmatize prostitution, allowing women to make money without societal shame. That is absolutely a worthy goal. Women (and men) should not be judged for "selling themselves." As this book has hopefully illustrated, there are a litany of reasons why people come to sex work, and rarely, if ever, it is because they simply have loose morals or poor character.

However, that is one of the major weaknesses of both decriminalization and legalization—they fail to address the personal and societal pressures that send people into sex work in the first place. If a woman truly desires, at the bottom of her soul, to "sell herself," it's difficult to argue she is being exploited. But as the evidence overwhelmingly shows, that is rarely the case for American prostitutes. People enter prostitution when they're desperate. Remember the therapists' line, *No little girl dreams of being a prostitute?* Any reforms we enact should seek to make people's lives better, happier, and more fulfilled, not merely allow them to scrape by and hate themselves in the process.

More troubling, decriminalization and legalization both could make life *easier* for sex traffickers like Mally. Supporters argue that if prostitution were legal or decriminalized, girls and women would have no need for pimps, that they could band together in female collectives and reap all the economic rewards themselves. This is a wonderful dream—but that is all it is, a dream. As it is now, some women working in legal strip clubs are being illegally trafficked. They dance, collect tips, and then at the end of the night turn over all their earnings to a pimp. This can occur outside the purview of the club's managers, who have little incentive to delve into the personal lives of their strippers. In fact, some pimps actually prefer this form of pimping. In a strip club, working legally, their girls have less risk of being arrested. But they're still raking in cash night after night.

Of course, pimps who beat or blackmail or defraud legal prostitutes (or strippers) could still, in theory, be prosecuted for crimes under existing laws. But if prostitution were legal or decriminalized, would any law enforcement agency ever pursue such cases? As Don's experiences show, many in law enforcement don't view prostitution as a major priority today—and it's illegal almost everywhere in the US. If cops and prosecutors have such little empathy now, imagine how little they'll have if prostitution is legal or decriminalized in more places. As Don is fond of saying, *It would be open season for pimps, who will be laughing all the way to the bank.*

Another reform proposal that seeks to capture the benefits of decriminalization and legalization while also holding traffickers and johns accountable is something known as the Equality Model[1] or the Nordic Model, so called because it's been adopted by the Nordic countries of Sweden, Iceland, and Norway. Under the Nordic Model, the selling of sex is decriminalized, but the buying of sex and pimping remain illegal. Meanwhile, a third prong of the Equality Model establishes a robust social service network to help girls and women get out of prostitution, when they're ready.

Ideally, this model would foster better, stronger relationships between law enforcement, service providers, and prostituted women, which, in turn, would be used to hold pimps and other traffickers accountable for their abhorrent, criminal behavior. But Don believes the Nordic Model is flawed in this regard. As we've already established, making cases against traffickers is difficult. Almost always, successful prosecution of a trafficker requires a victim to testify and many simply are not willing to do it. Victims' understandable lack of cooperation is a major impediment to holding sex traffickers accountable. One critical way around this obstacle is to develop a circumstantial case (as Metro originally tried to do with Mally), based on a trafficker's lifestyle without a known source of income and on the trafficker's association with known prostitutes. But if the selling of sex is decriminalized, police would have no reason to track prostitution in their community. And if cops don't track prostitutes, they can't establish a circumstantial case against sex traffickers.

One supporter of the Nordic Model I turned to for consultation on this section acknowledged that this scheme removes a tool from the police's toolbox. But she argued what is gained in return—the destigmatization of prostitutes, who will have greater opportunities outside of The Game without the burden of a criminal record—far outweighs that loss.

It's tricky, balancing these competing ideals. I can't say I know what deserves the most weight or what is the right answer.

To put it another way, the devil in this discussion is in the details. For sex trafficking reform to be truly successful, it's going to have to be carefully implemented, and nuanced. As you might imagine, both Don and Angela have some ideas on reform and, despite them having only met each other once, at a lunch I organized in January 2020, their ideas are remarkably similar.

Both Angela and Don believe prostitution should remain illegal—and that prostitutes should continue to be criminally charged. Angela is as passionate on this point as Don, if not more so. "When I went to jail, I felt relieved," Angela told me.[2] She agrees with Don's assessment that jail time gives prostitutes a much-needed break from their traffickers—although this is not a widely agreed upon point. Some in the anti-trafficking community believe jail time for prostitution is immoral and that the long-term negative implications of arrest and incarceration far outweigh any of their benefits.

Don calls prostitution a problem with three prongs: supply (prostitutes), demand (johns), and management (pimps). Both he and Angela believe enforcement must be applied about equally to all three to fix the problem. They think the disparity in prostitute and john arrests I found on the Las Vegas Strip is abhorrent and must change. Don can't understand how anyone could justify heavily policing the supply side but ignoring the demand.[3]

Of course, Don and Angela think sex traffickers should be the top focus of any enforcement scheme. Stamping out pimps would go a long way toward drying up the supply, they say, and the arrest or conviction of a big trafficker always sends shockwaves through the prostitution subculture. Angela favors anything that would make it easier for prosecutors to convict sex traffickers. Don thinks the key is educating everyone—police, district attorneys, and the general public—about sex trafficking. He said one of the biggest hurdles to prosecuting pimps is prosecutors' own ignorance about sex trafficking. District attorneys often are judged by their conviction rates, so they're hesitant to take on cases they don't think they can win. The more prosecutors know about sex trafficking, the more willing they'll be to take on pimps, Don believes. Initially when Don was in Vice, he and the other officers in the section would hand deliver their cases to prosecutors and then meet with them regularly thereafter to ensure they were fully prosecuted. Then the Clark County District Attorney's office got wise and started asking certain prosecutors to specialize in sex trafficking cases. Those attorneys developed an expertise in sex trafficking and suddenly getting convictions got a little easier.

The same goes for the public. Don believes if the general population better understood the brainwashing prostitutes endure, juries would be more apt to convict pimps without a victim's testimony, and that would at least start to put sex traffickers on their heels.

Both Angela and Don are concerned about the messages the public receives about sex trafficking, because that messaging largely comes from nonprofits, and they believe a great deal of them are run by people with no real knowledge about the prostitution subculture. Nothing gets Angela fired up more than talking about sex trafficking nonprofits. She finds most of them to be worthless, headed by wannabe do-gooders who glommed onto sex trafficking because it's trendy; they suck up available resources and give little of value to survivors. When I relayed Angela's thoughts to Don, he chuckled. "I don't disagree," he said.

As is probably clear by now, I deeply respect Angela and Don. Policymakers the country over should listen to them and the opinions of others who have wrestled directly with this issue—other victims, survivors, direct-support service providers, and law enforcement officers who have actually busted traffickers. But people like Angela and Don are unique in that they've thought a lot about this issue. Sadly, it appears, most American policymakers have not.

I'm not saying that proposals contrary to Angela and Don's should be rejected either. As mentioned, there are those in the anti-trafficking community who passionately argue that prostitutes (or as some call them "prostituted people") should never be arrested, and I have the utmost respect for their thinking on the matter. As I indicated before, this is not a simple problem with easy answers. Well-meaning people are going to disagree and in a serious, thorough debate of policy options effective solutions eventually will trickle out.

But in order for that to actually happen, there needs to in fact be a serious discussion, and if there's one thing that I've learned from struggling with this issue myself for the last several years, it's that it's not being taken seriously by nearly enough people at all levels of our society. Frequently, the plight of sex trafficking victims gets lost in the petty squabbles of advocates or outright ignored by our business and political leaders. So, my personal recommendation is far more modest.

If America is going to combat domestic sex trafficking, its policymakers need to first make it a top priority and then approach the topic with the utmost humility. To craft good, effective policies, they need to disregard political ideologies and listen closely to the stories of survivors and empathetic cops and knowledgeable advocates. Too often discussions about sex trafficking, pimping, and prostitution seem to devolve into hypotheticals. But this is not a hypothetical problem. This is a real, devastating affliction in our society, and it needs to be taken seriously, with policies designed to work in the real world, not to appease a political base or an ideology.

This is modern-day slavery—a nonpartisan, human-rights issue if there ever was one—and it's time its eradication becomes a part of the American political agenda.

ACKNOWLEDGMENTS

Ever since I read *The Drunkard's Walk: How Randomness Rules Our Lives* by Leonard Mlodinow, I've been convinced that luck is the most powerful force in the universe. My experience writing this book did nothing to change that. I was extremely lucky to get this book done given the pandemic and other obstacles I faced. There are so many ways this project could have gone sideways, and almost did, but I was fortunate to have had the support of a small, but dedicated group of people.

My good luck started, of course, with Angela Williams and Don Hoier. I've worked as a journalist for about twenty years, and it just so happens that the two best sources I've ever encountered turned out to be the protagonists of the biggest story I've ever tackled. How's that for dumb luck? Both Don and Angela were incredibly generous with their time, each devoting countless hours to talk and meet with me, and putting in countless more to find me records or other people to interview. Any success this book achieves is a testament to them and their courage to speak out when so many others choose to stay silent. Telling Angela's story has been one of the greatest honors of my life, and I'm humbled by the trust Don showed in me when he had every reason to distrust a journalist. They are both heroes in my eyes and I just hope I've done them justice on the page. I can't thank either of them enough. They will be my friends for life.

I was also very lucky, through a series of random events, to enlist the author Charles Bock as my writing coach. (Check out his novels *Beautiful Children* and *Alice & Oliver* and his new memoir *I Will Do Better.*) Charles is without a doubt the best writer I've ever worked with or even encountered, and his guidance shaped this story in innumerable ways. I don't think it's at all a stretch to say Charles is a genius and I'm grateful for his friendship and mentoring.

Likewise, I was blessed when I landed Rita Rosenkranz as my literary agent, because she stuck with this project even when it looked like it was going nowhere. Her counseling through this process has been invaluable and her enthusiasm for what I was trying to do was invigorating, especially after the many doors that were slammed in my face. And it was Rita, of course, who put this project into the hands of my editor at Rowman & Littlefield, Becca Beurer, who proved to be tailormade for this book, with her deep experience in criminology and her heart for the downtrodden. For a rookie author trying to write a book in his spare time while struggling to support his family, I sure lucked into a pretty stellar literary team.

Once I knew this book was going to become a reality, I needed to get help with a variety of tasks, one being seeking comments from my ex-colleagues at the *Review-Journal,* who I figured would not be interested in talking to me. As luck would have it, while I was working on this book, I reconnected with an old intern of mine from the *Orange County Register,* Timothy Sandoval, who agreed to act as my go-between with the *R-J* folks. Timothy is one of the most honest and forthright people I know. He was perfectly suited to the task and I'm grateful for his help in handling this sensitive matter.

Thank you also to Kathryn Belgiorno, for her help with fact checking this book; Reno attorney Jason Guinasso, who provided a pro bono legal review of the book's manuscript; and the long list of "beta" readers who reviewed an early draft manuscript, including Dennis Brooks, my bodyguard who previously worked in the hip-hop business; my friend Camille Cravero; UNLV professor and sex trafficking researcher Dr. Alexis Kennedy; my opinionated friend David Kennedy (or as I like to call him, "Angry Dave"; no relation to Dr. Kennedy); Pulitzer-Prize winning investigative reporter Susan Kelleher; reporter Aaron Kessler, my closest friend in journalism; Susan Roske, a retired attorney from the Clark County Public Defender's Office in Las Vegas; my cousin Amy Roseland; investigative journalist and editor Mc Nelly Torres; and Judge William Voy (retired).

I put in a lot of time and enlisted a lot of help trying to ensure that the material in this book was not only factually accurate but presented in a sensitive and appropriate manner. In an environment today where even the slightest misstep can invalidate a book, story, or person, I've spent quite literally years worrying over how to prevent that from happening here, so as not to distract from the needs of survivors. If this book succeeds in that effort, it's a credit to all the tremendous help I received. But if, however, something in these pages proves to be incorrect, or if a topic was inappropriately framed, that failure is mine and the blame rightfully belongs to me alone.

Now, even with all the help I've already mentioned, this book wouldn't have crossed the finish line without the support, both financial and emotional, of my family and a couple of very special friends. Thank you to my friends Kay Landwehr and Howard Kaiman (the latter of whom sadly died in April 2023 while I was drafting this manuscript), and to my cousins Julie Kestner and Dr. Steve and Marilyn Tipp for your donations to this project. Your support of my work is so appreciated.

Of course, the three people who supported this project the most were my wife, Buu, and my parents, Dr. Les and Sharon Joseph. I had many conversations with them about the risks of pursuing this book and at every turn they encouraged me to keep going. My wife, despite the financial uncertainty facing us, allowed me to tap our savings to fund part of this book and my parents essentially covered the rest—which was a lot. I simply couldn't have done this without them. Their financial support was critical, but their emotional support may have been even more important. As I mentioned in chapter 17, the events of this book enflamed my anxieties fairly seriously. My wife and parents helped me through the most troubled times of my life and enabled me to finish this book. (It feels ridiculous writing that, knowing the kind of trauma sex trafficking victims have experienced. But it's the truth for my generally privileged life.)

In closing, I'd like to say a few words to my daughter Zoey, who was only an infant when I began researching sex trafficking and now, at the time of this writing, is in the second grade. Zoey, you might not have known it, but you helped me through these tough years as well, with your smiles and giggles and hugs. For now, you're still far too young to read this book. But when the day comes that you are old enough to understand it, I hope this reads like something from the distant past, that the events depicted here seem strange and inconceivable, because sex trafficking has been eradicated from our society.

Resources

Angela didn't really understand the kind of resources that were available to people like her when she first learned about sex trafficking in 2008, after watching that Diane Sawyer special. This section is an attempt to prevent that from happening to anyone reading this book. What follows is a list of vetted places where victims and survivors can go to for help as well as information for people who may suspect that their friends or loved ones are being trafficked.

Where You Can Get Help

Thankfully, today there are many organizations and agencies across the country that can and do assist sex trafficking victims and survivors. But, as Angela discovered, not all of these organizations are as responsive as they could be, or as survivors would like them to be.[1] As such, this is not intended to be an exhaustive list of agencies that could help survivors. Rather, the entities listed here have been vetted by myself and several leaders in the anti-trafficking community.[2] I have confidence that if a victim were to contact one of these agencies for help, they'd be heard.[3]

Nationwide

Elevate Academy, the largest online school for survivors of human trafficking in the world. elevate-academy.org, elevate@rebeccabender.org.

F.R.E.E. (Find, Restore, Embrace, Empower) International, a Las Vegas-based nonprofit that provides social and legal services to survivors as well as organizes rescue operations for sexually exploited people. free-international.org, 702-423-6105, info@freeinternational.org.

National Human Trafficking Hotline, operated by Polaris, an anti-human trafficking nonprofit, offers a twenty-four/seven toll-free hotline, SMS text lines, and an online chat function for victims and survivors in more than two hundred languages. humantraffickinghotline.org, 888-373-7888, help@humantraffickinghotline.org.

National Trafficking Sheltered Alliance, a network of organizations offering services to sex trafficking victims and survivors; its Alliance Referral System connects survivors with residential programs across the country. shelteredalliance.org, 443-453-5037, referral@shelteredalliance.org.

Refuge for Women, a faith-based nonprofit offering a two-year continuum of care for female survivors of sex trafficking and commercial sexual exploitation. Locations in Chicago, Kentucky, Las Vegas, North Texas, Pittsburgh, and the Texas Gulf Coast. refugeforwomen.org, 940-331-0042, refugeweb@refugeforwomen.org.

Shared Hope International, a nonprofit with a threefold mission to prevent the conditions that foster sex trafficking, restore survivors of sex trafficking, and bring justice to vulnerable children; it offers training, intervention, and legislative activities that confront sex trafficking in communities throughout America. sharedhope.org, 866-437-5433, save-lives@sharedhope.org.

StreetLightUSA, a nonprofit organization based in Arizona, providing residential services for at-risk, highly suspected, and confirmed female, adolescent victims of child sex trafficking and child sexual exploitation. streetlightusa.org, 623-435-0900, info@streetlightusa.org.

Together Freedom, a non-profit organization providing long- and short-term care, including food, shelter, clothing, education, and access to legal services for girls who have become victims of sex trafficking in the United States. togetherfreedom.org, 951-399-3332, connect@together-freedom.org.

United Abolitionists, a network of first responders fighting human trafficking in the United States. stophumantrafficking.com, 407-495-5846, info@stophumantrafficking.com.

Alaska

Abused Women Aid in Crisis, or *A.W.A.I.C.*, an Anchorage-based nonprofit offering a 24–7 shelter and intervention for victims of domestic violence. awaic.org, 907-272-0100, development@awaic.org.

Advocates for Victims of Violence Inc., a Valdez-based nonprofit offering shelter, a 24-hour crisis line, legal advocacy, and other services for victims of domestic and sexual violence. avvalaska.org, 907-835-2999, avv@avvalaska.org.

Alaska Family Services, a Palmer-based organization offering a multitude of services, including a shelter for victims of domestic and sexual violence and a 24-hour hotline. akafs.org, 907-746-4080, info@akafs.org.

Alaska Network on Domestic Violence and Sexual Assault, a network of programs across Alaska providing shelter, 24-hour hotlines, advocacy, and other services to victims of domestic and sexual violence. andvsa.org, andvsa@andvsa.org.

Cordova Family Resource Center, a domestic violence shelter with a 24-hour hotline. cordovafamilyresourcecenter.org, 907-424-5674, info@Cordovafamilyresourcecenter.org.

Interior Alaska Center for Non Violent Living, a Fairbanks-based nonprofit offering housing, legal aid, and other programs for victims of domestic and sexual violence. iacnvl.org, 907-452-2293 or 800-478-7273, iac@iacnvl.org.

Kodiak Women's Resource and Crisis Center, a nonprofit serving survivors of domestic or sexual violence, offering a twenty-five-bed shelter and a 24-hour crisis line. kwrcc.org, 907-486-3625 or 888-486-3625, outreach@kwrcc.org.

LeeShore Center, a Kenai-based, thirty-four-bed emergency shelter for women and children who have been victims of domestic violence and sexual assault; also offering legal advocacy, transitional living assistance, and more. leeshoreak.org, 907-283-7257 (crisis line), 907-283-9479.

Safe and Fear-Free Environment, or *S.A.F.E.*, a Dillingham-based shelter for victims of domestic and sexual violence. safebristolbay.org, 907-842-2320, director@safebristolbay.org.

South Peninsula Haven House, a Homer-based organization offering emergency shelter, a twenty-four-hour crisis line, and other programs for victims of domestic or sexual violence. havenhousealaska.org, 907-235-7712, 907-235-8943 (24-hour crisis line) admin@havenhousealaska.org.

Tundra Women's Coalition, a Bethel-based nonprofit offering a forty-three-bed shelter, 24-hour crisis line and legal advocacy for victims of sexual violence. tundrapeace.org, 907-543-3456 or 1-800-478-7799, TWC@TWCpeace.org.

Unalaskans Against Sexual Assault & Family Violence, a nonprofit operating a shelter and a 24-hour crisis line for people impacted by domestic and sexual violence and other life crises. usafvshelter.org, 907-581-1500 or 1-800-478-7238, usafved@arctic.net.

Women in Safe Homes, or *W.I.S.H.*, a Ketchikan-based nonprofit operating a thirty-two-bed shelter for victims of domestic violence and sexual assault. wishak.org, 907-225-9474 (shelter), 800-478-9474 (twenty-four-hour crisis line), info@wishak.org.

California

After Hours Ministry, a faith-based organization in Los Angeles serving victims of sexual exploitation. afterhoursministry.org, 323-524-8044, info@afterhoursministry.org.

Alabaster Jar Project, a faith-based nonprofit offering housing and resources for sex trafficking victims in San Diego. alabasterjarproject.org, 858-598-3238, info@AlabasterJarProject.org.

Bay Area Women Against Rape, or *B.A.W.A.R.*, an Oakland-based crisis center providing 24-hour services to survivors of sexual violence. bawar. org, 510-800-4247, bawar@bawar.org.

Children of the Night, a Los Angeles nonprofit with a nationwide and global reach dedicated to rescuing sexually exploited children. childrenofthenight.org, 818-908-4474 or 800-551-1300 x 0 for twenty-four/seven service lois@childrenofthenight.org.

Community Solutions, a nonprofit agency offering services for survivors of human trafficking, intimate partner abuse, and sexual violence, serving Santa Clara and San Benito counties. communitysolutions.org, 1-877-363-7238, info@communitysolutions.org.

Journey Out, a Van Nuys nonprofit assisting victims of sex trafficking and commercial sexual exploitation. journeyout.org, 818-988-4970, info@journeyout.org.

San Francisco SafeHouse, an organization providing services, transitional housing, and other safe spaces for survivors of sexual exploitation and trafficking. sfsafehouse.org, 415-643-7861, info@sfsafehouse.org.

Saving Innocence, a Los Angeles-based nonprofit organization dedicated to the recovery and restoration of child and adult victims of human trafficking by providing crisis response, advocacy, case management, and foster families. savinginnocence.org, 323-379-4232, info@savinginnocence.org.

Women's Resource Center, an Oceanside nonprofit offering counseling, a 24-hour crisis line, a twenty-eight-day emergency shelter, a two-year transitional housing program, and advocacy for victims of domestic violence and child abuse. wrcsd.org, 760-757-3500.

East Coast

EVA Center, based in Boston, helps individuals exit prostitution, offering emergency housing, among other services. evacenter.org, 617-779-2133, info@evacenter.org

FAIR (Free Aware Inspired Restored) Girls, a Washington, DC, organization providing intervention and holistic care to female survivors of human trafficking; operates a 24-hour, toll-free crisis line. fairgirls.org, 202-520-9777 (main number) or 855-900-3247 (crisis line), info@fairgirls.org.

HER Resiliency Center, a Washington, DC and Baltimore, Maryland-based, survivor-led organization serving vulnerable women ages eighteen to twenty-five with the support, skills, and resources they need to make life-changing positive decisions and thrive. herresiliency.org, 844-4HER-NOW, info@herresiliency.org.

Living in Freedom Together, or *LIFT,* a nonprofit in Worcester, Massachusetts, offering programs for survivors of the sex trade. liftworcester.org, 508-762-9660, lift@liftworcester.org.

Reset180, a Christian nonprofit in Virginia seeking to help human trafficking survivors in Arlington, Fairfax, Fauquier, Loudoun, and Prince William counties as well as the cities of Alexandria, Fairfax, Falls Church, Manassas, and Manassas Park. reset180.com, 703-634-6061, info@reset180.com.

Sasha Bruce Youthwork offers emergency housing and supports for home-less and runaway children as well as victims of sex trafficking in the greater Washington, DC region. SashaBruce.org, 202-547-7777 (emer-gencies), info@sashabruce.org.

The University of Maryland Support, Advocacy, Freedom, and Empowerment (SAFE) Center for Human Trafficking Survivors, a direct services, research, and advocacy center that provides free legal, social, economic empow-erment, and behavioral health services to human trafficking survivors. umdsafecenter.org, 301-314-7233, safecenter@umaryland.edu.

TurnAround, Inc. serves survivors of intimate partner violence, sexual vio-lence, and human trafficking in Baltimore County and Baltimore City, and serves survivors of human trafficking in Howard County. turnaroundinc. org, 410-377-8111 or 443-279-0379 (twenty-four/seven helpline), 410 498-4956 (twenty-four/seven text line), info@turnaroundinc.org.

Florida

Abuse Counseling & Treatment, Inc. (ACT), a Fort Myers-based nonprofit serving sex trafficking victims with free and confidential treatment services and a twenty-four-hour hotline. actabuse.com, 239-939-3112, act@actabuse.com.

Glory House of Miami offers wrap-around services to adult survivors of human trafficking, including case management, life skills, trauma coun-seling, mentorship, medical and mental health care, spiritual guidance, and legal support. gloryhouseofmiami.org, 786-505-4681, info@glory-houseofmiami.org.

Redefining Refuge, a Tampa-based specialized service provider and non-profit advocacy agency for commercially exploited and trafficked children. redefiningrefuge.org, 813-778-4916, info@redefiningrefuge.org or referral@redefiningrefuge.org.

Refuge House, based in Tallahassee, operates a crisis hotline, emergency shelter, transitional housing, and legal assistance, among other programs, for victims of domestic and sexual violence, and sex trafficking. refugehouse.com, 1-800-500-1119 or 888-956-7273, receptionist@ refugehouse.com.

Midwest

Ascent 121, an Indianapolis-based nonprofit offering a full continuum of therapeutic care, including residential placements and home-based services, for teen survivors of sex trafficking and commercial sexual exploitation. ascent121.org, 317-759-0067, info@ascent121.org.

Breaking Free, a survivor-led, non-profit provider of housing to sex trafficking survivors and their children in St. Paul, Minnesota. breakingfree. net, 651-645-6557 or 651-219-9287 (after hours), breakingfree@breakingfree.net.

New Name, a faith-based, Chicago-area nonprofit offering services to women in the sex industry. new-name.org, 630-465-0802, anne@new-name.org.

Pathfinders Milwaukee, Inc., offers basic needs, shelter/housing, and anti-violence services for youth and young adults (ages eleven to twenty-five years old) in crisis. pathfindersmke.org, 414-271-1560 or 866-212-7233 (twenty-four/seven), info@pathfindersmke.org.

RAHAB Ministries, a faith-based organization in Canton, Ohio, offering mentoring and housing for sex trafficking survivors. rahab-ministries.org, 330-819-3326, believe@rahab-ministries.org

Sacred Beginnings, a survivor-led, peer-mentored program for sex trafficking victims based in Grand Rapids, Michigan. sbtp.org, 616-443-6233, leslieking@sbtp.org.

SAFE on Main, based in Lebanon, Ohio, provides shelter, legal advocacy, and therapy to human trafficking survivors and victims of domestic and sexual violence. safeonmain.org, 888-860-4084 (crisis line), 513-695-1185 (office).

Veronica's Voice, a Kansas City–based nonprofit offering two years of free transitional housing to sex trafficking survivors. veronicasvoice.org, 816-483-7101 or 913-214-1401, admin@veronicasvoice.org.

Nevada

Awaken, a faith-based, anti-trafficking nonprofit offering housing, a drop-in center, and assistance for girls and women looking to leave The Life, based in Reno. awakenreno.org, 775-393-9183, info@awakenreno. org

Cupcake Girls, a nonprofit providing confidential support to those in the sex industry as well as trauma-informed outreach, advocacy, and referrals; offices in Las Vegas and Portland, Oregon. thecupcakegirls.org, 702-879-8195 (Las Vegas), 207-200-8094 (Portland), info@thecupcake-girls.org.

Eddy House, a Reno nonprofit offering a daytime drop-in center and overnight shelter for homeless, runaway, foster, and other at-risk youth. eddyhouse.org, 775-384-1129, info@eddyhouse.org.

The Embracing Project, a Las Vegas nonprofit offering a drop-in center, advocacy, mentorship, and other wrap-around services to youth survivors of violence and sexual exploitation. theembracingproject.org, 702-463-6929, tep_info@rop.com.

Nevada Partnership for Homeless Youth, a Las Vegas nonprofit providing housing and services for youth in crisis. nphy.org, 702-383-1332, info@nphy.org.

Signs of H.O.P.E. (Healing, Options, Prevention, Education), a Clark County nonprofit serving victims of sexual violence; it operates a 24/7 hotline and a counseling center, among other services. sohlv.org, 702-366-1640 or 888-366-1640, community@sohlv.org.

The Children's Cabinet, a statewide nonprofit serving parents and children with offices in Reno, Carson City, Las Vegas, and Elko. Programs vary by city, contact for more information: childrenscabinet.org, 775-856-6200, mail@childrenscabinet.org.

Xquisite, a nonprofit in Northern Nevada designed to bring freedom to survivors of sex trafficking, sexual assault, and domestic violence by helping them to live healthy, flourishing lives. xquisite.org, 775-434-7255 (emergency hotline).

New York

Girls Educational and Mentoring Services, Inc., or *G.E.M.S.*, an anti-trafficking nonprofit offering housing, education, court advocacy, and survivor leadership, based in New York City. gems-girls.org, 917-837-0357, info@gems-girls.org.

LifeWay Network Inc., an anti-trafficking nonprofit offering housing, mentorship, and education based in Tarrytown, New York. lifewaynetwork.org, 718-779-8075, help@LifeWayNetwork.org

Restore NYC, an anti-trafficking nonprofit offering counseling, housing, and economic-empowerment solutions to survivors based in New York City. restorenyc.org, (212) 840-8484, info@restorenyc.org.

Safe Horizon, a victims' assistance nonprofit offering shelter, legal aid, counseling, and other programs based in New York City. safehorizon.org, 800–621-HOPE or 212-577-7700, website@safehorizon.org.

The South

A Safe Place, a Wilmington, North Carolina nonprofit providing trauma-informed services and housing to sex trafficking survivors. asafeplacetogo.com, 855-723-7529 ext. 3, info@asafeplacetogo.com.

BeLoved Atlanta, a nonprofit providing safe homes and a two-year restoration program for women overcoming sex trafficking. belovedatlanta.org, 770-630-7765, info@belovedatlanta.org.

Partners Against Trafficking Humans or PATH, an anti-trafficking organization with a hotline based in Little Rock, Arkansas. pathsaves.org, 501–301-HELP (4357), info@pathsaves.org.

Street Grace, a nonprofit that serves child sex trafficking victims in Georgia, Tennessee, and Texas. streetgrace.org, 678-809-2111 or 888-373-3223, info@streetgrace.org.

The Institute for Shelter Care, a national faith-based organization based in Louisville, Kentucky, offering mentorship, research, and support to organizations who are operating residential programs for the sexually exploited. instituteforsheltercare.org, info@instituteforsheltercare.org.

The WellHouse, an Odenville, Alabama-based organization offering residential and therapeutic programs to female sex trafficking victims. the-wellhouse.org, 205-306-6058 and 800-991-0948, info@the-wellhouse.org.

Wellspring Living, an Atlanta nonprofit providing recovery services for domestic sex trafficking victims and those at risk. wellspringliving.org, 404-948-4673.

Unshackled by Love Ministries, a Lexington, Kentucky, faith-based nonprofit offering housing and trauma-informed rehabilitation services for sex trafficking victims. unshackledbylove.org, 859-509-6421, info@unshackledbylove.org.

Texas

New Day for Children, an Alamo nonprofit that raises and provides financial support for restorative care for sex trafficked children; its funding provides a safe and secure living environment, school tuition, therapy, medical/dental care, equine therapy, and other essential needs. newdayforchildren.com, moreinfo@newdayforchildren.com.

Redeemed operates a faith-based, trauma-informed, long-term residential program for sex trafficking survivors around Houston. redeemedtx.org, 832-447-4130, info@redeemedtx.org

The Landing, an anti-trafficking nonprofit with a drop-in center for minor and adult trafficking survivors in the Houston area. thelanding. org, 713-766-1111, hello@thelanding.org

The West

Gospel Rescue Mission, a faith-based organization offering shelter for people in crisis in Tucson, Arizona. grmtucson.com, 520-740-1501, web@grmtucson.com.

Mirror Ministries, a faith-based organization serving sex trafficking victims in Tri-Cities, Washington. mirror-ministries.org, info@mirror-ministries.org, local twenty-four/seven hotline is 509-212-9995

Organization for Prostitution Survivors, a Seattle-based social services organization led by survivors of commercial sexual exploitation. seattleops.org, 206-337-6155, info@seattleops.org.

Phoenix Dream Center, a faith-based nonprofit devoted to ending human trafficking and childhood hunger. phoenixdreamcenter.org, 602-516-0033.

Real Escape from the Sex Trade or REST, a direct service provider in Seattle. iwantrest.com, 206–451-REST for services, info@iwantrest.com.

Shelter From the Storm, a La Grande, Oregon, nonprofit serving victims of violence and sexual assault. unioncountysfs.org, 541-963-7226 or 541-963-9261.

Voluntad, a Denver, Colorado, organization providing services and support to human trafficking survivors. voluntad.org, 303-433-2712, services@Voluntad.org.

POSSIBLE SIGNS YOUR FRIEND OR LOVED ONE IS BEING SEX TRAFFICKED

Like domestic violence, sex trafficking is the product of an abusive relationship, and relationships, obviously, aren't tangible things. Still, there are some common red flags that could indicate that someone you love is being sex trafficked.[4]

Fear and/or submission. One major character trait that is common among sex trafficking victims is the presence of excessive fear or anxiety or paranoia. This can manifest in obvious ways, such as shaking or crying, or in less obvious ways, like submission. As illustrated in this book, sex trafficking victims frequently live under the thumbs of their traffickers. As such, sex trafficking victims may defer to their traffickers before giving information to another person or may not even have access to their own identification documents, like their birth certificate or driver's license.

Inappropriate, excessive sexuality. Provocative attire or behavior alone is not a sign of sex trafficking. (Indeed, police on the Las Vegas Strip have gotten in trouble for assuming as much.) But an adolescent girl acting or dressing overly sexual for her age is a potential sign, as is a woman wearing little clothing given the weather conditions. Remember the anecdote in Chapter 15 about Angela in the cold Chicago weather? She was staying at a high-priced hotel but didn't have a coat to keep her warm. Angela said the people at the hotel looked at her like she was crazy, walking around with just a sweater. This sort of mismatch between a woman's clothing and the environmental conditions could be a sign of trafficking.

Injuries and/or tattoos. As documented extensively in this book, many pimps beat their prostitutes and many also brand them with tattoos, marking them as their property. These two physical signs might be among the strongest indicators that someone you know is being trafficked. For tattoos, you'll want to especially be on the lookout for ink depicting money, sex, or pimp slang (see below).

Unexplained and/or unusual behaviors or possessions. The most obvious example in this category is when a girl or woman suddenly shows up with luxury items like jewelry, shoes, or phones without a new source of income. But that's not the only possible sign. Another could be a girl or woman with multiple phones and/or multiple social media accounts on the same platform, for no obvious or explained reason. Another could be a person who works long or excessive hours or who is always "on demand" or at a particular person's beck and call. A particularly concerning sign is a girl or woman who lives at a massage parlor or similar business or who is not free to leave wherever she is staying.

Unaccompanied or evasive minors. While not discussed at length in this book, some sex traffickers prey on underage girls or, in rarer cases, boys. Signs that a minor may be trafficked can include minors who are unaccompanied at nighttime, particularly in places typically reserved for adults, or who falter or try to avoid answering questions about who they are with or what they are doing.

Use of prostitution-related slang. Another sign that a friend or loved one may be a victim of sex trafficking is if they use certain terms from the pimp-prostitute subculture. Here is a glossary of several common terms used in The Game.[5]

Glossary Terms

Bottom or *Bottom Bitch*: This is a pimp's top prostitute, the woman (or girl) who serves as the pimp's right hand, helping him collect money and/or train other women in his stable.

Catch a date: To secure and perform services for a sex buyer.

Choosing up: This is the process by which a prostitute submits to serve a pimp. It can be as subtle as making eye contact or as formal as paying a fee. Prostitutes working for one pimp can choose up with another rival, a dynamic portrayed in depictions of the pimp-prostitute subculture. ("Your bitch chose me.")

Dry serve: When a non-pimp pretends to act like a prostitute's pimp (sometimes so that prostitute can get away from an abusive pimp).

Ducks: Black women.

Exit Fee: A fee a pimp will demand if a prostitute tries to leave him.

Family or *Folks:* This is how prostitutes may refer to other people who work under or with their pimp.

Greek: Anal sex.

Gorilla (or Guerilla): A pimp who uses violence to control his prostitutes.

Knock: The process by which a pimp recruits a prostitute into his servitude.

Out of pocket: When a prostitute is disobeying her pimp.

Quota: The amount of money a pimp expects his prostitute to earn every day.

Reckless eyeballing: When a prostitute is looking around instead of looking at the ground. Pimps expect their prostitutes to keep their eyes on the ground, otherwise they may interact with other pimps who could steal them away.

Renegade: A prostitute who doesn't work for a pimp.

Romeo: A pimp who controls prostitutes through psychological manipulation, often by showering them with affection.

Snow Bunny: A white prostitute.

Stable: A group of prostitutes working for a pimp.

The Game or *The Life*: A shorthand label for the pimp-prostitute subculture.

Track or *Blade* or *Ho Stroll*: A stretch of road where prostitutes walk to pick up sex buyers.

Trick: Another word for a john or sex buyer.

Turn out: The act of a pimp making a woman or girl work as a prostitute.

Wifey or *Wife-in-Law* or *Sister Wife*: This is what prostitutes may call each other when they work for the same pimp.

Notes

Introduction

1. Domestic sex trafficking in the United States takes many forms, including pimp-controlled trafficking, trafficking by gangs, and even familial trafficking, in which parents traffic their children or a husband traffics his wife. There is no data on which of these forms is the most prevalent.

2. Some in the anti-trafficking community believe the term "prostitute" is labelling and offensive and prefer descriptions like survivors, survivors of commercial sexual exploitations (or trafficking), women involved in the sex trade, or people who were prostituted. I understand and respect that position, but I will sometimes use in this book the term "prostitute" as well as occasionally its street synonyms "ho" and "bitch" to reflect the way some people speak in the United States. This is intended to reflect the pimp-prostitute subculture and not to offend or label anyone.

3. Pimpin' Ken Ivy with Karen Hunter, *Pimpology: The 48 Laws of the Game* (New York: Gallery Books, 2008).

4. At least some states also have laws against pimping, which is generally defined as living from the earnings of a prostitute.

5. "Attorney General Masto Announces Bill to Combat Sex Trafficking Signed Into Law," Nevada Attorney General Press Release, June 6, 2013, accessed August 19, 2022, https://ag.nv.gov/News/PR/2013/Human_Trafficking /Attorney_General_Masto_Announces_Bill_to_Combat_Sex_Trafficking _Signed_Into_Law/#:~:text=Assembly%20Bill%2067%20establishes%20the ,supporters%20at%20the%20bill%20signing.

Chapter 1

1. Angela was the primary source for this chapter.

2. Like many victims of sex trafficking or trauma in general, Angela sometimes struggles with her memory. This came into play as we attempted to pin down exactly when she arrived in Las Vegas with her pimp Dallas. We determined that her nervous walk down The Strip occurred in mid-2006 based on several data points. First, she remembered listening to Suga Free's album *Just Add Water* during their drive to Las Vegas. That album was released on May 9, 2006. That suggests Angela's harrowing road trip with

Dallas occurred after that date. However, as documented in Julia Beverly's book, *Sweet Jones: Pimp C's Trill Life Story*, Angela briefly worked for the pimp Ocean Fleming after leaving Mally Mall around Christmas 2006. Angela also distinctly remembers that it was warm enough in Las Vegas that she didn't need to wear a coat the night she walked The Strip. By October, temperatures generally fall in Las Vegas. Thus, we determined that her first night in Las Vegas probably occurred sometime between mid-May and September 2006.

3. Prostitutes who solicit sex buyers in Las Vegas casinos are said to "work the carpet" (as in the carpeted floor of the casino) as opposed to "working the street" or "working the corner."

4. This statement is not intended as a negative, racial stereotype. Rather, it's widely understood in the world of prostitution that street pimps in particular are big, Black men.

5. *State of Texas v. Angelina Garcia Delgado* (name later changed to Angelina Delgado Koudas), Case No. 486538, (Texas 183rd District Court, Harris County, Texas, June 22, 1988).

6. The National Student Clearinghouse confirmed Angela attended Houston Community College.

7. The National Student Clearinghouse confirmed Angela attended Sanford-Brown College in Houston.

8. In the trafficking survivor community, it's not considered appropriate to name a prostituted person without their permission. As I could not track down Angela's friend in this case, I elected not to provide her first name in this book.

9. Andre McDaniels and five others were indicted in August 2009 for multiple counts of sex trafficking in connection with commercial sex businesses disguised as spas and massage parlors in Houston. McDaniels entered a guilty plea in September 2012 and was sentenced to ninety-six months in federal prison. *USA v. Butler, et al*, Case No. 4:09-cr-00453, (United States District Court Southern District of Texas, Houston Division, August 4, 2009).

10. *State of Texas v. Angela Delgado*, Case No. 967125 (Texas 262nd District Court, Harris County, Texas, November 5, 2003).

CHAPTER 2

1. Angela was the primary source for this chapter. The description of the mansion was corroborated by Donald Hoier; ex-stripper and ex–porn star Sandi Jackmon, who described an encounter she had with Mally in her 2020 book *The Rise and Fall of Sandi Jackmon*; an ex-Metro officer who asked for anonymity out of concern for the effect speaking out would have on this person's family; a music blogger who asked to remain anonymous because he didn't want to be connected to Mally or any other artist; and a person who was positioned to know Mally well but asked to remain anonymous for fear of retaliation. (This person's relationship with Mally was independently confirmed by documents.) The mansion description was further corroborated by court documents and Instagram posts by Mally Mall and by *The Rise and Fall of Sandi Jackmon*. Sandi J., *The Rise and Fall of Sandi Jackmon*, independently published, 2020. In the trafficking survivor community, it's not considered appropriate to name a prostituted person without their

permission. As I could not speak with J. in this case, I elected not to provide her name in this book.

2. While the general area where the mansion is located is drab, there are other large, fancy houses on the street currently, although the propertyn clearly stands out among the rest of the homes on the block.

CHAPTER 3

1. Angela was the primary source for this chapter.

2. Angela said Mally didn't refer to himself as a "pimp," but rather as a manager of prostitutes on a higher level than a mere pimp.

CHAPTER 4

1. Angela was the primary source for this chapter. Some descriptions in this chapter were corroborated by a person who was positioned to know Mally well but asked to remain anonymous for fear of retaliation. (This person's relationship with Mally was independently confirmed by documents.) Some of them were also corroborated by Las Vegas Metropolitan Police Department, Officer's Report for Search Warrant Service at 2857 Paradise Road, Tower 2, Apartment 106, Las Vegas, NV 89109, Event No. 100427–2886, April 28, 2010, at 11:00 hours and Las Vegas Metropolitan Police Department, Officer's Report for Service of a Search Warrant at Metropolis Condominiums, 360 E. Desert Inn, #807, Las Vegas, NV 89109, Event No. 100427–2886, April 27, 2010 (Both obtained through a public records request.) Some descriptions were also corroborated by Mally's later federal court case, *United States of America v. Jamal Rashid*, Case No. 2:19-cr-00246-GMN-NJK, (U.S. District Court for the District of Nevada, Las Vegas, September 25, 2019).

2. Angela says her clients included famous comedians and a reality television star who once snorted cocaine off her ass. She and I debated for years on whether to name these celebrities, to hold them accountable for their behavior. However, revisiting memories like that are incredibly painful for Angela. As such, she's fuzzy on some of the details and these celebrities, with their wealth and lawyers, could attack her credibility based on that. Never mind that it's typical for women in Angela's position to have difficulty remembering details of such encounters, or that the prevailing ethic in American society today is that we should "believe women." The truth is, Angela and I knew we'd face an uphill battle if we publicized the identities of her celebrity clients. So, ultimately, we decided not to name her famous clients in this book, although someday Angela may revisit that decision.

3. Jennifer Paone did not respond to requests to be interviewed for this book.

4. Julie's attorney, federal public defender Jason Hannan, did not respond to my emails requesting an interview with her. In fact, he apparently had his secretary hang up on me whenever I'd call his office and identify myself. Multiple times, I was put on hold and disconnected when I tried calling him in May 2023. When I kept calling back, his secretary finally said he didn't want to talk to me but confirmed he had been receiving my emails.

5. Repeated attempts to talk with various Bone Thugs-N-Harmony representatives over several months were unsuccessful. One eventually declined to comment.

6. Las Vegas Metropolitan Police Department, Officer's Report on Search Warrant Service at 2857 Paradise Road, Tower 2, Apartment 106, Las Vegas, NV 89109, Event No. 100427–2886, April 28, 2010, at 11:00 hours. (Obtained through a public records request.)

7. Julia Beverly, *Sweet Jones: Pimp C's Trill Life Story* (Atlanta, GA: Shreveport Ave Inc., 2015), 455, 458, 477, 478. Ocean Fleming declined to be interviewed for this book.

8. The anecdotes describing Angela's experiences with Ocean Fleming originate from descriptions in *Sweet Jones: Pimp C's Trill Life Story*. In that book, she is identified under the alias Jada.

9. The Public Information Office of the Las Vegas Metropolitan Police Department declined to participate in this book.

10. Vic Vigna declined to be interviewed for this book, saying he wanted to save his stories for his own book. I emailed him a detailed description of everything this book would say about him, but he never responded.

CHAPTER 5

1. This chapter draws on interviews with Don Hoier; former Metro police officer Roger Barrera; former Metro Sgt. Norm Jahn; and an ex-Metro officer who asked for anonymity out of concern for the effect speaking out would have on this person's family. The material in this chapter is also corroborated by an internal document authored by Karen Hughes, the former head of the Vice Section, entitled "Background Notes inception [sic] of Rashid investigation," which was written at the request of a deputy chief in 2014. (Obtained from Don.)

2. Felicia Mello, "Nevada ranks among worst for integrity in state government," The Center for Public Integrity, November 9, 2015, accessed September 5, 2023, https://www.reviewjournal.com/local/local-nevada/nevada-ranks-among-worst-for-integrity-in-state-government/

3. Julie Bindel, "A Ballot on the Brothels of Nevada," *The New York Review of Books*, July 13, 2018, accessed July 29, 2022, https://www.nybooks.com/daily/2018/07/13/a-ballot-on-the-brothels-of-nevada/.

4. Michelle L. Price, "Pandemic makes prostitution taboo in Nevada's legal brothels," Associated Press, February 20, 2021, accessed July 29, 2022, https://apnews.com/article/prostitution-taboo-nevada-coronavirus-c0647f194e2c7bf76743d671843cac4d

5. Prostitution is also illegal in Washoe County, Nevada, home to Reno, although the county does not have a population of more than 700,000. A county ordinance bans brothels.

6. "History of the Department," Las Vegas Metropolitan Police Department, accessed July 29, 2022, https://www.lvmpd.com/en-us/Pages/HistoryoftheDepartment.aspx

7. Christopher Baughman declined to be interviewed for this book.

8. Christopher Baughman, *Off the Street* (Lake Forest, CA: Behler Publications, 2011); Chris Baughman, *Off the Street: Redemption*. (Lake Forest, CA: Behler Publications, 2014).

9. The Associated Press, "Teens shot at Las Vegas school bus stop," *The Guardian*, December 12, 2007, accessed August 23, 2022, https://www.theguardian.com/world

/2007/dec/12/usgunviolence.usa; "One suspect arrested in shootings at bus stop," *Las Vegas Review-Journal*, December 13, 2007, accessed August 23, 2022, https://www.reviewjournal.com/news/one-suspect-arrested-in-shootings-at-bus-stop/; "Suspect in shooting at school bus stop to return to Nevada," *Las Vegas Review-Journal*, December 15, 2007, accessed August 23, 2022, https://www.reviewjournal.com/news/suspect-in-shooting-at-school-bus-stop-to-return-to-nevada/; "Three more arrested," *Las Vegas Review-Journal*, December 19, 2007, accessed August 23, 2022, https://www.reviewjournal.com/news/three-more-arrested/

10. Karen Hughes declined to be interviewed for this book.

11. "Clearly, I wasn't thinking," Barrera says now when describing why he told his acquaintance about the investigation into Mally. Barrera is no longer with the Metro but says he has second-guessed his behavior that night many times. Barrera said he was investigated by the department and no wrongdoing was found. He was never charged with any criminal wrongdoing.

CHAPTER 6

1. Don was the primary source for this chapter. Some descriptions in this chapter were corroborated by an ex-Metro officer who asked for anonymity out of concern for the effect speaking out would have on this person's family.

2. *Barbara Dapper v. Las Vegas Metropolitan Police Department, Officer Donald M. Hoier, Officer Troy D'Ambrosio, Officer Juanita Goode, Does I-X and Roe Corporations XI-XX*, Case No. CV-S-96–00223-LDG (United states District Court, District of Nevada, March 13, 1996).

3. Warren Gray declined to be interviewed for this book.

4. Don told me he wasn't aware of any escort service operating in Las Vegas that wasn't actually a front for prostitution. When he led an enforcement team for Vice, he and another officer once posed undercover in a hotel room as johns and requested two escorts from a service. The women came to the door and said, *Just so we're clear, we're not prostitutes.* Don replied, *Well, that's too bad, because we want prostitutes,* and slammed the door in their faces. A couple seconds later, the women knocked on the door and said, *Well, actually, we are prostitutes.* The women had initially said they weren't prostitutes as a sort of screening technique to avoid undercover cops.

5. Karen Hughes, internal Metro document entitled "Background Notes inception [sic] of Rashid investigation," which was written at the request of a deputy chief in 2014. (Obtained from Don.)

CHAPTER 7

1. Don was the primary source for this chapter. Events in this chapter were corroborated by an ex-Metro officer who asked for anonymity out of concern for the effect speaking out would have on this person's family. Some of the material in this chapter was also corroborated by an internal document authored by Karen Hughes entitled "Background Notes inception [sic] of Rashid investigation," which was written at the request of a deputy chief in 2014. (Obtained from Don.)

2. The basic details about Mally's mansion—its address, square footage and number of bathrooms and bedrooms—were derived from a lawsuit Mally filed against State Farm after a May 2016 fire. *Jamal Rashid v. State Farm Fire and Casualty Company and Matthew Keim*, Case No. 2:19-cv-01483-APG-EJY (U.S. District Court of the District of Nevada, Las Vegas, August 26, 2019). After the case was remanded to a Nevada state court, the parties stipulated to a dismissal with prejudice, which was entered into the court in late September 2022.

3. Las Vegas Metropolitan Police Department, Property Report for 4311 E. Oquendo Road, Las Vegas, NV 89122 [sic], Event No. 100427–2886, April 28, 2010 at 23:00 hours; Las Vegas Metropolitan Police Department, Property Report for 4311 E. Oquendo Road, Las Vegas, NV 89122 [sic], Event No. 100427–2886, April 28, 2010 at 20:00 hours; Las Vegas Metropolitan Police Department, Property Report for 4311 E. Oquendo Road, Las Vegas, NV 89120, Event No. 100427–2886, April 28, 2010 at 22:50 hours; Las Vegas Metropolitan Police Department, Property Report for 4311 E. Oquendo Road, Las Vegas, NV 89122 [sic], Event No. 100427–2886, April 28, 2010 at 20:00 hours, revised on May 5, 2010. (All obtained through a public records request.)

4. At another location that Metro raided, officers found among Mally's things the business card of a New York-based FBI special agent.

5. David Logue did not respond to requests to be interviewed for this book.

CHAPTER 8

1. This chapter draws on interviews with hip-hop scholar and cultural critic Michael A. Gonzales; Angela; retired Lodi Police Det. Dale Eubanks; rapper Luce Cannon who said Mally managed him for five years; people who were positioned to know Mally well, but asked to remain anonymous for fear of retaliation (These relationships with Mally were independently confirmed by documents); and a music blogger who asked to remain anonymous because he didn't want to be connected to Mally or any other artist. Some of the material in this chapter is also corroborated by Las Vegas Metropolitan Police Department, Officer's Report on Search Warrant Service at 2857 Paradise Road, Tower 2, Apartment 106, Las Vegas, NV 89109, Event No. 100427–2886, April 28, 2010, at 11:00 hours. (Obtained through a public records request.)

2. Ruth Mazo Karras, *Common Women: Prostitution and Sexuality in Medieval England.* (New York: Oxford University Press, 1996), 57–58.

3. Jesse Sheidlower, "A History of Pimping," *Slate*, February 11, 2008, accessed September 15, 2023, https://slate.com/human-interest/2008/02/a-brief-history-of-the-verb-to-pimp.html

4. Elizabeth and James Vorenberg, "The Biggest Pimp of All," *The Atlantic*, January 1977, accessed June 9, 2022, https://www.theatlantic.com/magazine/archive/1977/01/the-biggest-pimp-of-all/305057/

5. Emma Goldman, "The Traffic in Women," in *Anarchism and Other Essays* (New York: Mother Earth Publishing Association, 1910), 183–200.

6. Jessica Pliley, "Prostitution in America," *Oxford Research Encyclopedia of American History*, November 27, 2018.

7. "Iceberg Slim: Life lessons from a pimp-turned-luminary," CBC Radio, September 3, 2015, accessed July 29, 2022, https://www.cbc.ca/radio/q/schedule-for-thursday -september-3-1.3212964/iceberg-slim-life-lessons-from-a-pimp-turned-luminary-1 .3212971

8. A. D. Carson, "Hip-hop holiday signals a turning point in education for a music form that began at a back-to-school party in the Bronx," *The Conversation*, August 9, 2021, accessed July 29, 2022, https://theconversation.com/hip-hop-holiday-signals-a -turning-point-in-education-for-a-music-form-that-began-at-a-back-to-school-party -in-the-bronx-165525

9. Michael A. Gonzales, "Cashmere Thoughts," in *Beats, Rhymes & Life: What We Love and Hate About Hip-Hop*, ed. Ytasha Womack, et al. (New York: Harlem Moon, 2007).

10. Snoop Dogg, whose real name is Calvin Cordozar Broadus Jr., claimed in a 2013 *Rolling Stone* article that he worked as a pimp in 2003 while on a *Playboy* tour. "I did a *Playboy* tour, and I had a bus follow me with 10 bitches on it," he told the magazine. "I could fire a bitch, fuck a bitch, get a new ho: It was my program. City to city, titty to titty, hotel room to hotel room, athlete to athlete, entertainer to entertainer." Snoop claimed that he let his women keep the money from servicing clients, who he said included professional athletes. (He specifically name dropped the Denver Broncos and the Denver Nuggets.) "I'd act like I'd take the money from the bitch, but I'd let her have it," he said. "It was never about the money; it was about the fascination of being a pimp. . . . As a kid I dreamed of being a pimp, I dreamed of having cars and clothes and bitches to match. I said, 'Fuck it—I'm finna do it.'"

11. Ice-T (sometimes written as Ice T), whose real name is Tracy Lauren Marrow, worked as a pimp and a jewel thief before he got into rapping and, later, the larger entertainment business. Ice-T appeared in the 1998 HBO documentary *Pimps Up, Ho's Down*, which depicted American pimps' annual "Players Ball," where one sex trafficker is honored as "Pimp of the Year."

12. Julia Beverly, *Sweet Jones: Pimp C's Trill Life Story* (Atlanta, GA: Shreveport Ave Inc., 2015), 455, 458, 477–78.

13. Pimp C dissed Mally on a song he recorded with BankRoll Jonez called "Pedigree." On the song, Pimp C makes fun of Mally for allowing some of his girls to take home 50 percent of their earnings:
Niggas say they not trickin' and sucking them hoes' cocks
Lettin' them keep half the money, playin' the shortstop
I was quarterbackin', nigga, puttin' the bitch out on the track
Makin' her get down for the grind and bring all the money back.

14. Several posts online list Mally Mall's birthday as July 7, 1977 (which would make his birthdate 7/7/77), but that's not true. His Nevada driver's license, a copy of which was made public through *Jamal Rashid v. State Farm Fire and Casualty Company and Matthew Keim*, Case No. 2:19-cv-01483-APG-EJY (United States District Court, District of Nevada, Las Vegas, August 26, 2019) shows that his date of birth was July 3, 1975.

15. Justin Hunte, "Mally Mall did 'Love & Hip Hop' Because He Kept Getting Mistaken for Marley Marl," *HipHopDX*, April 12, 2016, accessed June 22, 2022, https:

//hiphopdx.com/news/id.38309/title.mally-mall-did-love-hip-hop-because-he-kept
-getting-mistaken-for-marley-marl#.

16. Mally's lawyers in a court filing as well as a person who was positioned to know Mally well both say that his mother abandoned him (Angela, who believes Mally tells lies, is skeptical of this story).

17. Information about Mally's arrest for statutory rape and his interview with the California State Fire Marshal come from a lengthy declaration by former Lodi Police Department Det. Kenneth K. Melgoza, which was filed as an exhibit in a Search Warrant and Seizure Order issued as part of the department's investigation into Mally's sale of cloned phones, as described in the subsequent paragraphs.

18. SOCIAL TV, "SOCIAL Magazine's Dre Dynasty Interview's Mally Mall," YouTube, January 10, 2016, accessed April 3, 2024, https://www.youtube.com/watch?v=OC7Zu2_hY6A&t=194s.

19. The information about Mally's involvement with cloned phones comes from search warrant documents obtained from San Joaquin County Superior Court.

20. Mally ultimately pleaded no contest in this case. Later he moved to have his plea changed to not guilty and the matter expunged. His motion, according to the available documents, was granted.

21. *The People of the State of California v. Jamal Fayeq Rashid*, Case No. SC062160A (San Joaquin County Superior Court, September 15, 1997); *The People of the State of California v. Jamal Rashid*, Case No. SC062161A, (San Joaquin County Superior Court, September 15, 1997) Please note, I obtained more than 220 pages of court records about Mally from the San Joaquin County Superior Court in California. The records stretch from the 1990s into the 2000s and while they include a lot of specific details about the investigation of Mally's sale of cloned phones, they also are confusing and contradictory in parts. For example, according to the records provided, Mally was initially charged in the clone phone case on June 5, 1997, in the Municipal Court of California, County of San Joaquin, Lodi Judicial District, in Case No. LP-97–6329, DA Case COM 0281116. In that complaint, Mally was charged with six total counts. An amended complaint was filed for that same case number and DA number on July 16, 1997. On July 29, 1997, a complaint was filed against Mally in the Municipal Court of California, County of San Joaquin, Stockton Judicial District, under Case No. SP97–28011, charging him with one count of Sale/Possession of a Device to Defraud the Phone Company. (This document was date-stamped twice, the second date being September 5, 1997.) Then, on September 16, 1997, two separate Informations were filed against Mally in the Superior Court of California, County of San Joaquin. One case, No. SC62160A, DA Case INF 0285631, charged Mally with one count of Sale/Possession of a Device to Defraud the Phone Company. The other case, No. SC62161A, DA Case INF 0281116, charged Mally with several counts and enhancements. It's unclear why two Informations were filed against Mally in this case on the same day by the San Joaquin County District Attorney. The DA's office declined to answer any questions about the cases. However, it appears from subsequent court filings that Mally was sentenced to five years' probation in both Case No. SC0621610A and SC062161A on March 23, 1998. In fact, subsequent documents in which Mally sought to have that matter expunged list the case numbers together.

22. *The People of the State of California v. Jamal Rashid*, Case No. LF004495A (San Joaquin County Superior Court, May 5, 1999).

23. *Lindsey Morin v. Jamal Rashid*, Case No. 311604 (San Joaquin County Superior Court, October 6, 1999).

24. HipHopDX, "Mally Mall talks Mac Dre & Details Drake recording 'The Motto'," YouTube, April 12, 2016, accessed August 16, 2022, https://www.youtube.com/watch?v=qxP-B1mk7BQ.

25. Many times, women who find themselves in prostitution end up staying in The Life because, even though it's toxic, they find it better than their previous experiences, such as abusive childhoods.

26. A representative for Poo Bear did not respond to several interview requests. Poo Bear also did not respond to direct attempts to contact him through his Instagram account.

27. Bianca Torres, "Giant Records' Shawn 'Tubby' Holiday Shares Advice on Artists Obtaining Longevity, What Makes a Hit Record and More," *XXL*, July 29, 2021, accessed August 17, 2022, https://www.xxlmag.com/shawn-holiday-interview/

28. Of course, you could argue that there are many in the music business who are fakes. Also, whatever criticisms he may face as a legitimate artist, Mally boasts sixteen Grammy nominations, four Grammy Awards, and nearly 50 singles reaching Billboard's Hot 100 List, according to a July 2023 press release he put out.

29. Devin, "Drake Celebrates 25th Birthday In Las Vegas," Rap-Up, October 23, 2011, accessed July 29, 2022, https://www.rap-up.com/2011/10/23/drake-celebrates-25th-birthday-in-las-vegas/

30. Joshua Espinoza, "T-Minus Explains How He Crafted the Beat for Drake's 'The Motto,'" *Complex*, December 8, 2017, accessed July 29, 2022, https://www.complex.com/music/2017/12/t-minus-breaks-down-creating-beat-for-drake-motto

31. Billboard Staff, "Drake's 'Thank Me Later' Debuts At No. 1 On Billboard 200 With 447,000," Billboard, June 23, 2010, accessed July 29, 2022, https://www.billboard.com/music/music-news/drakes-thank-me-later-debuts-at-no-1-on-billboard-200-with-447000-1204818/

32. Chris Malone, "How Many Grammy Awards Does Drake Have?," Showbiz CheatSheet, September 4, 2021, accessed July 29, 2022, https://www.cheatsheet.com/entertainment/how-many-grammy-awards-does-drake-have.html/

33. Andy James, "Beat Break: T-Minus Shares the Story Behind His 5 Biggest Songs," *DJBooth*, May 15, 2018, accessed July 29, 2022, https://djbooth.net/features/2018-05-15-t-minus-beat-break-interview

34. Joshua Espinoza, "T-Minus Explains How He Crafted the Beat for Drake's 'The Motto.'"

35. Andy James, "Beat Break: T-Minus Shares the Story Behind His 5 Biggest Songs."

36. Through a representative, DJ Franzen declined to be interviewed for this book.

37. Brian "Z" Zisook, "One Take Drake: The Backstory Behind 'The Motto,'" *DJBooth*, March 19, 2018, accessed March 9, 2023, https://djbooth.net/features/2018-03-19-drake-the-motto-one-take; djvlad, "Mally Mall Talks About Getting Justin Bieber a Monkey & Relationship w/ Drake," YouTube, May 6, 2013, accessed March 9, 2023, https://www

.youtube.com/watch?app=desktop&v=FFBx9jSLm3k&lc=UgiktG1xFHr9FngCoAEC; Eileen Shapiro, "Mally Mall: 'Conversation With A Global Anomaly,'" by Eileen Shapiro and Gabriel Evan, Louder Than War, June 20, 2021, accessed March 9, 2023, https://loudenthanwar.com/mally-mall-conversation-with-a-global-anomaly-by-eileen-shapiro-and-gabriel-evan/

38. Andy James, "Beat Break: T-Minus Shares the Story Behind His 5 Biggest Songs."

39. Devin, "New Music: Drake F/ Lil Wayne – 'The Motto,'" Rap-Up, October 31, 2011, accessed July 29, 2022, https://www.rap-up.com/2011/10/31/new-music-drake-f-lil-wayne-the-motto/

40. Oliver, "Drake—The Motto Feat. Lil Wayne," November 1, 2011, accessed July 29, 2022, http://octobersveryown.blogspot.com/2011/11/drake-feat-lil-wayne-motto.html

41. "Week Ending Oct. 6, 2013. Songs: Adele Reaches A Milestone," Yahoo! Entertainment, October 9, 2013, accessed July 29, 2022, https://www.yahoo.com/entertainment/blogs/chart-watch/week-ending-oct-6-2013-songs-adele-reaches-192150577.html

42. "Chart History: Drake," Billboard, accessed July 29, 2022, https://www.billboard.com/artist/drake/chart-history/bsi/

43. Amanda London, "'The Motto' by Drake (ft. Lil Wayne and Tyga)," Song Meanings + Facts, August 4, 2021, accessed July 29, 2022, https://www.songmeaningsandfacts.com/the-motto-by-drake-ft-lil-wayne-and-tyga/

44. "Year-End Charts: Hot 100 Songs," Billboard, accessed July 29, 2022, https://www.billboard.com/charts/year-end/2012/hot-100-songs/

45. Benjamin R. Freed, "Wale Nominated for Best Rap Song Grammy Award," DCist, December 6, 2012, accessed July 29, 2022, https://dcist.com/story/12/12/06/wale-nominated-for-best-rap-song-gr/

46. HipHopDX, "Mally Mall talks Mac Dre & Details Drake recording 'The Motto,'" YouTube, April 12, 2016, accessed August 16, 2022, https://www.youtube.com/watch?v=qxP-B1mk7BQ

47. Kyle Eustice, "Mally Mall Credits Justin Bieber for Changing His Life," HipHopDX, June 7, 2018, accessed July 29, 2022, https://hiphopdx.com/news/id.47190/title.mally-mall-credits-justin-bieber-for-changing-his-life#

48. djvald, "Mally Mall Talks About Getting Justin Bieber a Monkey & Relationship w/ Drake," YouTube, May 6, 2013, accessed May 23, 2024, https://www.youtube.com/watch?v=FFBx9jSLm3k; djvald, "Mally Mall Shows Off His Exotic Animals (Flashback)," YouTube, April 8, 2019, accessed May 23, 2024, https://www.youtube.com/watch?v=Y3kw0V1Am74.

49. Meghan Mabey, "Justin's Roman Numeral Tattoo on his Chest/Shoulder," PopStarTats.com, January 16, 2013, accessed July 29, 2022, http://www.popstartats.com/justin-bieber-tattoos/jb-chest/roman-numeral-1975/

50. Ellie Hall, "Everything You Need To Know About Justin Bieber And His Monkey," Buzzfeed News, April 3, 2013, accessed July 29, 2022, https://www.buzzfeednews.com/article/ellievhall/everything-you-need-to-know-about-justin-bieber-and-his-monk

51. Sean Michaels, "Justin Bieber gives up on Mally the monkey," The Guardian, April 24, 2013, accessed July 29, 2022, https://www.theguardian.com/music/2013/apr/24/justin-bieber-gives-up-on-mally-monkey

52. Laura Smith-Spark, "Justin Bieber's monkey starts new life in German zoo," CNN, June 27, 2013, accessed July 29, 2022, https://www.cnn.com/2013/06/27/world/europe/germany-justin-bieber-monkey/index.html

53. Associated Press, "Mally Mall Sentenced to Prison in Las Vegas Prostitution Case," Billboard, May 13, 2021, accessed July 29, 2022, https://www.billboard.com/pro/mally-mall-sentenced-prison-las-vegas-prostitution-case/

54. Producers appearing on songs and in music videos has been a point of contention in hip hop since at least the 1995 Source Awards, when Death Row Records co-founder Suge Knight dissed Sean "Puffy" Combs for being an "executive producer trying to be all in the videos, all on the record, dancing." Combs, now known as Diddy, of course has since established himself as a legitimate rapper, not only an executive and a producer. There's at least a couple of fairly spirited debates online over whether the producer Lil Jon also qualifies as a rapper. The comedian Dave Chappelle famously made fun of his simple lyrics ("What?" "Yeah!") on his classic Comedy Central show.

55. Representatives of VH1 declined to be interviewed for this book.

56. Nikki Mudarris declined to be interviewed for this book.

57. Counts here and elsewhere of the number of songs for which Mally has received credit were calculated from a spreadsheet I made by hand from information pulled from Genius, a website that lists songs lyrics and songwriting and producing credits. I found Mally's songs on the website by using the search function on the homepage, genius.com, and entering "Mally Mall." Several songs associated with Mally did not have a release date; they therefore were not included in any calculations presented in this book. Mally also received credit through this website for several songs that were apparently remixes of other songs he had worked on. For calculation purposes, I only counted those songs once. I should also note that while I made every attempt to ensure that the information I scraped from the website was copied and pasted accurately into my spreadsheet, I did do this by hand for nearly 200 songs. It's possible that some small errors were entered and subsequently missed upon review.

CHAPTER 9

1. Don Hoier was the primary source for this chapter.

2. Christopher Baughman, *Off the Street* (Lake Forest, CA: Behler Publications, 2011).

3. Al Beas declined to be interviewed for this book.

4. Alisha Grundy spoke with me for this book.

5. *The State of Nevada v. Raymond Sharpe*, Case No. C-11-274805-1 (Clark County, Nevada, July 15, 2011).

6. I wrote to Raymond Sharpe in prison, to inform him I'd be mentioning him in this book. He had a friend of his call me to say that he can prove that this description of his case, which I drew from court records and from speaking with Alisha Grundy, is entirely untrue. His friend said about the only thing that was true was that Sharpe and Grundy had a child together. I told his friend I would gladly look at the proof. His friend promised to talk with Sharpe again and said someone would get back to me. No one ever did.

7. Attempts to reach April Millard through her attorneys were unsuccessful.

8. *The State of Nevada v. Ocean Fleming*, Case No. C-11-276866-1 (Clark County, Nevada, October 14, 2011).

9. Don describes Fleming's August 2012 trial as "a circus" and told me the story of what happened over those seven days could be a book of its own. An associate of Fleming's was arrested at court, in an apparent attempt to cause a mistrial. On Day 4 of the trial, 25 Xanax pills were discovered in a suit jacket brought for Fleming to wear in court. It was thought that Fleming might have intended to overdose, with the idea of either killing himself or getting sent to the hospital, where he'd try to escape. The situation became so volatile Vice officers were tasked with escorting witnesses to and from court and a contingent of Gang Section officers were asked to be on hand as well. To avoid intimidation, jurors had to be snuck in and out of the building through backdoors and their lunches were brought to them at the courthouse. "It was fucking nuts," Don said.

10. In letters entered into the court record that Fleming addressed to his attorney Robert Draskovich, Fleming wrote that he talked with Sharpe while he was awaiting trial in jail in the spring of 2012. In those letters, Fleming refers to Baughman as a "crooked" cop and says Sharpe has shown him text messages between Baughman and Alisha Grundy, the woman who pounded on the neighbors' doors for help getting away from Sharpe. The text messages were flirty, suggesting to Fleming she and Baughman had a romantic relationship. Grundy told me that she tipped Sharpe off to the text messages, because while he hurt her, he is also her baby's father. Grundy said she did not have a romantic relationship with Baughman.

11. Liz Mercer did not respond to requests to be interviewed for this book. Later, in 2023, while Christopher Baughman debated whether to talk to me for this book, he asked me to stop reaching out to Mercer, who by then was his wife. I honored his request.

12. Trying to reach Aaron Cohen for comment was a bizarre odyssey. His LinkedIn page, https://www.linkedin.com/in/aaron-cohen-chasen-06ab648/, accessed July 22, 2022, among other dates, listed him as the managing director of the Abolish Slavery Coalition from January 2009 to March 2022 and as the executive director of Ukraine Disaster Relief from March 2022 to present. Both of those organizations are associated with someone named Dawn Adams. I emailed both organizations seeking Cohen's contact information. Through the email address for Ukraine Disaster Relief, I connected with a Dawn Adams who first asked me (among other questions) if I had money to pay Cohen because, she said, he rarely does unpaid interviews. When I explained that as a journalist I don't pay for interviews, she said I could e-mail her some questions that she would forward to Cohen because "he hasn't done live interviews in years due to mission security." When I e-mailed her questions, she responded, "You mentioned you were writing a book about sex trafficking and human trafficking. All of your questions are pertaining to Mr. Cohen's [sic] work and no questions regarding the subject of human trafficking on its own platform. The questions that you have presented will not be forwarded to Mr. Cohen as this is not what you were originally implying. For these reasons . . . we are declining the interview." I said that was fine, at least Cohen knows what I'm writing about. Then she responded that actually Cohen is not declining my interview, rather she is refusing to forward my questions to him and that I need to find some other way to contact him. So, I again returned to his LinkedIn page, where he also claimed to have served as a senior

policy advisor to the Bexar County Commissioners Court in Texas from March 2020 to March 2022. A public information officer told me in actuality he worked for Bexar County from March 2020 to April 2021, and his title was senior executive assistant (to Precinct 4 Commissioner Tommy Calvert). I tracked down three phone numbers and five email addresses for Cohen using the online people search tool SignalHire. Of the phone numbers, one was disconnected, and one was a wrong number. The third I never heard back from. Of the email addresses, one email bounced, another was delayed. However, an email sent to a Gmail account went through and that Gmail account was tied to a picture of Cohen. Cohen's publisher later told me that email address is the same one it had on file for Cohen. I never heard back from the email I sent, which laid out detailed, fact-checking questions to Cohen. I also sent the same questions to Cohen through a LinkedIn message. On August 1, 2022, someone named "Eliza" who apparently manages Cohen's LinkedIn profile responded to me. Eliza wrote, "Wanted to thank you for your inquiry and let you know that Mr. Cohen hasn't been doing interviews for some time. Appreciate your concern for the issue of human trafficking. Best wishes."

13. *Tiersa Baughman v. Christopher M. Baughman*, Case No. D-13–478162-D (Clark County, Nevada, April 5, 2013).

14. The events described are based primarily on Don's recollection. Marc Schifalacqua, now a senior assistant city attorney for the city of Henderson, declined to be interviewed for this book.

15. *The State of Nevada v. Arman Izadi*, Case No. C-13-289719-1 (Clark County, Nevada, May 10, 2013). Arman Izadi declined to be interviewed for this book.

16. "Izadi talks; Money, Ho's, Vegas and His Rap Career," Swagg News, accessed April 20, 2024, https://swaggnews-blog.tumblr.com/post/10622549027/izadi-talks-money-hos-vegas-and-his-rap-career/amp; "Izadi," ReverbNation, accessed April 20, 2024, https://www.reverbnation.com/artist/video/8756567.

17. CIs are not supposed to be committing crimes while working as a CI. CIs trade information to get out of a specific set of charges. If CIs continue to commit crimes, those crimes should be investigated. In the case of Izadi, once Don received word Izadi might be involved in criminal activity, he became a target for investigation. Don said if he had ever gotten similar information about Mally after he became a CI, Don would have opened an investigation on him, too. "I was praying I would get something like that," Don said.

18. Las Vegas Metropolitan Police Department, Arrest Report for Arman Izadi, ID/Event No. 2825076, April 24, 2013, 2700 South Las Vegas Boulevard, Unit 4305, Las Vegas, NV 89109. (Obtained through a public records request.)

19. Chris Baughman, *Off the Street: Redemption* (Lake Forest, CA: Behler Publications, 2013).

20. "Slave Hunter: Freeing Victims of Human Trafficking," MSNBC, November 11, 2013, accessed June 3, 2022, https://www.msnbc.com/documentaries/watch/slave-hunter-freeing-victims-of-human-trafficking-62335555826; "Slave Hunter: 'You're Making Me Nervous," [sic]" M.S.N.B.C., November 26, 2013, accessed June 3, 2022, https://www.msnbc.com/documentaries/watch/slave-hunter-youre-making-me-nervous

-74186819943; "Slave Hunter," MSNBC, November 26, 2013, accessed June 3, 2022, https://www.msnbc.com/documentaries/watch/slave-hunter-74278979790

21. Melissa Farley, Kenneth Franzblau, M. Alexis Kennedy, "Online Prostitution and Trafficking," *Albany Law Review*, 77(3) 2014: 1039–94, accessed September 19, 2023, https://www.albanylawreview.org/article/70164-online-prostitution-and-trafficking. The authors of this study reported that "according to estimates from eighteen sources including research studies, government reports, and nongovernmental agencies, on average 84% of women in prostitution are under third-party control or pimped or trafficked." The study looked at prostitutes worldwide.

22. "Slave Hunter," MSNBC, November 26, 2013, accessed July 29, 2022, https://www.msnbc.com/documentaries/watch/slave-hunter-74278979790

23. By MSNBC staff, "New MSNBC Series- Slave Hunter," N.B.C. News, November 12, 2013, accessed September 18, 2023, https://www.nbcnews.com/id/wbna53534382

24. Letter to Deb Finan, Vice President, Production & Programming at MSNBC from New York Anti-Trafficking Network, Washington Anti-Trafficking Response Network, International Rescue Committee, FB Consulting, Sex Workers Outreach Project-Denver, Women's Law Center of Maryland, Sex Workers Outreach Project-New York, Sex Workers Outreach Project-Chicago, Best Practices Policy Project, Freedom Network USA, Worker Justice Center of New York, Tapestri, Inc., Walter Leitner International Human Rights Clinic, International Institute of Buffalo, The Coalition to Abolish Slavery & Trafficking, Sex Worker Outreach Project-Las Vegas, Asian Pacific Islander Legal Outreach, Sex Worker Outreach Project-Bay Area, Americans for Immigrant Justice, Sex Workers Outreach Project-USA, Get EQUALNV, The PROS Network (Providers Offering Resources to Sex Workers), New York Harm Reduction Educators, Gay and Lesbian Community Center of Southern Nevada, and Sex Workers Project at the Urban Justice Center, sent on December 9, 2013, accessed May 22, 2022, http://www.bestpracticespolicy.org/2013/12/09/msnbc-launches-new-offensive-program-slave-hunter/

25. Anna Merlan, "Sex Workers Project Asks MSNBC to Pull Show on 'Sex Slaves,'" *Jezebel*, July 14, 2015, accessed September 27, 2022, https://jezebel.com/sex-workers-project-asks-msnbc-to-pull-show-on-sex-slav-1717782506; Mark Joyella, "Activist Groups Ask MSNBC to Cancel 'Sex Slaves in America,'" *Adweek*, July 15, 2015, accessed September 27, 2022, https://www.adweek.com/tvnewser/activist-groups-ask-msnbc-to-cancel-sex-slaves-in-america/267505/; Sex Workers Project at the Urban Justice Center; New York Anti-Trafficking Network; Freedom Network, National; FB Consulting; Helping Individual Prostitutes Survive (HIPS); MISSSEY, Inc.; Project SAFE; Abeni; KlaasKids Foundation; Advocating Opportunity; Women's Law Center of Maryland; STEPS to End Family Violence; Sex Workers Outreach Project-New York City; Sex Workers Outreach Project-San Antonio; Sex Workers Outreach Project-Las Vegas; Sex Workers Outreach Project-Tampa Bay; Sex Workers Outreach Project-Seattle; New Jersey Red Umbrella Alliance; letter to Timothy E. Smith, Senior Producer, MSNBC Documentaries, July 21, 2015, accessed September 27, 2022, https://sexworkersproject.org/downloads/2015/20150712-msnbc-sex-slaves-letter-sign-ons.pdf

26. A sex tape of Nikki Mudarris and Mally Mall was once leaked online.

27. "Love and Hip Hop' Star Mally Mall—FBI Raids Vegas House in Criminal Investigation,"TMZ, September 29, 2014, accessed May 23, 2022, https://www.tmz.com/2014/09/29/mally-mall-fbi-raids-las-vegas-house-love-and-hip-hop-search-warrant/

28. Joe Dickey declined to be interviewed for this book.

29. Cited elsewhere in this book, this document was entitled "Background Notes inception [sic] of Rashid investigation." (Obtained from Don.)

30. Brian Evans declined to be interviewed for this book.

CHAPTER 10

1. Don was the primary source for this chapter. Events in this chapter were corroborated by Don's wife, Dr. Shera Bradley, and his attorney, George Kelesis.

2. Joe Lombardo, who became governor of Nevada in January 2023, declined to be interviewed for this book.

3. Joe Schoenmann, "In Clark County sheriff race, Joe Lombardo, Larry Burns will pit police brass against police union," *Las Vegas Sun*, June 27, 2014, accessed July 29, 2022, https://lasvegassun.com/news/2014/jun/27/clark-county-sheriff-race-joe-lombardo-larry-burns/

4. Joe Schoenmann, "In Clark County sheriff race, Joe Lombardo, Larry Burns will pit police brass against police union," *Las Vegas Sun*, June 27, 2014, accessed July 29, 2022, https://lasvegassun.com/news/2014/jun/27/clark-county-sheriff-race-joe-lombardo-larry-burns/

5. Mike Blasky and Francis McCabe, "Lombardo wins Clark County sheriff's race," *Las Vegas Review-Journal*, November 5, 2014, accessed July 29, 2022, https://www.reviewjournal.com/news/lombardo-wins-clark-county-sheriffs-race/

6. In addition to treating sex trafficking survivors, Bradley also advocated for them in court. She fought a court order that would have compelled her to make the counseling records of one of her patients available to the fifteen-year-old girl's pimp, who was charged with sex trafficking. Bradley fought the court order all the way to the Nevada Supreme Court and won, upholding that psychologist-patient communications are privileged. That ruling was published, setting a citable precedent. See *Dr. Shera D. Bradley, Petitioner, v. The Eighth Judicial Court of the State of Nevada, in and for the County of Clark; and the Honorable Douglas W. Herndon, District Judge, Respondents, Dontae Hudson, an Individual; and the State of Nevada, By and Through Steven B. Wolfson, in his Official Capacity as District Attorney for the County of Clark, Real Parties in Interest*, Case No. 70522 (Nevada Supreme Court, November 22, 2017).

7. *Ocean Fleming v. The State of Nevada*, Case No. 62167 (Nevada Supreme Court, July 17, 2014).

8. *The State of Nevada v. Robert Sharpe, III*, Case No. C-14-301364-1, (Clark County, Nevada, October 3, 2014); *Autumn Richards v. Robert Sharpe*, Case No. A-16-742880-C (Clark County, Nevada, September 5, 2016). Robert Sharpe III was ultimately convicted of 12 criminal counts and sentenced to life in prison. He was found dead in his cell in High Desert State Prison in an unincorporated part of Clark County, Nevada in May 2017.

9. The detective mentioned here and in chapter 16 specifically asked not to be named for fear of personal and professional repercussions. The detective also declined to be interviewed for this book.

10. Kevin White did not respond to requests to be interviewed for this book.

11. Don's girlfriend got him a list of possible attorneys through a rider on her professional liability insurance, which she carried as a psychologist. She was able to go to her insurance carrier and lay out the parameters of Don's case, and the insurance company provided her a list of attorneys best suited to handle it. George Kelesis was the only name Don recognized on the list and the first attorney he called.

12. Cristina Silva, now a federal judge, did not respond to requests to be interviewed for this book.

13. Don knew this because, in July 2012, he had attended an Innocence Lost Coordinators Conference in Chicago. After he gave a presentation about the difficulties of taking Las Vegas cases federally, the agent in charge of the event said that if the local US Attorney's office was unwilling to move forward with a case, it should be forwarded to the Washington, DC, office for consideration.

14. When he initially walked into the meeting, Don thought there were so many DC attorneys there either because the Nevada office had concerns about White's case or simply because it was common practice for DC to take an interest in cases like that. He wasn't entirely sure which it was, but he became convinced it was the former after Silva cut off White's questioning.

15. Alisha Grundy told me that Baughman also once texted her "I love you" and sent her a link to a song and said, "This is our song." She said twice Baughman got a hotel room and asked her to visit him there. Grundy said she didn't meet him at the room either time, but she believes Baughman asked her to go there for sex. She said she did not have a sexual relationship with Baughman.

16. Don wanted to say something about his surprise. But he didn't want to start a pissing contest with White. So out of respect and decorum, he kept his mouth shut.

17. "Whitey Bulger," The Mob Museum, accessed July 29, 2022, https://themobmuseum.org/notable_names/whitey-bulger/

CHAPTER 11

1. Don Hoier was the primary source for this chapter.

2. George Knapp and Matt Adams, "I-Team: Former cop, suspected pimp linked together in FBI investigation," https://www.8newsnow.com/news/i-team-former-cop-suspected-pimp-linked-together-in-fbi-investigation/ KLAS-TV, November 11, 2016, accessed May 26, 2022.

3. "George Knapp," KLAS-TV, accessed September 20, 2023, https://www.8newsnow.com/author/george-knapp/

CHAPTER 12

1. I was the primary source for this chapter. Some of the events and descriptions in this chapter were corroborated by Matt Isaacs, a reporter on the *Frontline* documentary;

my wife, Buu Joseph; and former colleagues of mine at the *Las Vegas Review-Journal* who asked to remain anonymous for fear of retaliation.

2. Brian Joseph, "The Brief Life and Private Death of Alexandria Hill," *Mother Jones*, February 26, 2015, accessed May 23, 2022, https://www.motherjones.com/politics/2015/02/privatized-foster-care-mentor/

3. I chose not to name in this book the editors I worked for at the *Review-Journal*, not because I was afraid of them or because I was writing anything inaccurate, but because I wanted to try to avoid the sort of petty, pissing matches that frequently come out of reporting on journalism, which I thought would only distract from the plight of sex trafficking victims. Through an intermediary, *Review-Journal* editors specifically referenced in this book were told exactly what this book would say about them and given a chance to comment. Their responses, when they were given, are reflected in virtually their entirety in the endnotes of this book, with some light editing for ease of reading. (One editor, no longer with the *R-J*, did not respond.) In the interest of not debating my former employer, I've elected to let their statements stand on their own, without taking the time to refute their comments that I believe to be inaccurate. I think readers will be able to see where we disagree and can determine for themselves who to believe.

4. "EDITORIAL: Why we want to stop printing the Las Vegas Sun," *Las Vegas Review-Journal*, August 30, 2019, accessed July 29, 2022, https://www.reviewjournal.com/opinion/editorial-why-we-want-to-stop-printing-the-las-vegas-sun-1837661/

5. The Adelson family maintained that it always intended to publicly announce its ownership. "We understand the desire of the hard-working staff at the *R-J* and others in the community to know the identity of the paper's new owners, and it was always our intention to publicly announce our ownership of the R-J," the family said in a statement printed by the *Review-Journal* on December 17, 2015. James DeHaven, Howard Stutz, and Jennifer Robison, "Adelson son-in-law orchestrated family's purchase of Las Vegas Review-Journal," *Las Vegas Review-Journal*, December 17, 2015, accessed May 23, 2022, https://www.reviewjournal.com/local/local-las-vegas/adelson-son-in-law-orchestrated-familys-purchase-of-las-vegas-review-journal/

6. James DeHaven, Howard Stutz, and Jennifer Robison, "Adelson son-in-law orchestrated family's purchase of Las Vegas Review-Journal," *Las Vegas Review-Journal*, December 17, 2015, accessed May 23, 2022, https://www.reviewjournal.com/local/local-las-vegas/adelson-son-in-law-orchestrated-familys-purchase-of-las-vegas-review-journal/

7. Molly Ball, "Why Did Sheldon Adelson Buy Nevada's Largest Newspaper?," *The Atlantic*, December 17, 2015, accessed July 29, 2022, https://www.theatlantic.com/politics/archive/2015/12/why-did-sheldon-adelson-buy-nevadas-largest-newspaper/421035/

8. "With Adelson as Owner, Las Vegas Paper Needs Independent Public Editor," Common Cause, December 22, 2015, accessed July 29, 2022, https://www.commoncause.org/media/adelson-owner-las-vegas-review-journal-needs-independent-editor/.

9. Laura Wagner, "More Journalists Leaving 'Las Vegas Review-Journal' After Sale To Billionaire," NPR, May 9, 2016, accessed July 29, 2022, https://www.npr.org/sections/thetwo-way/2016/05/09/477423367/more-journalists-leaving-las-vegas-review-journal-after-sale-to-billionaire

10. David Folkenflik, "The Vegas Columnist And The Newspaper Owner Who Once Sued Him For Libel," NPR, January 14, 2016, accessed July 29, 2022, https://www.npr.org/2016/01/14/463070783/casino-magnate-and-new-newspaper-owner-has-history-of-suing-reporters

11. Lloyd Grove, "Why Did Frontline Kill Lowell Bergman's Gambling Documentary?," *The Daily Beast*, July 6, 2015, accessed July 29, 2022, https://www.thedailybeast.com/why-did-frontline-kill-lowell-bergmans-gambling-documentary

12. The editor referred to here said in a statement, "I have no recollection of asking the investigative team as a whole to come up with a 'big story' for the redesign launch. Of course I cared what the story would be and I never said I didn't. In fact we knew long before the redesign launch that the LVCVA investigation suggested by [then an investigative reporter at the newspaper] Jeff German would be our first A1 centerpiece for our new look."

13. John Dougherty, "NPRI's Transparency Project on the LVCVA," December 3, 2008, accessed August 1, 2023, https://www.npri.org/nevadajournal/npris-transparency-project-lvcva/

14. Arthur Kane, Brian Joseph, and Jeff German, "LVCVA spends millions to wine and dine but some question spending," *Las Vegas Review-Journal*, April 3, 2017, accessed May 23, 2022, https://www.reviewjournal.com/local/local-las-vegas/lvcva-spends-millions-to-wine-and-dine-but-some-question-spending/

15. Mario R. García, "It's a new look for the Las Vegas Review Journal," The Mario Blog, April 3, 2017, accessed July 29, 2022, https://garciamedia.com/blog/its-a-new-look-for-the-las-vegas-review-journal/

16. This reporting eventually led to an audit of the Las Vegas Convention and Visitors Authority, which found executives at the agency misused Southwest Airlines gift cards. This, in turn, led to criminal charges being filed, which were settled in 2020 and 2021, and to a change in the agency's leadership.

17. An editor referred to in this book said in a statement, "I have no knowledge of whether Sheldon Adelson was copied on a letter from the authority's president complaining about Brian."

18. Richard N. Velotta, "Review-Journal defends reporting tactics criticized by LVCVA executive," *Las Vegas Review-Journal*, April 20, 2017, accessed May 23, 2022, https://www.reviewjournal.com/local/local-las-vegas/review-journal-defends-reporting-tactics-criticized-by-lvcva-executive/

19. An editor referred to in this book said in a statement that if Adelson received such a letter, "it was of no consequence to the RJ."

20. Richard N. Velotta, "Review-Journal defends reporting tactics criticized by LVCVA executive," *Las Vegas Review-Journal*, April 20, 2017, accessed May 23, 2022, https://www.reviewjournal.com/local/local-las-vegas/review-journal-defends-reporting-tactics-criticized-by-lvcva-executive/

21. The editor referred to here said in a statement, "This is completely false. I never discussed any such letter with Adelson, and, to repeat, have no idea if Adelson received any such letter. In fact, I never discussed the LVCVA [Las Vegas Convention and Visitors Authority] story, at all, with Adelson. Nor did I ever pull Brian aside and say the things

[attributed] to me." The editor also said in a statement, "I never had any discussions about the LVCVA story, or any follow-up letter, with Adelson, and never had this discussion with Brian, so this entire premise is erroneous."

22. Paul Farhi, "How a Las Vegas newspaper quickly mobilized to cover a tragedy," *Washington Post*, October 2, 2017, accessed August 1, 2023, https://www.washingtonpost .com/lifestyle/style/how-a-las-vegas-newspaper-quickly-mobilized-to-cover-a-tragedy /2017/10/02/c37149c0-a794-11e7-850e-2bdd1236be5d_story.html

23. An editor referred to in this book said in a statement, "There was nothing solitary about our endeavor to cover the worst mass shooting in US history. Dozens of *RJ* journalists worked overnight to pull together a very complete report, given the timing factor (for instance, the shooting of concert-goers did not begin until 10:05 p.m. and it wasn't until after 2 a.m. when Sheriff Lombardo held a press conference to inform media that the death count had risen dramatically). There was no mystery to the reporters who were working the live story what their immediate assignments were. Brian wasn't called immediately because he was not one of the reporters we chose to have on the story during that first night. We had reporters and photographers on the scene within minutes of learning of the shooting (even getting into Mandalay Bay before it was locked down)."

24. An editor referred to in this book said in a statement, "We did have calls going out to many staffers on deadline. Brian just wasn't one of them. The story broke after 10 pm on a Sunday night, and it is incorrect for Brian to suggest we weren't talking to many reporters from that point on. Of course some staffers might have learned on their own because of the nature of the breaking story. Many, if not all, of the reporters who learned on their own before hearing from the newsroom informed the newsroom what they had heard, and we put them to work immediately. Just because Brian goes to bed relatively early and was oblivious to what was happening, and just because he was not one of the reporters called that night, doesn't mean we weren't in full-scale coverage mode."

25. An editor referred to in this book described this description as "uninformed." In a statement, he said, "In fact, many, many next-day story assignments had been given out overnight while Brian was sleeping. Many reporters were out and about during the morning doing in-person interviews and gathering facts. A few key editors went home to grab a few winks and change clothes after 16-hour shifts, but a next-day game plan was solidly in place when Brian would have wandered in to work."

26. The idea was to scour social media for people talking about the shooting and to piggyback off of other media's interviews with the family members of victims.

27. An editor referred to in this book said in a statement, "It might have seemed like hours to Brian that editors were in planning meetings, but he knows full well it wasn't anywhere near that long. We appreciate Brian's concern for the victims' families, but there wasn't a media outlet covering the story that wasn't scrambling to be first with family members' reactions. The necessities of the news meant we had to try to track down sources as quickly as possible. Brian clearly lacked the competitive instincts that needed to be in place when the NY Times, WaPo, WSJ, AP, LAT, CBS, CNN, ABC, NBC, Fox News had flown teams into town to cover the story. I don't recall anyone creating a spreadsheet to list which reporters where [sic] calling whom, but it is disappointing to hear he may

have wasted time on a spreadsheet when the newsroom needed help tracking down leads in a hurry."

28. Anita Hassan, Brian Joseph, and Colton Lochhead, "One family's path through horror of shooting on Las Vegas Strip," *Las Vegas Review-Journal*, October 8, 2017, accessed May 23, 2022, https://www.reviewjournal.com/local/the-strip/one-familys-path -through-horror-of-shooting-on-las-vegas-strip/. An editor referred to in this book said in a statement, "Again, a mischaracterization by Brian. In covering a monster story such as this one, there will always be stories that don't pan out. The direction given was not that the story should be 'flashy,' but we did want a big, meaningful story. The reporters were not told what story to write. It was their job to think like reporters, and dig around like reporters and come up with ideas. But, of course, editors ensured it was what the news-paper was looking for. In the end, the Sunday story was an excellent one, with reporters Anita Hassan and Colton Lochhead really stepping up, and Brian working on it, too."

29. Brian Joseph, "Las Vegas shooting tragedy spurs fake fundraising," *Las Vegas Review-Journal*, October 20, 2017, accessed July 29, 2022, https://www.reviewjournal .com/crime/shootings/las-vegas-shooting-tragedy-spurs-fake-fundraising/

30. An editor referred to in this book said in a statement, "Again, in covering a monster story such as this one, there will always be stories that don't pan out. These passages of Brian's assertions reek of sour grapes from someone who was eventually fired for poor performance. He was assigned, but failed to produce, an all-encompassing sex-trafficking story for the RJ. After well more than a year, Brian never gave us a story that was publish-able or one that reached the quality of work we expect at the RJ. As for his role during the Oct. 1 coverage, it appears that Brian is unhappy that he was not the center of attention or a dependable 'go-to' reporter."

31. *The State of Nevada v. Robert Sharpe III*, Case No. C-14-301364-01 (Clark County, Nevada, October 3, 2014); *The State of Nevada v. Shatni Stimpson*, Case No. C-15-307069-1 (Clark County, Nevada, June 4, 2015); *The State of Nevada v. Rickey Allen Jones III*, Case No. C-14-295752-1 (Clark County, Nevada, February 6, 2014); *The State of Nevada v. Craig Rodgers*, Case No. C-16-316167-1 (Clark County, Nevada, June 30, 2016); *The State of Nevada v. Mario Lamont Jones II*, Case No. C-14-299101-1 (Clark County, Nevada, June 30, 2014).

32. The Polaris Project has gone by just the name Polaris since 2014, but its website remains polarisproject.org. I hadn't realized the organization had shortened its name when I first contacted it in early 2017.

CHAPTER 13

1. Don Hoier and I were the primary sources for this chapter. Events in this chap-ter were corroborated by Don's wife, Dr. Shera Bradley.

2. George Knapp and Matt Adams, "I-Team: Accused pimp claims he was set up by former cop," KLAS-TV, November 18, 2016, accessed February 19, 2024, https://www .8newsnow.com/news/i-team-accused-pimp-claims-he-was-set-up-by-former-cop/; George Knapp and Matt Adams, "I-Team: Former club promoter opens up about LV nightclub industry," KLAS-TV, November 22, 2016, accessed May 23, 2022, https:// www.8newsnow.com/news/i-team-former-club-promoter-opens-up-about-lv-nightclub

-industry/; George Knapp and Matt Adams, "I-Team: FBI probe leads to changes in Metro's vice unit," KLAS-TV, April 13, 2017, accessed May 23, 2022, https://www.8newsnow.com/news/i-team-fbi-probe-leads-to-changes-in-metros-vice-unit/; George Knapp, "I-Team: Convicted pimp's hearing could include interesting testimony," KLAS-TV, July 18, 2017, accessed May 23, 2022, https://www.8newsnow.com/news/i-team-convicted-pimps-hearing-could-include-interesting-testimony/; George Knapp and Bill Roe, "I-Team: 2 pimps seek new trials, allege police corruption," KLAS-TV, August 17, 2017, accessed May 23, 2022, https://www.8newsnow.com/news/i-team-2-pimps-seek-new-trials-allege-police-corruption/; George Knapp, "I-Team: Metro hires law firm to prevent testimony of vice cops in pimp's appeal," KLAS-TV, October 12, 2017, accessed May 23, 2022, https://www.8newsnow.com/news/i-team-metro-hires-law-firm-to-prevent-testimony-of-vice-cops-in-pimps-appeal/;George Knapp and Matt Adams, "I-Team: Explosive testimony in police corruption case," KLAS-TV, November 17, 2017, accessed May 23, 2022, https://www.8newsnow.com/news/i-team-explosive-testimony-in-police-corruption-case/; George Knapp and Matt Adams, "I-Team: New evidence in alleged police corruption case," KLAS-TV, February 12, 2018, accessed May 23, 2022, https://www.8newsnow.com/news/i-team-new-evidence-in-alleged-police-corruption-case/; George Knapp and Matt Adams, "I-Team: Witnesses in police corruption case to testify soon," KLAS-TV, April 11, 2018, accessed May 23, 2022, https://www.8newsnow.com/news/i-team-witnesses-in-police-corruption-case-to-testify-soon/; George Knapp and Matt Adams, "I-Team: Pimp offered plea deal, state avoids hearing into possible police corruption," KLAS-TV, May 14, 2018, accessed May 23, 2022, https://www.8newsnow.com/news/i-team-pimp-offered-plea-deal-state-avoids-hearing-into-possible-police-corruption/

3. *The State of Nevada v. Arman Izadi*, Case No. C-13-289719-1 (Clark County, Nevada, May 10, 2013).

4. *The State of Nevada v. Ocean Fleming*, Case No. C-11-276866-1 (Clark County, Nevada, October 14, 2011).

5. Janiece Marshall declined to be interviewed for this book.

6. Adam Gill declined to be interviewed for this book.

7. Attempts to reach Jessica Gruda through her attorneys were unsuccessful.

8. Statements Millard made in her April 16, 2018, affidavit conflict with statements she made in an October 29, 2013, affidavit that was also produced during Fleming's appeals. In the 2013 affidavit, for example, Millard said "the District Attorney" told her Fleming had put three hits out on her. In the 2018 affidavit, she said Baughman told her Fleming had put three hits out on her. In 2013, Millard said she lost Fleming's child when she had a miscarriage. In 2018, she said she had an abortion.

9. Less than two years later, in May 2019, Don Ramos provided a declaration in the appeal of another pimp, Charles Adrian Ford, aka Charley Mac or Charlie Mac. Like Fleming, Ford was trying to get out of prison, and he claimed that he was set up by corrupt officers in Vice colluding with Mally. Ramos's declaration in Ford's case differs from the one he gave in Fleming's. In Ford's case, Ramos claimed that Mally had a "hit list" of rival pimps, which included Fleming, Ford, and a pimp known as Wheelchair Mike, aka Big Mike. He goes on to state that "in order to eliminate the competition, Mally Mall

would work with LVMPD officers to have rival pimps arrested, charged with assault, and sentenced to prison for many years. As part of his plan to have these pimps arrested and imprisoned, Mally Mall would have a woman from his 'stable' infiltrate another pimp's operation in order to get close to the competitor. Once in the inner circle of this operation, the women would contact police officers and allege beatings and sexual abuse from the competitor pimp in order to have them arrested, prosecuted, and removed from the streets." Ramos also declared to have seen the Vice officer who arrested Ford visit Mally's home on multiple occasions. Ramos never mentioned this particular officer in his affidavit in the Fleming case, despite naming several other officers, and also never referred to a pimp "hit list," or to Mally's alleged scheme of infiltrating rival pimp's stables with girls, all of which would have presumably been salient to Fleming's case. Don believes the differences in Ramos's declarations make his testimony uncredible. He's also disturbed that pimps are trying to use the allegations around Mally to get themselves out of jail.

10. Through his law clerk, Judge Michael Villani declined, via email, a request to be interviewed for this book. Villani announced his retirement from the District Court bench in July 2022.

11. Vanessa Murphy, "I-Team: Local judge reveals troubles with vice cops," KLAS-TV, April 12, 2018, accessed February 19, 2024.

12. Doug Poppa, "EXCLUSIVE: Las Vegas Grand Jury evidence hints convicted felon 'Suga' Shane Valentine is a snitch," *Baltimore Post-Examiner*, August 5, 2019, accessed September 25, 2023, https://baltimorepostexaminer.com/exclusive-grand-jury-evidence -hints-convicted-felon-suga-shane-valentine-is-a-snitch/2019/08/05

13. Judge Melanie Andress-Tobiasson resigned from the bench in May 2021 after she was hit with ethics charges, including that she involved herself personally in the unsolved double murder investigation. Tobiasson killed herself in January 2023.

14. The pimp Raymond Sharpe, busted by Chris Baughman around the same time as Ocean Fleming, also tried to use allegations against Baughman to get his charges overturned. His efforts, however, took much longer than Fleming's to bear fruit. In early 2024, all 18 felony charges against him were dropped and Sharpe pleaded guilty to three other charges: possession of a firearm by an ex-felon, second-degree kidnapping, and coercion with force. With the time he had already served, Sharpe was released from prison in February. Sharpe's defense attorney, Jean Schwartzer, negotiated Sharpe's release with Joshua Tomsheck, who replaced Adam Gill as the special prosecutor on the case. Schwartzer declined to speak about the specifics of the case but said that in her negotiations on behalf of Sharpe she was focused primarily on ineffective assistance of counsel, including some failure to present evidence attacking Baughman's credibility.

15. The practice of criminally charging minors with prostitution has since been discontinued in Clark County.

16. Brian Joseph, "Review-Journal goes to court for Las Vegas sex trafficking records," *Las Vegas Review-Journal*, May 31, 2018, accessed May 23, 2022, https://www .reviewjournal.com/crime/sex-crimes/review-journal-goes-to-court-for-las-vegas-sex -trafficking-records/

17. When I conducted this research, buyers and sellers of sex were charged with the same violation in Nevada. In 2021, the Silver State created separate criminal code numbers for sex buyers and sellers.

18. Prior to 2006, johns were cited, not arrested, in Clark County.

19. Police departments also need female officers willing to work undercover as prostitutes in order to arrests johns. Not many female officers volunteer for that duty, and when they do, negotiating for their use within the chain of command can be difficult because they may be volunteering from another section or unit within the police department. These challenges severely limit Metro's ability to target johns.

20. Brothers Lorenzo and Frank Fertitta III are the majority owners of Station Casinos. Their cousin, Tilman Fertitta, owns the NBA's Houston Rockets and the downtown Las Vegas casino the Golden Nugget. When we spoke, Young talked about working for the "Fertittas" and about the good influence he felt the family had on Sin City.

21. I interviewed Bill Young again on July 28, 2022, shortly after he started a new job as the director of community engagement at Hope for Prisoners, a Las Vegas nonprofit that provides training and support to former prisoners. (He had left Station Casinos by then.) I wanted to interview him again in part to re-establish everything he had previously told me, so the *Review-Journal* couldn't claim that I was using research gathered on their dime, and in part to see if his sentiments on prostitution enforcement had changed. They hadn't. He told me arresting johns "isn't helping this town" because all it does is discourage men from coming to Las Vegas for conventions. In fact, he said prostitution is part of the fabric of Nevada, noting that if it wasn't someone would have passed a law banning prostitution statewide. He said he didn't expect such a law to be passed in his lifetime. At one point while we were talking, he started to refer to prostitutes as "whores," then caught himself. (Don later told me a lot of old-timers on the police force would refer to prostitutes as whores. For them, it wasn't necessarily an insult. It was just how they referred to prostitutes.) Young said the Las Vegas police should focus its limited resources on activities to combat the most heinous crimes, like child pornography and child prostitution. (Young apparently didn't stay with Hope for Prisoners very long. A receptionist for the nonprofit, who had said she had been with Hope for Prisoners for months, said in late October 2023 that she had never heard the name Bill Young associated with the organization.)

CHAPTER 14

1. I was the primary source for this chapter. Events in this chapter were corroborated by T. J. Moore, former madam of the Love Ranch South and Alien Cathouse brothels, and Judge William Voy of the Eighth Judicial District Court's Family Division (retired).

2. Brian Joseph, "Judge slams Las Vegas police for keeping sex trafficking records secret," *Las Vegas Review-Journal*, August 8, 2018, accessed May 23, 2022, https://www.reviewjournal.com/crime/courts/judge-slams-las-vegas-police-for-keeping-sex-trafficking-records-secret/

3. I've tried my best in these paragraphs to describe the chronological progress of my reporting on these story ideas. But as anyone who has attempted to develop any idea knows, it's a muddled process that doesn't often have discrete steps. You think of

something, you have some conversations, you do some research, you think some more. It's sometimes difficult to pinpoint the exact moment in time when a vague notion in your head becomes a crystal-clear idea or goal. The descriptions of my reporting process are informed by the numerous notes I took (and when they were dated) as well as an extensive log I maintained of contacts I made with sources and records for when I downloaded or saved certain documents or reports.

4. Dennis Hof died on October 16, 2018, while he was running for the Nevada State Assembly.

5. Brian Joseph, "Weak safeguards make Nevada companies easy targets for fraud," *Las Vegas Review-Journal*, May 18, 2018, accessed May 23, 2022, https://www.reviewjournal .com/investigations/weak-safeguards-make-nevada-companies-easy-targets-for-fraud/

6. There is a sort of chicken-and-egg problem with analyzing solicitation arrests on The Strip by casino. Does a high number of arrests at a casino mean that there is a problem with prostitution there? Or does it mean that Vice is patrolling that area more, perhaps because the casino management allows officers to set up shop there more often for their undercover busts?

7. The editor referred to here said in a statement, "The allegation that I described the Venetian as 'the worst place in Las Vegas' in any meeting at any time is wrong. I have never thought or felt such a sentiment and would not be inclined to make any statement."

8. "Sunshine Week," News Leaders Association, accessed July 29, 2022, https://www .newsleaders.org/sunshine-week-about

9. Brian Joseph, "How Las Vegas Metro police kept sex trafficking records under wraps," *Las Vegas Review-Journal*, March 10, 2019, accessed May 23, 2022, https:// www.reviewjournal.com/investigations/how-las-vegas-metro-police-kept-sex-trafficking -records-under-wraps-1614880/

10. The editor referred to in this case said in a statement, "I recall that I worked through the managing editor and the investigations editor to assign the story to Brian, rather than me assigning it to him directly. The story was written, and the quote attributed to me is accurate. Brian's characterization of the story he wrote as a 'simple regurgitation' of what the newspaper already reported is disappointing because it seems to represent a lackluster effort by him– the kind of effort Brian would display with regard to the sex trafficking project."

11. My reporting strategy with victims and survivors, whatever their age, was to learn about their experiences first, then determine whether they (and, if appropriate, their parents) wanted to be named in the newspaper. At the beginning of working with a victim or survivor, I'd come to an understanding with them that I'd like for them to consider whether they'd be comfortable having their name published, but I promised I'd circle back with them later on for a final decision. Given the sensitivity of the topic and how long I knew the reporting would take, I didn't think it would be appropriate to lock any victim or survivor into going public until we were much closer to having a publication date. (People's circumstances change, as do their thoughts and feelings on something this serious.) When we were closer to a publication date, I thought victims and survivors would be better able to assess the potential impacts of revealing their identities. But, in the meantime, learning the intricacies of their personal stories was valuable to me as I tried

to understand the realities of the pimp-prostitute subculture. It was only much later into my research that I learned that victims or survivors who speak out could possibly become the targets of violence from random pimps they didn't even know. That made me think that we as a newspaper would have to reassess our approach to naming victims. However, from the beginning, it was my understanding that the editors wanted me to try to name as many victims and survivors as possible, regardless of their age. Newspapers typically have policies about naming minors involved in crimes, but the *R-J*'s policy, whatever it may have been at the time, was never discussed with me, as I understood that the editors were hoping we could do something unique and groundbreaking with this project. I always thought the implications of naming victims and survivors would be thoroughly discussed with *R-J* editors as we got closer to a publication date. I worked on this research for a long time and frequently updated my direct editor of the progress I was making. As far as I knew, everyone was onboard with what I was doing, although I don't know what the communication was like between the lower-level editors at the newspaper and those in upper management.

12. Max Michor, "Review-Journal takes most total awards in Best of the West contest," *Las Vegas Review-Journal*, April 26, 2019, accessed July 29, 2022, https://www.reviewjournal.com/local/local-las-vegas/review-journal-takes-most-total-awards-in-best-of-the-west-contest-1650531/

13. The editor referred to here said in a statement, "I disagree with the assertion that I 'rarely' spoke with Brian. I walked around the newsroom often and said hello to anyone I came in contact with. I recall speaking with Brian regularly, particularly when I visited the area of the investigative team. And, yes, it is true that I congratulated Brian on his Best of the West award. I initiated that conversation."

14. The editor referred to here said in a statement, "The editor under whom Brian worked had been pressing Brian for a long time to show sufficient progress on the sex trafficking investigation he had spent years on without producing a story, and Brian had distinguished himself throughout the process for all the wrong reasons. He always had an excuse for why the story couldn't be completed, and he had reversed course on previous understandings and agreements he had with his editor. Notably, the project was undertaken with the understanding that the *Review-Journal* would not identify juvenile sex trafficking victims who were still juveniles, but would pursue on the record interviews with adults who had been victims as juveniles and were willing to lend their names to provide more power to the story. We said from the start that the story had to have the names of real people if it was going to have credibility and impact. However, when Brian was fired, no one said he should have named juvenile victims. Rather, his failure to pursue adults who had been juvenile victims and were willing to talk on the record was discussed. When Brian submitted a draft of the story, it noted that no victims or family members would be identified. Brian had not received approval from editors up the chain for this approach. Brian had made various other promises to his editors, such as getting the cooperation of detectives, or being able to get trafficking data from Family Court Judge William Voy. But Brian kept moving the goalposts, and it became clear that the longer Brian spent on the story, the weaker it would become. After working on the story for about two years, Brian had nothing in his draft that reflected interviews from

coalitions or victim advocacy groups. His story was thousands of words in length and had merely a half-dozen on-the-record sources, nearly all of them public officials. His story was unpublishable. Brian was familiar with all of the problems surrounding the writing of this story. His editor had counseled him extensively and told him the story needed to be better and that he needed to deliver something reflective of two years of work." Another editor referred to in this book said in a statement, "I never suggested Brian name a sex trafficking victim who was underaged at the time the story was being written, and, to my knowledge, neither did anyone else. The story's quality was unacceptable for a laundry list of reasons."

15. The Human Resources representative here said in a statement that she did not cut me off and denied that the editor present said he was disappointed that I did not name juvenile sex trafficking victims.

16. The editor referred to here said in a statement, "I was professional when I terminated Brian's employment. . . . I certainly did not shut the door in Brian's face. I watched him leave the building through two sets of glass doors with a vestibule in between them. The doors close automatically at a set rate. Brian walked through the first set of doors, through the small vestibule and through the second set of doors, and then walked toward the parking lot. His back was to the doors and he was walking toward his car when the outside door closed automatically."

CHAPTER 15

1. Angela Delgado was the primary source for this chapter. Descriptions in this chapter were corroborated by a person who was positioned to know Mally well but asked to remain anonymous for fear of retaliation. (This person's relationship with Mally was independently confirmed by documents.) The Las Vegas Metropolitan Police Department has no record of Angela's arrest or incarceration in May 2007. This is likely because Angela was using fake IDs at the time, and she was initially detained under an alias. Don said that during his time at Metro prostitutes would often be booked under their fake names and the records would never be updated to reflect the women's real names, even after the department learned it. As such, it's proved impossible to obtain documentation of Angela's arrest during this time. Even the Harris County District Clerk's office in Houston, where Angela's drug charge originated, was unable to find any information about this arrest, incarceration, or her fugitive warrant.

2. I asked the Texas Attorney General's office if it could confirm these time frames—twenty-five days if a subject waived the extradition hearing, ninety days if not—but the Attorney General's press office said it was "unable to provide a comment at this time."

3. Among many of the difficulties women face when they leave The Life is the realization that their labor is not worth more in traditional society. Even though prostitutes typically do not get to keep much, if any, of the money they earn, they become accustomed to bringing in lots of cash and that becomes a part of their self-worth, their ability to earn large sums of money. So, while on the surface it may seem odd to say Angela was "addicted to the money" when she wasn't pocketing much (if any) of the money herself, in the pimp-prostitute subculture this actually makes sense.

4. When she was travelling, Angela said Mally's network would permit her to keep a little money for food and incidentals. But she said it was never very much and she was instructed precisely how much to keep and how much to deposit.

5. Chicago Police Department Arrest Report for Angela Delgado, October 23, 2007. Chicago Police Department Vice Case Report and Supplementary Report for Angela Delgado, October 23, 2007, RD No. HN665505. Chicago Police Department, Extradition Records for Angela Delgado. Cook County Sheriff detention records for Angela Delgado at the Cook County Jail, October–November 2007, Case No. 07–137422. (All obtained through a public records request.)

CHAPTER 16

1. Angela Delgado was the primary source for this chapter.

2. ABC News confirmed that the two-hour special originally aired on March 21, 2008, when Angela would have been in prison. It's believed that the special was repackaged for rebroadcast and it possibly aired on WE TV, although WE TV declined to speak to me to confirm.

3. To Don Hoier, this interaction suggests Mally was fishing for information about other pimps in his role as a criminal informant. Don also feels that this undercuts accusations that Mally was paying police officers to knock out his competition in the pimp game, because this suggests he didn't know critical things about these other pimps. If he was so concerned about his rivals that he wanted them taken out, wouldn't he keep close tabs on them?

4. I wrote Tyree Wright a letter in prison, telling him that he'd be mentioned in this book and what it would say about him. He never responded to me.

5. *The State of Nevada v. Tyree Kenneth Wright*, Case No. C-17-321009-1, (Clark County, February 1, 2017).

6. Kenny Red died in early September 2022.

7. Christopher King, "Domestic-abuse survivor fears ex-boyfriend's plea deal puts her in danger," KTNV-Las Vegas, March 2, 2018, accessed July 29, 2022, https://www.ktnv.com/news/domestic-abuse-survivor-fears-ex-boyfriends-plea-deal-puts-her-in-danger

8. Angela testified under oath before a grand jury that Wright robbed her, but he denied it. While Wright was originally charged with two robbery counts, those charges were eventually dismissed as part of his plea deal.

CHAPTER 17

1. Angela, Don, and I were the primary sources for this chapter. Events in this chapter were corroborated by Dr. Stephany Powell, formerly of Journey Out, an anti-trafficking organization that was contacted prior to the 2019 raid on Mally's Encino mansion; and my wife, Buu Joseph.

2. *Jamal Rashid v. State Farm Fire and Casualty Company and Matthew Keim*, Case No. 2:19-cv-01483-APG-EJY (U.S. District Court of the District of Nevada, Las Vegas, August 26, 2019).

3. "Mally Mall Furious Over Dead Exotic Cat Pic," TMZ, May 27, 2016, accessed July 29, 2022, https://www.tmz.com/2016/05/27/mally-mall-dead-cat-house-fire-photo/

4. Mary Stringini, "LAPD raids hip-hop producer Mally Mall's home for exotic animals, human trafficking," Fox 11, April 4, 2019, accessed July 29, 2022, https://www.foxla.com/news/lapd-raids-hip-hop-producer-mally-malls-home-for-exotic-animals-human-trafficking; Sha Be Allah, "SWAT Raids Home of 'Love and Hip Hop' Star Mally Mall for Human Trafficking and Exotic Pet Violations," The Source, April 3, 2019, accessed July 29, 2022, https://thesource.com/2019/04/03/swat-raids-home-of-love-and-hip-hop-star-mally-mall-for-human-trafficking-and-exotic-pet-violations/.

5. George Knapp, "I-Team: LAPD's raid on Mally Mall's home could be tip for more legal trouble for music producer," KLAS-TV, April 3, 2019, accessed July 29, 2022, https://www.8newsnow.com/news/local-news/i-team-lapds-raid-on-mally-malls-home-could-be-tip-for-more-legal-trouble-for-music-producer/

6. Michael Saponara, "Mally Mall Wasn't Arrested After Police Raid of His Home for Exotic Animals & Human Trafficking, Lawyer Says," Billboard, April 4, 2019, accessed July 29, 2022, https://www.billboard.com/music/rb-hip-hop/mally-mall-police-raid-exotic-animals-human-trafficking-lawyer-8505745/

7. "Hip Hop Producer 'Mally Mall' Pleads Guilty To Unlawful Prostitution Business," U.S. Attorney's Office, District of Nevada and the U.S. Department of Justice, October 21, 2019, accessed July 29, 2022, https://www.justice.gov/usao-nv/pr/hip-hop-producer-mally-mall-pleads-guilty-unlawful-prostitution-business

8. *United States of America v. Jamal* Rashid, Case No. 2:19-cr-00246-GMN-NJK, (U.S. District Court for the District of Nevada, Las Vegas, September 25, 2019).

9. Greg Haas, "I-Team: Mally Mall pleads guilty to federal prostitution charges," KLAS-TV, October 21, 2019, accessed May 23, 2022, https://www.8newsnow.com/i-team/mally-mall-pleads-guilty-to-federal-prostitution-charges/

10. Vanessa Murphy, "UPDATE: I-Team learns convicted pimp will be freed from prison," KLAS-TV, October 17, 2019, accessed July 29, 2022, https://www.8newsnow.com/news/local-news/i-team-convicted-felon-could-soon-be-freed-from-prison/.

11. Severance Agreement and General Release drafted by the *Las Vegas Review-Journal* for Brian Joseph, dated April 10, 2019, unsigned. It also included a clause that would have given me two weeks of additional pay in return for signing it.

12. An HR representative of the newspaper confirmed in a statement that I had tried to obtain the rights to my sex trafficking research, but the paper refused to give them up, reiterating what she had told me before: "anything that you worked on during your employment is the property of the Review Journal and will not be released."

13. I know at least one reporter who said he was allowed to take his ongoing research with him when he left the employment of a news organization.

14. *Las* Vegas *Review-Journal v. Las Vegas Metropolitan Police Department*, Case No. A-18–775378-W, (District Court, Clark County, Nevada, May 31, 2018).

15. One editor referred to in this book said in a written statement, "The settlement the Review-Journal obtained from Metro was simply the recovery of some of the legal expenses the newspaper incurred to obtain some of the records Brian was supposed to use in his reporting. The recovery of fees is provided for under the state's public records law.

It is true that the Review-Journal did not publish anything resulting from Brian's work. What Brian produced was not publishable. Of course, Brian was paid for years for the work the Review-Journal had hoped he would do to produce a story the news organization could publish. Although Brian's work could not be published, the newspaper regularly reports on sex trafficking. A search of the newspaper's online archive shows at least 200 stories about sex trafficking and related arrests since Brian was fired." Another editor referred to in this book wrote in a statement, "We never published any stories related to Brian's reporting because it was flawed and unpublishable . . . The Review-Journal continues to regularly cover news of sex trafficking stings, arrests and other matters." A third editor mentioned in this book said in a statement, "Brian was not able to deliver a publishable story about sex trafficking in two years. In addition, any newspaper would have fought for reimbursement, as granted by statute, of legal expenditures spent trying to get records we were entitled to under state law."

16. While writing this book, I was very careful not to disclose specific findings from the reporting I did while at the *Review-Journal*, in the event the newspaper wanted to try to claim that it owned that research. The narrative I relay here about my time at the *R-J* sets up the circumstances of my termination—and I never signed a non-disparagement agreement, so the newspaper can't stop me from writing about that. As an example of the work I did to avoid disclosing specific findings, I did not report in this book the specific ratio of prostitute-to-john arrests on The Strip. Instead, I merely reported that I discovered that "hundreds and hundreds of prostitutes were arrested on The Strip, but only dozens of johns," a vague generality. I mention generally about the things I reported on without specifically talking about any investigative findings. I also took the time to re-interview every relevant source I spoke to during my time at the *R-J*, including Don, former sheriff Bill Young, retired juvenile court Judge William Voy, and former brothel madam T. J. Moore.

17. Brian Joseph, "Nevada brothel owner steps in to defend legal sex trade," *Las Vegas Review-Journal*, March 29, 2019, accessed July 29, 2022, https://www.reviewjournal.com /news/politics-and-government/nevada/nevada-brothel-owner-steps-in-to-defend-legal -sex-trade-1629352/.

18. Letter from Angela Williams (née Delgado) to United States District Court for the District of Nevada Judge Gloria M. Navarro, July 12, 2020.

19. Gordon Dillard declined to be interviewed for this book. His reference letter stands out as particularly strange. Written on Maverick Management letterhead, it's dated August 19, 2019, more than two months before Mally's plea agreement was announced by the US Department of Justice. The letter is addressed to "To Whom It May Concern" and refers to Mally as "Mally," not by his real name, as all the other letters do. Dillard wrote, "Mally is a genuinely humble and generous human being. He considers those he works with to be his family, and there is quite literally nothing Mally won't do for them, particularly in their times of need." Another reference letter, from Stacey Henley, the commissioner of the Crenshaw Rams Youth Football and Cheerleading Organization, which participates in rapper Snoop Dogg's youth football league, is dated August 1, 2019, and lauds Mally for serving as a mentor and coach. Henley wrote, "I am confident that this will remain a one-off incident for Mr. Rashid from which he has taken the time to

reflect on his actions and is remorseful." These letters underscore that Mally and his law-yers were apparently negotiating a plea agreement with the feds for some time.

20. Wack 100 declined to be interviewed for this book. In the past, he has been out-spoken in his disdain for "snitches."

21. After I contacted Roc Nation in March 2023 to ask about this letter, the company filed a motion to intervene in Mally's federal criminal case, saying that it wanted the letter stricken from the record. "In March 2023, the existence of the Letter was brought to the attention of management at Roc Nation, and it was quickly determined that the use of Roc Nation's name on the Letter was not authorized by anyone at Roc Nation," the company wrote in a June 2023 court filing. "Moreover, further inquiry revealed that the Letter contains false information about Roc Nation's relationship with Mr. Rashid, as Roc Nation did not then have—and never has had—a professional relationship with Mr. Rashid. In sum, Mr. [Nima] Nasseri did not have authority to submit the Letter on Roc Nation's letterhead, particularly as it conveyed false information." Sean Mulvehill, chief financial officer of Roc Nation, said in an accompanying affidavit, "Roc Nation has a stellar reputation and the misuse of our letterhead in support of Mr. Rashid, particularly given the nature of the criminal charges for which he was sentenced, is unacceptable." In a filing in response, Mally said he didn't oppose Roc Nation's motion to strike the letter but claimed it "was submitted in good faith and without knowledge as to whether Nas-seri had permission or access to letterhead." Mally said at the time the letter was written, Nasseri worked for Roc Nation and managed an artist known as Gashi with whom he had collaborated. As part of the record, he included a screenshot of the credits for a Gashi song called "Don't OD," in which Mally is listed as a producer and writer. Roc Nation responded effectively that it didn't care about Mally's "unauthenticated apparent screenshot" or whether he knew if Nasseri lacked authorization to submit the letter. It just wanted the letter stricken, which a judge did on June 14, 2023.

22. *The State of Nevada v. Tyree Kenneth Wright*, Case No. C-17-321009-1 (Clark County, February 1, 2017).

23. I supplemented the reporting for this section with a transcript of the hearing I obtained from the court reporter.

24. Nicholas Dickinson declined, via email, a request to be interviewed for this book.

25. Special Agent Megan Beckett, who was involved in the Mally case, died shortly after Mally's hearing, in Costa Rica, on August 1, 2021. She was forty-eight.

26. Through her courtroom administrator, Judge Gloria Navarro declined, via email, a request to be interviewed for this book.

27. Mally later tried, unsuccessfully, to get that date pushed back. He also apparently didn't turn himself in to the US Marshals. Instead, he seems to have reported directly to the federal prison in Sheridan, Oregon, where he asked to be housed. The US Marshal for the District of Nevada, Gary Schofield, told me on August 13, 2021, that he had no record of Mally turning himself in. But Schofield said Mally technically didn't have to turn himself in to the Marshals; he could report directly to the prison where he was assigned. I called one of Mally's attorneys that day to ask if Mally had turned himself in to the prison in Sheridan, but he hung up on me without giving me an answer. A short while later, the Bureau of Prisons' website listed Mally as an inmate at Sheridan.

CHAPTER 18

1. I was the primary source for this chapter.

2. This interview was conducted in April 2023.

3. Knapp acknowledged the events involving Mally and Baughman tarnished the whole police department. But he disagreed that it had any significant, lasting impact on Metro or the Vice Section's reputation. He said Las Vegans have short memories and have moved on to the next local scandal. Don and I agreed that hasn't been our experience in talking with Las Vegas sex trafficking victim advocates over the last several years. Not long before I met with Knapp, I attended the screening of a sex trafficking documentary with Don. There, I watched him talk with a high-profile advocate, a survivor. While they were talking a man who knew the advocate walked up. She introduced Don as a former Vice cop and when the man grimaced, she quickly added, *He's one of the good ones.*

4. I emailed Arman Izadi a detailed description of everything this book would say about him. He declined to speak with me on the record.

5. Through his attorney Janiece Marshall, I sent Fleming a detailed description of what would be said about him in this book—with one exception. Angela was willing to fact check every allegation she made against Fleming directly with him, but she was not comfortable with me sending those allegations to him in writing, for fear that the information could be repurposed out of context. So in the message I sent to Fleming through his attorney I also noted I had items I wanted to go over with him about a woman who used to work for him, as documented in Julia Beverly's book *Sweet Jones: Pimp C's Trill Life Story*. I said the woman wanted me to discuss those matters with him verbally and offered to set up a time to do. No one followeded up with me on that offer.

6. Will Sommer, "New Member of YouTube Star Logan Paul's Crew Is a Convicted Pimp," *The Daily Beast*, July 27, 2018, accessed April 15, 2023, https://www.thedailybeast.com/new-member-of-youtube-star-logan-pauls-crew-is-a-convicted-pimp; In 2020, the FBI raided both Jake Paul and Izadi's homes in connection with an alleged looting and vandalizing incident at a Scottsdale, Arizona, mall. The whole matter was later dropped.

7. Most of those cases apparently never went anywhere. But in October 2012, Izadi pleaded guilty to attempted battery with substantial bodily harm for attacking a videographer and was sentenced to some prison time for the felony. *The State of Nevada v. Arman Izadi*, Case No. C-12-284747-1, (Clark County, October 9, 2012).

8. Vanessa Murphy, "I-Team: Convicted pimp freed from prison," KLAS-TV, January 2, 2020, accessed October 13, 2023, https://www.8newsnow.com/i-team/i-team-convicted-pimp-freed-from-prison/; Vanessa Murphy, "I-Team: Convicted pimp back in custody after being freed from prison," KLAS-TV, January 2, 2020, updated February 28, 2020, accessed April 15, 2023, https://www.8newsnow.com/investigators/i-team-convicted-pimp-freed-from-prison/; Vanessa Murphy, "I-Team Exclusive: Formerly convicted pimp, DA speak out after case dismissed," KLAS-TV, March 3, 2020, accessed October 13, 2023, https://www.8newsnow.com/investigators/i-team-exclusive-formerly-convicted-pimp-da-speak-out-after-case-dismissed/; Dana Gentry, "D.A. drops all charges against Ocean Fleming," *Nevada Current*, March 3, 2020, accessed April 15, 2023, https://www.nevadacurrent.com/2020/03/03/d-a-drops-all-charges-against-ocean-fleming/#:~:text=By%3A%20Dana%20Gentry%20%2D%20March%203%2C%202020

%203%3A13%20pm&text=Clark%20County%20District%20Attorney%20Steve
,coerced%20by%20police%20and%20prosecutors.

9. Knapp made a point in our conversation to stress that he didn't think Izadi or Fleming were totally innocent, that they were guilty of some wrongdoing. He also stressed to me that he thought sex trafficking was awful and that women who go through it suffer greatly, in part because of the sex-obsessed culture of Las Vegas. In fact, he said that the reason he was willing to talk to me for this book was because I was focusing on the plight of trafficking victims.

10. Bianca Torres, "Giant Records' Shawn 'Tubby' Holiday Shares Advice on Artists Obtaining Longevity, What Makes a Hit Record and More," *XXL*, July 29, 2021, accessed August 17, 2022, https://www.xxlmag.com/shawn-holiday-interview/

11. I interviewed Kirk Riddle in late September 2021. He said he partied with Mally's girls on numerous occasions. One of those girls, he said, was Tia. Riddle pleaded no contested to two felony counts of theft and paid back the money he stole. He was sentenced to 90 days in jail. Pioneer Press, "Company credit allegedly used for escort service," *St. Paul Pioneer Press*, June 6, 2013, accessed October 13, 2023, https://www.twincities.com/2013/06/06/company-credit-allegedly-used-for-escort-service/; Associated Press, "Former Kohler employee gets 90 days in theft case," *Wisconsin Law Journal*, January 19, 2014, accessed October 13, 2023, https://wislawjournal.com/2014/01/19/former-kohler-employee-gets-90-days-in-theft-case/

12. Before March 2023, when I'd make initial contact with people in the entertainment industry and ask about Mally, I'd keep it vague, saying generally I was doing research on him. I never told the publicist who originally passed my information on to Tia that I was working on a book.

13. I sent Baughman a detailed description of everything this book would say about him, but he never responded.

14. I sent Gray a detailed description of everything this book would say about him, but he never responded.

15. When I was working for the *Las Vegas Review-Journal*, a sex trafficking survivor I interviewed told me about an FBI agent named Kevin White who was looking into Metro's Vice unit. She passed along to me the same phone number Don had for White. (This was long before I had ever connected with Don, let alone looked into Mally Mall.) The survivor recommended I give White a call; she said he might be able to help me with my research into sex trafficking in Las Vegas. But she warned that if White was willing to talk to me, he'd likely call me back late at night. That's when he liked to talk on the phone, she said. So, one day I dialed the number she gave me and left a voicemail. A while later, at about 9:00 or 9:30 p.m., I got a call from a blocked number. The caller was a young-sounding man who refused to give him his name but said I could figure out who he was. The caller, who only talked with me for a few minutes, told me he believed Metro's Vice unit was lazy in their investigations into sex trafficking victims. It's hard to say for certain, given the number of years that passed in between (and that I'm relying solely on my memory for this anecdote), but it certainly seemed to me that the anonymous voice that called me and the young-sounding man who picked up White's phone in March 2023 could be the same person.

16. In rejecting my appeal, an associate chief of the US Department of Justice's Office of Information Policy wrote in an August 2022 letter, "If you are dissatisfied with my action on your appeal, the FOIA [Freedom of Information Act] permits you to file a lawsuit in federal district court."

17. In total, I received 795 pages of records pertaining to Mally Mall, Ocean Fleming, and Arman Izadi. It took Metro more than a year to fulfill the request.

18. Las Vegas Metropolitan Police Department, Case Report No. LLV201200083358; Las Vegas Metropolitan Police Department, Voluntary Statement (written), Event No. LLV201200083358; Las Vegas Metropolitan Police Department, Voluntary Statement (interview transcript), Event No. LLV201200083358. (All obtained through a public records request.)

19. Ex-stripper and ex–porn star Sandi Jackmon also described a similar encounter with Mally in her 2020 book, *The Rise and Fall of Sandi Jackmon*. In the book, she refers to Mally by his first name, Jamal, and by the nickname "M&M," but in an interview with me in July 2023 she confirmed that the person she's talking about is indeed Mally. As Jackmon described in her book and confirmed to me in our conversation, she met Mally in 2006 while she was working as a stripper in Las Vegas. She said she knew immediately he was a pimp and wanted nothing to do with him. But she said she put up with him because he would tip her well when she'd perform on stage and because he had good weed. Over time, she said they became friends and would hang out occasionally, but they were never particularly close. One night in 2008, Jackmon said she walked out of the strip club where she was working to find her car had two flat tires. She was going to call a cab, but Mally pulled up just then in his Maybach. Her offered her a ride and a shot of liquor. Jackmon said she threw back the drink and the next thing she knew she woke up many hours later in one of Mally's guest bedrooms. In the days that followed, she said, she started having dreams of Mally raping her. A short while later, she collapsed on stage and was rushed to the hospital, where she discovered she was pregnant. Jackmon was living as a lesbian at the time; she said she wasn't having sex with any men at that point in her life. She confronted Mally. As she wrote in her book, "I called his phone. He answered like everything was OK. 'Hello??" Out of anger and disbelief I yelled, 'Jamal, the night I passed out at your house you fucked me!!' He said yes [*sic*] he followed that yes with 'and I recorded it.' My heart dropped. Tears ran down my face. I went on to tell him I was pregnant. He got real quiet and hung up." For the next several months, Jackmon said Mally pressured her to get an abortion. When she was about five months pregnant, she said Ocean Fleming and another one of Mally's goons beat her up at the strip club. She said her unborn baby became so badly injured she then agreed to have an abortion.

20. Chanda Tresvant, an unsigned singer/songwriter who has performed under her own name and the name "Trapanese," said that Mally assaulted her at his Las Vegas mansion in August 2020. She said a friend had introduced her to Mally at his Encino mansion that same month. In fact, she said she watched Mally receive oral sex from another woman during her first conversation with him. That's when she said she played him some of her music. After hearing one of her songs, "Don't Look at Me," Tresvant said Mally paid for her to fly to Las Vegas to record with him. But Tresvant said that when she arrived at Mally's Las Vegas home, he wasn't there. Instead, she said she encountered a couple of

"run down" women she thought looked like prostitutes. Later, she said, Mally showed up and stashed her luggage in his closet, where she couldn't access her stuff. She also said Mally offered her a plate of coke and badgered her about setting up an account on Only-Fans, where he wanted her to perform sexual acts on camera with another woman. Then, at one point during her visit, she said Mally suddenly pushed her down in his closet and pulled down her pants, in what she took to be an attempt to rape her. Tresvant said she ran out of the closet into the living room and, using her phone, booked the first flight she could back to California. "I'm literally on that plane crying," Tresvant said of her flight home. After that incident, Tresvant said she released a song called "Count to a Million" on which she rapped over one of Mally's beats. (Mally-produced songs often feature at the beginning an echoey, woman-sounding voice saying "Mally Mall" before the actual artist starts rapping or singing. "Count to a Million" has that tag.) Tresvant said that while Mally did provide her with the beat, she didn't record her vocals with him.

21. Nothing ever came of the investigation, apparently. No charges were brought.

22. *Quashay Davis v. Jamal Rashid, et al*, Case No. 2:20-cv-00288-RGK-AGR (U.S. District Court, Central District of California, January 10, 2020).

23. "The Reason For Mally Mall's Raid," TMZ post on Facebook, April 4, 2019, accessed October 13, 2023, https://www.facebook.com/watch/?v=390660578154165.

24. "MALLY MALL SUED FOR SEXUAL BATTERY . . . Accused of Drugging and Raping Model," TMZ, January 10, 2021, accessed October 13, 2023, https://www.tmz.com/2020/01/10/mally-mall-sexual-battery-lawsuit/. Davis says now that she believes what she witnessed at Mally's Encino mansion was a pimping operation. "I think he was trying to recruit me," she told me when we spoke in July 2023. Davis said that while she was at Mally's mansion there were numerous women hanging around, some she saw give oral sex to Mally, others she heard having sex behind closed doors. Davis said one of the girls told her, "He don't let us leave." And indeed, while she was there, Davis said she felt trapped. She said Mally had several armed bodyguards patrolling the house, and one even took her cell phone. She also said that Mally told her, "If you walk out of my door, I'm going to kill you." Davis said she feared for her life and went along with whatever Mally demanded of her. She told me that after Mally sexually assaulted her, he took her to a restaurant where they hung out with Fereidoun Khalilian, aka "Fred Khalifa Khalilian" aka "Prince Fred," a known party mate of Mally's. Later, after she got back to Texas, she said Khalilian called her and offered her money if she agreed to keep quiet about what happened with Mally. I received a video showing an iPhone mid-call. The phone is set on "Speaker" mode, with the name "Fred Khalifa" scrolling across the top. A man with a slight accent says over the phone, "You can easily destroy his life," then adds, "If I can help, if the damage is not too severe, and I can help, I would love to financially take care of you." Davis said she didn't take him up on the offer. Khalilian, a former business partner of Paris Hilton, was arrested in June 2023 for allegedly masterminding a murder-for-hire conspiracy.

25. In re Rashid, Case No. 21–10121-nmc (U.S. Bankruptcy Court, District of Nevada (Las Vegas), January 13, 2021); In re Rashid, Case No. 21–14537-nmc (U.S. Bankruptcy Court, District of Nevada (Las Vegas), September 16, 2021) In the first bankruptcy case, Mally filed for Chapter 7 protection. In the second, he filed for Chapter 13 protection.

Chapter 7 bankruptcies help debtors sell their nonexempt property and give the proceeds to their creditors. Chapter 13 bankruptcies help debtors with regular income devise a plan for repaying their debts over time. The Chapter 7 bankruptcy case was closed on August 18, 2023. The Chapter 13 case was ongoing as of April 2024.

26. Ariela Anís, "Mally Mall Says Crooked FBI Agent Blackmailed Him Into Pleading Guilty In Prostitution Case: 'They Wanted Me To Snitch On My Friends, I Ain't 6ix9ine'," Hollywood Unlocked, May 13, 2021, accessed April 4, 2024, https://hollywoodunlocked.com/mally-mall-says-crooked-fbi-agent-blackmailed-him-into-pleading-guilty-in-prostitution-case-they-wanted-me-to-snitch-on-my-friends-i-aint-6ix9ine/; "Mally Mall Claims He's Blackmailed By Crooked FBI Agent Into Pleading Guilty In Prostitution Case," AceShowbiz, May 14, 2021, accessed April 4, 2024, https://www.aceshowbiz.com/news/view/00170839.html; Twila-Amoure McDaniel, "Mally Mall Turns Himself In To Start 33-Month Prison Sentence For Allegedly Running Prostitution Ring," The Jasmine BRAND, September 6, 2021, accessed April 4, 2024, https://thejasminebrand.com/2021/09/06/mally-mall-turns-himself-in-to-start-33-month-prison-sentence-for-allegedly-running-prostitution-ring/. Natasha Decker, "Hip-Hop Producer Mally Mall Sentenced To 33 Months In Prison Over Running A Prostitution Ring," MadameNoire, May 14, 2021, accessed May 10, 2024, https://madamenoire.com/1229162/mally-mall-scentenced/.

27. Tresure Price declined to be interviewed for this book. One of Price's representatives, who initially asked me how much I was willing to pay for an interview, said "Mally has never actually sex trafficked her" and that "she wasn't fully aware of his history in sex trafficking. She knew him as a music producer and later experienced some of his ways which were to her a surprise. However, she only feels she was a victim of not being aware of the seriousness of his charges . . . rather than actually having to go through what some of the other victims may have experienced." After I explained that I would not pay for an interview, Price's representative told me via e-mail, "After a-lot [sic] of thought Tresure has decided she does not want to speak on that situation. It is still very sensitive and a ball of emotions for her."

28. Regarding home confinement, the bureau wrote in an email, "Individuals in home confinement may be approved to leave their residence for a variety of programming reasons as determined by a BOP's RRM Office [Bureau of Prisons' Residential Reentry Management Office] and case managers overseeing their placement (e.g. work, religious activities, and social activities). Individuals who are placed in home confinement may be monitored via electronic monitoring equipment (including ankle bracelets), telephone, or in-person contacts. While we do not discuss internal security procedures, the frequency and type of monitoring are determined based on a number of factors, including security level, contract requirements, and behavior." The bureau also added, "While we do not discuss whether a particular inmate is the subject of allegations, investigations, or sanctions, we can tell you all inmates under the supervision of the BOP who are found to be in violation of the Inmate Discipline Program policy are subject to sanctions and may even lead to a possible transfer."

29. According to Clark County Assessor records, on August 10, 2021, three days before he went to prison, Mally transferred ownership of his home to "Tarnita Woodard, trustee

of THE JP MORGAN BRIDGE IRREVOCABLE TRUST." But that document was not recorded until March 1, 2022. The bankruptcy Mally filed on September 16, 2021, listed the mansion as being his property. A filing in that case made on April 27, 2022, once again listed the mansion as Mally's property. Mally continued to list the mansion as his principal residence as of a filing in that case on October 17, 2023.

30. When Mally first entered the federal prison in Sheridan, Oregon, in August 2021, the Bureau of Prison's website stated that he was scheduled to be released on December 15, 2023. If he had been released on that date, he would have spent only about twenty-eight months in prison, even though he was sentenced to thirty-three months. In the months that followed, his release date, according to the bureau's website, was repeatedly moved up, from September 6, 2023 to August 2, 2023, and then ultimately to July 14, 2023. The bureau said it wouldn't "discuss a specific inmate's release method," but noted that inmates "may earn good conduct time." The bureau said, "qualifying inmates will be eligible to earn up to 54 days of good conduct time for each year of the sentence imposed by the court," and that "inmates may release up to 12 months early if they complete" a bureau drug abuse program or if the court orders a compassionate release.

31. "The Return of Jamal 'Mally Mall' Rashid: Wiser and Stronger Than Ever Before!," 24–7pressrelease.com, March 29, 2023, https://www.24-7pressrelease.com/press-release/499685/the-return-of-jamal-mally-mall-rashid-wiser-and-stronger-than-ever-before, accessed March 29, 2023.

32. The Hip Hop Alliance, which advocates for the labor force working in hip-hop music, was founded by hip-hop legends Chuck D, Kurtis Blow, and KRS-One. Doug E. Fresh also serves as the group's chairman emeritus.

33. In that second meeting, Tia said that Mally wasn't at a halfway house but wouldn't confirm if he was staying at his mansion. All she would say is that Mally was in a "secure location."

34. There is no Bureau of Prisons policy prohibiting social media use for individuals in community custody. Some halfway houses restrict the use of cell phones and the internet, and some individuals have specific instructions from a Judgment & Commitment Order governing their internet usage. The bureau, however, declined to discuss with me any specifics about Mally's supervision with me.

35. A couple of times during our correspondence on Instagram, Tia and whoever was controlling Mally's account made reference to my family. I never knew if this was just an attempt to be polite or a veiled threat. (I certainly never told them I had a wife and daughter.) At one point, whoever was controlling Mally's account wrote, "We know exactly who you are."

36. I later used a website where you can view Instagram accounts anonymously.

37. Daphna Edwards Ziman is a TV executive and philanthropist who has donated to Democratic interests and even hosted a major campaign event for John Kerry's 2004 presidential bid at her Beverly Hills estate. Justice for Women International's Instagram page states that its goal is to "eradicate sex trafficking around the world." Ziman held a fundraiser for President Joe Biden's re-election campaign on Saturday, September 23, 2023, at her home, with Jill Biden in attendance. Reportedly, tickets to the event, which benefited Biden's re-election campaign, the Democratic National Committee, and state

parties, started at $6,600 and rose to $50,000 for co-chairs. The August 6, 2023, episode of the infomercial featured a segment in which Ziman talked directly to Mally over a FaceTime call. I reached out to Ziman through her Instagram page, telling her that she'd be mentioned in this book and what it would say about her. She never responded to me.

38. A "Robert Anderson," whose address is listed as the address of Mally's mansion, is among Mally's creditors in one of his bankruptcies.

39. On July 31, 2023, I sent Mally, Tia, and one of Mally's attorneys long emails describing in detail everything I intended to write about Mally and Tia in this book—with one exception. Angela was willing to for me to fact check every allegation she made against Mally and Tia directly with them, but she was not comfortable with me emailing her allegations in writing, for fear that they could be repurposed out of context. So, in those long emails I sent, I also noted that I had dozens of items I wanted to go over with them about a woman who used to work for Mally and Tia. I said that this woman was OK with me revealing her identity to them, but she wanted me to do so verbally. I wrote that I was willing to read off the items to them, or one of their representatives, over the phone and asked them to reach out to me to schedule a time to do so. No one ever followed up with me on that offer. However, on August 4, Tia did respond to my email saying, "A lot of your information isn't accurate." She said they'd "love" to give me accurate information, but they wouldn't be available to talk to me until sometime in November, adding "our schedule doesn't allow us to make this a priority." I told her that was too long to ask me to wait, considering I had originally requested interviews in late April and that they had already shown that they don't keep their promises when I was directed to contact Mally's Instagram account on July 11, and I was ignored. I told her I would be happy to set up a time to talk to them during the month of August. Tia responded with just one word: "Chill."

EPILOGUE

1. Adding to my disillusion with American media has been my realization, while researching this book, that it subtly perpetuates and promotes sex trafficking and the exploitation of women. In March 2023, for example, after the Las Vegas Raiders signed quarterback Jimmy Garoppolo, TMZ reported that two Chicken Ranch brothel workers were offering the signal caller free sex services (and a spokesperson for another brothel extended a similar invitation). Fox News and the sports website Outkick picked up the story. The articles provided the brothels with free, national advertising. On Twitter, on a thread underneath a posting about the free offers by TMZ, I saw one commenter write, "That's a hard pass for me—no pun intended. . . . They can keep those STDs . . . and I'm not talking about several touchdowns." Then someone responded, "Spoiler alert lol casual sex is worse for you than legal prostitution." Also receiving news coverage was a second offer from one of the same sex workers, this time to host a free orgy for Vegas Golden Knights players after they won the Stanley Cup in June 2023.

2. Peter G. Johnson, "Sheldon Adelson, Las Vegas Convention Visionary and Philanthropist, Dies at 87," *Las Vegas Review-Journal*, January 12, 2021, accessed September 20, 2022, https://www.reviewjournal.com/business/casinos-gaming/sheldon-adelson-las -vegas-convention-visionary-and-philanthropist-dies-at-87-2250326/

3. Sheldon Adelson died in January 2021. The company Adelson led, Las Vegas Sands Corp., completed its sale of the Venetian and Palazzo hotel and casino complex in Las Vegas about a year after his death, in February 2022.

4. David Ferrara, Briana Erickson, and Glenn Puit, "Police arrest county official in reporter's stabbing death," *Las Vegas Review-Journal*, September 7, 2022, accessed September 20, 2022, https://www.reviewjournal.com/crime/homicides/police-arrest-county -official-in-reporters-stabbing-death-2635486/

5. Investigative Reporters and Editors, or IRE as it's known, is based at the University of Missouri, Columbia, my alma mater. I worked on the staff of the non-profit organization while I was an undergraduate. After graduation, I was a dues-paying member of the organization for a long time but let my membership lapse in recent years.

6. "Announcing the 2022 IRE Award winners & finalists," https://www.ire.org/2022 -ire-award-winners/, accessed April 3, 2023.

7. *Angela Williams and Jane Doe v. Steve Sisolak, Governor of Nevada, in his official capacity; Aaron Ford, Attorney General of Nevada, in his official capacity; The city of Las Vegas, Clark County; Nye County; Chicken Ranch; Jamal Rashid; Mally Mall Music, LLC; Future Music, LLC; PF Social Media Management; LLC, E.P. Sanctuary Blu Magic Music, LLC; Exclusive Beauty Lounge, LLC; First Investment Property LLC; V.I.P. Entertainment, LLC; MP3 Productions, Inc.; and MMM Productions, Inc.,* Case No. 2:21-cv-01676-APG-VCF (U.S. District Court of the District of Nevada (Las Vegas), September 10, 2021).

8. Marissa Kynaston, "UPDATE: Standoff, sex-trafficking suspect breaks down in court," KTNV-Las Vegas, January 19, 2017, accessed July 29, 2022, https://www.ktnv .com/news/standoff-suspect-charged-with-attempted-murder

9. Angela also appeared in two other sex trafficking documentaries, *Buying Her*, which was screened in cities across the United States and Europe in 2023, and *High Class*, which premiered at the Newport Beach Film Fest in October 2023.

Policy Discussion

1. See "Equal Not Exploited," accessed May 26, 2024, https://www.equalitymodelus. org/.

2. By this comment, Angela is not saying that jail time was a vacation for her. Rather, she's saying that time in jail gave her permission to step away from the pressures of life in The Game—a life she deep down hated, but thought was the only life available to her.

3. It's for this reason that Don is skeptical of another reform option known as the "Agency" or "Accountability" or "Public Safety" Model, which is employed in Texas. Under this scheme, sex trafficking as well as the buying and selling of sex all remain criminalized, but johns face harsher penalties than prostitutes. Don obviously supports the arresting of johns and thinks, in general, it needs to be done more. But he worries there are constitutional concerns when there is a disparity in punishments for what is essentially the same crime.

RESOURCES

1. There were an additional fifteen organizations I wanted to include in this section, but representatives of those groups did not respond to more than two dozen of my attempts to contact them. Three of those organizations are based in Nevada.

2. The people consulted in crafting this were Angela, Don, sex trafficking survivor and advocate Bekah Charleston, lawyer Jason Guinasso, staff at the National Center on Sexual Exploitation, Judge William Voy of the Eighth Judicial District Court's Family Division (retired),; and Nicole Reilly, ombudsman for domestic violence, sexual assault, and human trafficking for the State of Nevada.

3. The agencies appearing on this list are provided solely as a resource to victims and survivors. Their inclusion does not mean that they have endorsed this book, nor does it constitute any sort of guarantee on my part or the part of anyone who advised me in compiling this list.

4. "Red Flags for Sex Trafficking," Texas Attorney General, accessed August 25, 2022, https://www.texasattorneygeneral.gov/human-trafficking-section/signs-trafficking/red -flags-sex-trafficking

5. "Trafficking Terms," Shared Hope International, accessed June 24, 2022, https:// sharedhope.org/the-problem/trafficking-terms/

Index

ABC News, 230n2
abuse and trauma, xiv–xv, 34–35, 103, 213n23
Adams, Dawn, 216n12
Adelson, Sheldon, 98–99, 222n17, 222n21; death of, 174; proceeding with caution against, 143; *Review-Journal* purchased by, 96, 221n5; *Review-Journal* questioned by, 100; in *Sharks in the Desert*, 97; The Venetian and, 120
adult attention, 6–7
advocates, 138
Air Supply, 86
Alice in Chains, 82
Alien Cathouse, 118
Amber Laura (rapper), 164
American Pimp (film), 44
Anderson, Robert, 169
Andress-Tobiasson, Melanie, 109–10, 226n13
anti-trafficking community, 182–83
April (pseudonym), 76
arrests: Delgado, Angela, report of, 230n5; Delgado, Angela, Texas warrant for, 29–30; Delgado, Angela, using fake ID's in, 229n1; investigative editor analyzing prostitute, 120; law enforcement with many, 45; law enforcement with pimp, 172–73; of Mally, 58–59; Mally's statutory rape, 212n17; prostitutes should not have, 183; prostitutes with repeat, 43, 226n19; prostitution and solicited, 113–14; of sex buyers, 226n19, 241n3; sex buyers and sellers targeted equally for, 114–15; The Strip sex soliciting, 117–18; tourists soliciting prostitutes, 115

bacterial infection, 129
bank account drops, 129–30
bankruptcy, 163, 238n24
Banks, Ant, 58
Banks, Tayvone, 21
Barrera, Roger, 36–37, 209n11
Baughman, Christopher, 40, 133; affidavit submitted by, 46; attention thirst of, 69;

corruption charges against, 142; daughter to meet Bieber, 90; escort service investigation of, 36; Fifth Amendment invoked by, 108; Fleming conviction and, 82–83; Grundy's text messages with, 216n10, 220n15; Knapp on dirty cop, 154; law enforcement job reapplication of, 77; law enforcement resignation of, 72; Mally's business relationship with, 89–90, 107; Mally's loan accepted by, 78–79, 83, 110; Mercer's marriage to, 108; Metro approach used by, 35; Metro not rehiring, 79–80; *Off The Street* by, 69–70; online ads for prostitutes studied by, 75; pimps indicted by, 70; PIT leader portrayed by, 155; realty television for, 71; self-promotion tactics of, 154

Bay Swag, 165

Beas, Albert, 70, 72, 109

Beckett, Megan, 150, 234n25

bedroom search, 50–51

Be on the Look Out (BOLO), 36

Bergman, Lowell, 97

"Best I Ever Had" (song), 66

Beverly, Julia, 57, 205n2, 234n4

Bible verses, 159

Biden, Joe, 240n37

Bieber, Justin, 66–67, 85, 90

"Big Pimpin" (music video), 56–57

Blackburn, Marsha, 167

Black Mafia Family, 163

BMF (television), 163

BOLO. *See* Be on the Look Out

Bone Thugs-N-Harmony, 25, 64

Boyd, Jason ("Poo Bear"), 63, 147

Bradley, Shera, 82, 87, 111, 219n6

brainwashing, of prostitutes, 44

branding, of prostitutes, 25, 43

Broadus, Calvin Cordozar, Jr. *See* Snoop Dog

Brooks, Dennis (executive protection), 168–69

brothels: Delgado, Angela, job at, 8–9; media providing advertising for, 241n1; Nevada with legal, 33–34; at Pahrump, 34, 118; regulated commercial sex in, 179; sex trafficking in, 113, 118–19, 122–23

Bulger, James Joseph ("Whitey"), 87

Burns, Larry, 81

business interests, xv

Butler, Chad, 57

Buying Her (documentary), 242n9

cancer, 41, 82–84

cars, Mally owning, 59, 63

Casino (film), 4

casinos, key cards for, 26

"Caught Up" (song), 63

CCDC. *See* Clark County Detention Center

celebrity identities, 205n2

Chappelle, Dave, 215n54

chemo treatments, 83–84
Chesnoff, David, 150–51
child prostitutes, 34, 112
Christianity, 176
Chuck D, 240n32
CI. *See* criminal informant
Clark County Detention Center (CCDC), 127
Clark County District Attorney, 171
Clark County Sheriff, 81
cloned phones, 59–60, 212n17
clothing, having proper, 129
Cohen, Aaron, 71, 75, 216n12
Collins, Chris, 81
Combs, Sean ("Puffy"), 2153n54
commercial sex, 179, 206n9
communications, psychologist-patient, 219n6
community cars, 24
compassion, for victims, 39–40, 46, 144–45, 173–74
consensual sex, 179
conservatives (the right), xvii–xviii
conviction appeal, of Fleming, 82–83
Cops (television), 69
coroner, 101
corruption: Baughman charges of, 142; Knapp on Vice Section, 107, 153–54; police, 86; public, 79, 90; Vice Section speculation of, 110–11
counselors, 138

"Count to a Million" (song), 237n19
COVID-19 pandemic, 145, 148–49
crackhead slumber party, 28
crime doesn't pay, 151
criminal charges, 7
criminal informant (CI), 60–61, 111–12, 217n16
Criminal Intelligence Section (Intel): dirty cops sought by, 79; information cultivated by, 40–41; Mally as criminal informant, 51–52, 60–61, 111–12; of Metro, 37; policy violations of, 74–75
culture shock, of Las Vegas, 99

Dallas (street pimp): Delgado, Angela, beat by, 10–11; Delgado, Angela, Las Vegas relocation by, 3–4; Delgado, Angela, meeting up with, 9–10; Delgado, Angela, pushed in trunk by, 10–11
"Dance with Me" (song), 63
Davis, Quashay, 163, 238n22
decriminalization, of prostitution, xvii–xix, 179–81
Delgado, Angela: adult attention sought by, 6–7; arrest report of, 231n5; arrests and fake ID's used by, 230n1; background of, 5–6; bacterial infection of, 129; basic skills relearned by, 138;

as better than other prostitutes, 25–26; CCDC detention of, 127; celebrity identities and, 207n2; daily earnings deposit by, 130; Dallas beating, 10–11; Dallas meeting up with, 9–10; Dallas pushing in trunk, 10–11; Dallas' relocation to Las Vegas of, 3–4; drug conviction of, 9; escort service job of, 11–12; Fleming violence against, 27, 155; freedom for, 177; help sought by, 133–34; as high-class lady of night, 23; illegal brothel job of, 8–9; incarceration of, 131, 241n2; as independent contractor, 15–16; jobs of, 7–8; john encounter of, 5; Joseph communications with, 145; Las Vegas return of, 135; life remaking process begun by, 137–38; Mally disillusionment of, 127–28; Mally hanging out with, 25; Mally hated by, 175–76; Mally hearing watched by, 149–50; Mally meeting, 18–19; Mally return of, 28; Mally's operation joined by, 19–20; Mally's profile seen by, 17; Mally's relationship with, 24–25; mansion stay of, 16; marriage of, 175; McDaniels desensitizing, 9; memory markers for, 205n2; money earned is self-worth of, 230n3; New York move of, 134–35; panic attack of, 148; parole of, 133; Pimp C's friendship with, 173; pimp protecting, 136; prostitution should remain illegal from, 181–82; Rolls-Royce ride of, 13–14, 18; as stripper and prostitute, 3; stubborn freewheeling impulses of, 27; in *Surviving Sex Trafficking*, 176–77; Texas extradition of, 131; Texas warrant arrest of, 29–30; traveling services by, 128–29, 133, 231n4; victim impact statement from, 146; victims helped by, 176; winter coat earned by, 146; Woodard meeting, 11–12, 15; Woodard requesting return of, 133; Wright meeting, 135–36; Wright robbing, 231n8; Wright savagely beating, 136–37, 176–77

Delgado, Angelina (mother), 6–7
Dickey, Joe, 78
Dickinson, Nicholas, 150
Dillard, Gordon, 147, 233n19
dirty cops, 51–52; Intel seeking, 79; Knapp on Baughman as, 154
divide and conquer, 24
DJ Franzen, 65
DJ Khaled, 67
document fight, 103–4
"Do It Again" (song), 64
domestic sex trafficking, 205n1

domestic violence, 138
"Don't Look at Me" (song), 237n19
"Don't OD" (song), 234n21
Drake (rapper), 64–66
Draskovich, Robert, 213
drug conviction, of Delgado, Angela, 9
drug trade, 60–61

education, on sex trafficking, 182
Edwards, Julie, 23
empathy, 180
empowerment, 26
Eros (online escort directory), 62
escort service: aggressive marketing used for, 22; Baughman's investigation of, 36; cash delivered to, 16; daily bank drops in, 129–30; Delgado, Angela, job at, 11–12; Delgado, Angela, traveling for, 128–29, 133, 231n4; Eros online directory for, 62; girl's quotas for, 22; of Mally, 61–62; marketing of, 22; online operations of, 128–39; Paone giving ride to, 15; referrals through, 134; screening process failure of, 130–31; sex buyers calling, 15; upselling skills for, 16
Eubanks, Dale, 60
Evans, Brian, 79
evidentiary hearing, on Fleming, 109–10

Exclusive Beauty Lounge, 24
exotic animals, 49–51, 63
expert witnesses, 82–83, 171
exploitation, 160

facial reconstruction surgery, 137
fake IDs, 29
Federal Bureau of Investigation (FBI): Mally's mansion raided by, 77–78, 135; public corruption investigation by, 79, 90; sex trafficking investigated by, 89
federal prisons, 234n27
felony convictions, of Wright, 138–39
female lieutenants, 23
Ferrell, Will, xiv
Fertitta, Frank, III, 115, 227n20
Fertitta, Lorenzo, 115, 227n20
Fertitta, Tilman, 115, 227n20
Fifth Amendment, 108
50 Cent, 57, 163
Finan, Deb, 76
Fleming, Ocean (pimp), 70, 225n8, 235n4; conviction appeal of, 82–83; deal accepted by, 110; Delgado, Angela, violence by, 27; evidentiary hearing on, 109–10; Hoier, D., on trial of, 216n9; indictment of, 71; Knapp's reporting on, 107–8; life in prison for, 71; prison release of, 142; as violent pimp, 155; White interviewing, 86

Flenory, Demetrius ("Big Meech"), 163
FOIA. *See* Freedom of Information Act
Ford, Charles Adrian ("Charley Mac"), 225n9
"Forever" (song), 66
Frankl, Viktor, 144
Freedom of Information Act (FOIA), 236n15
Fresh, Doug E., 240n32

"The Game Belongs to Me" (song), 57
Gashi (rapper), 234n21
German, Jeff, 174–75, 222n12
Gill, Adam, 108
Gillespie, Doug, 81
GoFundMe campaigns, 102
Goldman, Emma, 55
Graffiti Mansion, 155
Graham, Aubrey. *See* Drake
Gray, Warren, 46, 73–74, 79
Green Bay Packers, 111
Gruda, Jessica, 109
Grundy, Alisha, 70, 86, 215n6, 216n10, 2220n15
guilty plea, of Izadi, 235n6
guns, 50

Haines, George, 165
halfway houses, 239n34
Hannan, Jason, 207n4
Hansen, Chris, 69, 71
Hardy, Joe, Jr., 117

Hello Kitty music, 7
Henley, Stacey, 233n19
High Class (documentary), 242n9
hip hop: culture, 56; Mally in, 25, 58, 63–64; music, xvi; pimp culture in, 173
Hip Hop Alliance, 167, 240n32
Hof, Dennis, 118, 228n4
Hoier, Chris, 41–43
Hoier, Donald: background of, 41; brothers accident guilt of, 41–42; cancer diagnosis of, 82; CI information and, 217n16; education important from, 182; on Fleming's trial, 216n9; hours-long conversations with, 111; imprest money for, 45; at Innocence Lost Coordinators Conference, 220n13; Izadi as thorn in side of, 73–74; Kelesis name recognized by, 220n11; Knapp on, 235n2; Lombardo meeting, 81–82; on Mally fishing for information, 230n3; Marine Corps enlistment of, 42; Metro retirement of, 8; as PIT lead, 40; police strategies toward pimps from, 105; prostitutes conversations with, 44; prostitute sympathy from, 39–40; prostitution investigation assistance by, 112; prostitution should remain illegal from, 181–82; in Vice Section, 39, 43–44; Vice Section not trusted

by, 171–72; we're not prostitutes story of, 209n4; white
blood cell count of, 84; White's
interview of, 84–87; White's
message to, 83–84
Holiday, Shawn ("Tubby"), 18, 63,
156–57
home confinement, 165, 239n26
Hope for Prisoners, 227n21
ho stroll, 10
Hughes, Karen, 45, 72, 155; prostitutes as victims belief of, 40;
timeline created by, 78–79; as
Vice Section leader, 35
human impact, of Mally, 150
human rights, 184
Hunt for the Skinwalker
(Knapp), 89
Hustle & Flow (film), 57

Iceberg Slim (pimp), 55–56
Ice-T, 56, 211n11
imprest money, 45
incarceration: Delgado, Angela,
spending time in, 131; Delgado,
Angelina, release from, 6–7;
federal prisons and, 234n27;
Fleming's release from, 142;
juvenile, 119; of Mally, 163,
239n28; Mally's preparations
for release from, 164–65;
Sharpe, Robert, found dead in,
219n8
independent contractor, 15–16
in-depth interviews, 122, 155

indictments, 71, 137
information: CI, 217n17; Intel
cultivating, 40–41; Mally as
source for, 85; Mally fishing
for, 230n3; Mally providing law
enforcement, 109; White as
source for, 90
Innocence Lost Coordinators
Conference, 220n13
Instagram threats, 240n35
internal affairs report, 138
International VIP, 23
interviews: in-depth, 122, 155;
Mally's decision on, 170
investigations: escort service, 36;
FBI sex trafficking, 89; Hoier,
D., assisting prostitution, 112;
Mally as target of, 36; prostitution, 103–4, 112; *Review-
Journal* with no leader for, 102;
of sex trafficking, 230n15
investigative editor, 101, 120–21,
220n3
Investigative Reporters and
Editors (IRE), 242n5
Islam, Mally preaching about, 25
"It's Hard Out Here for a Pimp"
(song), 57
Ivy, Ken ("Pimpin'"), xiv–xvi
Izadi, Arman (pimp), 107, 232n5;
guilty plea of, 235n7; as Hoier,
D., nuisance, 73–74; records of
violence by, 155

J (psuedonym), 13

Jackmon, Sandi, 206n1, 237n19
jail cells, 28–29
JAY-Z, 56, 147
jobs, of Delgado, Angela, 7–8
johns. *See* sex buyers
Jones, Cash M., 147
Joseph, Brian: Delgado, Angela, communications with, 145; Knapp meeting with, 153; Las Vegas move of, 102; Mally's Instagram account and, 166–68; mansion visit of, 168–70; music industry ignoring, 157; no comment for book and, 161; *Review-Journal* research and, 232n12, 233n16; severance agreement of, 232n11; White hanging up on, 161; Woodard getting emails from, 239n39; Woodard meeting with, 158–61; Woodard's manipulation attempt on, 160
journalism: caution in, 143; on sex trafficking, 98
Journals (album), 66
Julien, Max, 56
Just Add Water (album), 203
Justice for Women International, 167–68
juvenile incarceration, 119
Juvenile Justice Services, 119
juvenile sex trafficking, 45, 82, 112, 118–22

Kardashian, Kim, 77

Keak da Sneak, 173
Kelesis, George, 84, 220n11
key cards, for casinos, 26
Khalilian, Fereidoun ("Prince Fred"), 238n24
Klobuchar, Amy, 167
Knapp, George: on Baughman as dirty cop, 154; Fleming reporting by, 107–8; on Hoier, D., 235n2; *Hunt for the Skinwalker* by, 89; Joseph meeting with, 153; mansion raid reported by, 141–42; on sex trafficking, 235n8; Vice Section corruption from, 107, 153–54; White as information source for, 90
Knight, Suge, 215n54
knock and move practice, 12
KRS-One, 240n32
Kurtis Blow, 240n32

Las Vegas: culture shock of, 99; Delgado, Angela, relocation to, 3–4; Delgado, Angela, return to, 135; Joseph's move to, 102; law enforcement in, 34–35, 227n21; Mally's move to, 61–62; *Review-Journal* in, 96; sex-obsessed culture of, 233n8; sex trafficking in, xvii, 102–3, 153; as Sin City, 33; the Strip of, 4
Las Vegas Concierge VS1, 23
Las Vegas Convention and Visitors Authority, 99, 222n16, 222n21

Las Vegas Metropolitan Police Department, 230n1

Latino men, 4

law-abiding citizen, 151

law enforcement, 6; Baughman reapplying for job with, 77; Baughman's resignation from, 72; Hoier, D., on strategies of, 105; juvenile sex trafficking and, 118–19; large arrest numbers for, 45; in Las Vegas, 34–35, 227n19; Mally providing information to, 109; pimps arrested by, 172–73; police corruption and, 86; prostitutes relationship with, 181; prostitution as low priority for, 33; public records from, 161; sex trade equal enforcement by, 182; sex traffickers as priority for, 182–84; undercover female officers in, 227n19; victims not priority by, 172

liberals (the left), xvi–xviii, 179

life remaking process, 137–38

Lil Baby, 165

Lil Wayne, 64, 66

LinkedIn, 95–96

LL Cool J, 56

Lloyd D. George Courthouse, 149

Logue, David, 51–52

Lombardo, Joe, 115, 154, 223n23; for Clark County Sheriff, 81; Hoier, D., meeting, 81–82; no comment from, 161

Love & Hip Hop (television), 68, 77, 156

Love Ranch South, 118

low income communities, xviii

low self-esteem, xv

Ludacris, 57

Mac Dre (rapper), 58

The Mack (film), 56

Mally Mall (pimp): arrests of, 58–59; background of, 58–59; bankruptcy filing of, 163, 238n24; Barrera recognizing, 37; Baughman accepting loan from, 78–79, 83, 110; Baughman's business relationship with, 89–90, 107; bedroom searched of, 50–51; birthdate of, 211n14; cars owned by, 59, 63; cloned phones sold by, 59–60; community cars of, 24; crime doesn't pay message to, 151; as criminal informant, 51–52, 60–61, 111–12; Davis suing, 163; Davis witnessing pimping operation of, 237n24; Delgado, Angela, disillusioned with, 127–28; Delgado, Angela, going back to, 28; Delgado, Angela, hanging out with, 25; Delgado, Angela, hating, 175–76; Delgado, Angela, joining operation of, 19–20; Delgado, Angela, meeting, 18–19; Delgado, Angela, relationship with, 24–25; Delgado, Angela, seeing profile of, 17; Delgado, Angela, watching hearing of, 149–50; Dillard on, 231n19; divide and conquer by, 24; drug trade involvement of, 60–61; escort services of, 61–62; Exclusive Beauty Lounge of, 24; federal prison check-in by, 234n27; female lieutenants of, 23; guilty plea of, 142; in hip hop, 25, 58, 63–64; hit list by, 225n9; Hoier, D., and fishing for information by, 230n3; Holiday on criminal activities of, 156–57; on home confinement, 239n28; human impact of, 150; humiliation forced by, 20; incarceration of, 163, 239n30; information to police by, 109; Instagram threats from, 239n35; interview decision by, 170; as investigation target, 36; on Islam, 25; Jackmon raped by, 237n19; Joseph contacting Instagram account of, 166–68; Joseph's emails sent to, 241n39; keeping himself out of prison, 87; kicked off *Marriage Boot Camp*, 164; Las Vegas move of, 61–62; mansion fire of, 141; mansion's ownership transferred by, 239n28; Metro and sex trafficking by, 162–63; Metro raiding properties of, 49; Metro's investigation of, 37; musical talent of, 147; music production by, 64, 66–67, 166, 213n28; new mansion of, 141–42; no one talking about, 156; no sentencing statement from, 152; Pimp C dissing, 211n13; plea agreement of, 144; press release about, 165; Price on, 239n27; pricing model employed by, 22; Priority Girls living arrangements of, 23–24; Priority Girls of, 21, 62; prison release preparations for, 164–65; property search sought for, 46–47; as prostitute manager, 207n2; prostitutes cash drops to, 47; public records on, 212n20; reality television of, 71, 145–46, 156, 168; restraining order against, 61; Roc Nation's relationship with, 234n21; as self-help guru, 16–17; sentencing hearing of, 145–48, 150–52; sentencing memo on, 148; as sex trafficker, 27, 63, 162–63; statutory rape arrest and, 212n17; strong case against, 51; television roles of, 68; Tresvant sexually assaulted by, 237n20; White accusation by, 163–64; White information source as, 85; women mentored by, 158; women recruited by, 62; women working for, 162–63;

Woodard on positive contributions of, 158; Woodard seeking support for, 160–61; Woodard's road to redemption of, 157–58; Woodard working with, 165

Mama Black Widow (Iceberg Slim), 56

Mandalay Bay Resort and Casino shooting, 100–102, 117, 223n23

manipulation: pimps using, xv–xv, 167; prostitutes using, 159; Woodard's attempt at, 160

mansion (of Mally): creepy vibe of, 51; Delgado, Angela, staying at, 16; description of, 14–15, 206n1, 210n2; federal agents raiding, 77–78, 135; fire at, 141; Joseph's visit to, 168–70; Knapp reporting on raid of, 141–42; Mally getting new, 141–42; Mally transferring ownership of, 239n29; Metro raid of, 49–50; public corruption squad and, 90; purchase of, 63; recording studio of, 63; security cameras of, 169; SWAT clearing, 50

Man's Search for Meaning (Frankl), 144

marginalized people, 103, 174

marijuana possession, 6

Marine Corps, 42

marketing, of escort services, 22

marriage, of Delgado, Angela, 175

Marriage Boot Camp (television), 145, 156, 164

Marshall, Janiece, 108, 234n5

Maupin, Robert Lee. *See* Iceberg Slim

McDaniels, Andre ("Dre"), 8–9, 206n9

media, 241n1

Melgoza, Kenneth K., 212n17

Menendez, Robert, 167

Mercer, Elizabeth, 71–72, 107–8, 216n11

methamphetamine, 59–60

Metro, 34; Barrera in, 209n11; Baughman not rehired by, 79–80; Baughman's approach used by, 35; Hoier, D., retired from, 8; Intel involved in investigation of, 37; Mally's properties raided by, 49; Mally's sex trafficking and, 162–63; mansion raid by, 49–50; prostitution laws enforced by, 113; record requests from, 117–18, 161–62, 236n17; *Review-Journal* lawsuit against, 143; Vice Section of, 35

Miami Vice (television), 33

Mickens, John ("Goldie"), 56

Millard, April, 70–71, 109, 225n8

Mitchell, Alvin, 73

"Molly" (song), 67

monkey, 50, 66–67

Moonlite Bunny Ranch, 118

Moore, T. J., 118, 227n1

"The Motto" (song), 66
MSNBC, 76–77
Mudarris, Nikki, 68, 77
Mulvehill, Sean, 234n21
musical talent, 147
music industry, 63, 157
music production, 64, 66–67, 166, 213n28

Nasseri, Nima, 147, 234n21
Navarro, Gloria M., 146, 151
The Neighborhood Talk, 163
New York Anti-Trafficking Network, 76
New York move, 134–35
Nita (Mally associate), 157
nondisparagement clause, 143
Nordic Model (Equality), 180–81

O'Boyle, Todd, 96
Odom, Lamar, 118
Off the Street (Baughman), 69–70
Off the Street (television), 75
OG Mally (monkey), 66–67
online operations, of escort services, 128–39
The Orange Show attraction, 7
The Other Guys (film), xiv
out of pocket, 10, 128

Paddock, Stephen, 100
Pahrump, Nevada, 34, 118
Palestine Liberation Organization, 60–61
pandering, xv–xvi

Pandering Investigations Team (PIT), 35, 46, 137; Baughman's portrayal of heading up, 155; Hoier, D., as head of, 40
panic attacks, 146, 148
Paone, Jennifer (Jen), 15, 23
paranormal activities, 89
parole, of Delgado, Angela, 133
Paul, Jake, 235n6
"Peaches and Cream" (song), 63
personal privacy, 161
Pimp (Iceberg Slim), 55–56
"P.I.M.P" (song), 57
Pimp C (rapper), 57–58, 173, 211n13
The Pimp Game (Royal), 44
Pimp My Ride (television), 56–57
Pimpology (Ivy), xv
pimps: Baughman indicting, 70; child prostitutes kept away from, 112; Delgado, Angela, protected by, 136; force and coercion used by, xv–xvi; hip hop reflecting culture of, 173; Hoier, D., on police strategies toward, 105; Ice-T as, 211n11; illegality of, 180–81; knock and move practice of, 12; law enforcement arresting, 172–73; mainstreaming of, 56–57; manipulation used by, xv–xvi, 167; prostitutes brainwashed by, 182; prostitute's road trips from, xix; prostitutes under control of, 75; prostitution recruitment

expected by, 5; scrutiny not welcomed by, 170; in sex trafficking, xv; sex trafficking victims in court facing, 148; slap, xiv; Snoop Dogg as, 211n10; strip clubs with, 180; violence used by, 137; white women desired by, 21; word origin of, 55. *See also* sex traffickers; *specific pimp*

Pimps Up, Ho's Down (film), 44

PIT. *See* Pandering Investigations Team

plea agreement, 144

Poker After Dark (television), 145, 156

Polaris Project, 133

police corruption, 86

policy violations, of Intel, 74–75

politics, sex trafficking and, xvii

popular culture, xiii

poverty, prostitution's connection to, 55–56

Powell, Stephany, 231n1

Price, Tresure (exotic dancer), 164, 239n27

pricing model, 22

Priority Girls, 21, 23–24, 62, 133–34

property search, 46–47

prostitutes: abuse and trauma suffered by, xiv–xv, 34–35, 103, 213n25; arrested over and over, 43, 227n21; Baughman and Cohen studying online ads for, 75; brainwashing of, 44; branding of, 25, 43; child, 34, 112; Delgado, Angela, as stripper and, 3; Delgado, Angela, feeling better than other, 25–26; fake IDs of, 29; Hoier, D., being told we're not, 209n4; Hoier, D., conversations with, 44; Hoier, D., sympathizing with, 39–40; ho stroll of, 10; Hughes on victims of, 40; incapable of love, 127; investigative editor analyzing arrests of, 120; in jail cells, 28–29; law enforcement's relationship with, 181; Mally as manager of, 207n2; Mally receiving cash drops from, 47; Mally with women working as, 162–63; manipulation used by, 159; McDaniels's recruitment of, 8; Nordic Model destigmatizing, 181; not arresting, 183; out of pocket, 10, 128; pimps and road trips by, xix; pimps brainwashing, 182; pimps controlling, 75; pimps expecting recruitment of, 5; Priority Girls tier of, 21; as prostituted person, xv–xvi; quotas for, 22; as renegades, 13; as robot sex slaves, 146; sex buyers targeted equally with, 114–15; sympathy and compassion for, 39–40, 46, 144–45, 173–74; as throwaway people, 33; tipping important for, 26; tourists arrested soliciting, 115; Vice Section targeting, 43; work the carpet by, 206n3. *See also* sex trafficking victims

prostitution: commercial sex and, 179, 206n9; consensual sex compared to, 179; decriminalization of, xii–xiv, 179–81; Delgado, Angela, and Hoier, D., on illegality of, 181–82; investigation, 103–4, 112; Metro enforcing laws on, 113; money earned is self-worth of, 230n3; Nevada criminal code for, 226n15; pimps expecting recruitment in, 5; as police low priority, 33; poverty's connection to, 55–56; soliciting arrests for, 113–14; on The Strip, 4–5, 233n16; tourists looking for, 34; as white slavery, 55; women desperate entering, 180

psychologist-patient communications, 219n6

public corruption, 79, 90

public integrity, 37

public-interest lawsuit, 176

public records, 161, 212n20

Public Safety Model, 242n3

Ramos, Don, 109, 225n9

rape, 212n17, 237n20

Rashid, Fayeq (Mally's father), 58

Rashid, Jamal. *See* Mally Mall

Ray J (R&B artist), 77

reality television, of Mally, 71, 145–46, 156, 168

The Real Mistresses of Atlanta (television), 134

recidivism rate, 43

recording studio, 63

record requests, 117–18, 161–62, 237n17

Red Rock Resort, 114

renegade, prostitutes as, 13

reporting process, 228n3

Residential Reentry Management (RRM), 164, 239n28

"The Return of Jamal 'Mally Mall' Rashid" (press release), 165

Review-Journal: Adelson purchasing, 96, 221n5; Adelson's question to, 100; big story wanted by, 99, 222n12; editors of, 220n3; Evans research for, 232n15; fired from, 122–23; investigative editor of, 101, 220n3; job with, 99; Joseph's research and, 232n13, 232n16; in Las Vegas, 96; Mandalay Bay shooting covered by, 100–102, 223n23, 223n24; Metro being sued by, 143; no investigative leader at, 102; reputation of, 174; research taking too long for, 117, 143; salary offered by, 98–99; victim's name publishing discussions with, 229n13

Riddle, Kirk, 159, 236n11

The Rise and Fall of Sandi Jackmon (Jackmon), 206n1, 237n19
robot sex slave, 146
Rock, Rick, 58
Roc Nation, 234n21
Rolls-Royce ride, 13–14, 18
Ross, Rick, 65
Royal, Mickey, 44
RRM. *See* Residential Reentry Management

San Joaquin County Superior Court, 212n19
Sawyer, Diane, 133
Schifalacqua, Marc, 73–74, 107
Schofield, Gary, 234n27
screening process failure, 130–31
scrutiny, pimps not welcoming, 170
security cameras, 169
self-esteem, xiv, 6
self-fulfillment, 26
self-help guru, 16–17
self-promotion tactics, 154
self-worth, 230n3
sentencing hearing, 145–48, 150–52
sentencing memo, 148
severance agreement, 231n11
sex buyers (johns), 15, 180–81; arresting, 226n19, 242n4; Nevada criminal code for, 226n15; prostitutes targeted equally with, 114–15; Riddle as, 159; the Strip with arrested, 115; as undercover cop, 130
sex industry, xiv, 19, 182
sex-obsessed culture, 236n9
sex traffickers: law enforcement priority of, 182–84; local court cases of, 104; pandering difference with, xv
sex trafficking: brothels with illegal, 113, 118–19, 122–23; business interests and, xvii; Clark County District Attorney and, 171; Cohen fighting, 71; domestic, 205n1; education on, 182; FBI investigating, 89; high-impact journalism on, 98; Holiday on, 156–57; human impact of, 150; juvenile, 45, 82, 112, 118–19, 121–22; Knapp on, 233n8; in Las Vegas, xix, 102–3, 153; low income communities and, xviii; of Mally, 27, 63, 162–63; media promoting, 241n1; no one wanting to talk about, 104; pimps and prostitutes in, xiv; politics and, xiii; in popular culture, xvii–xviii; *Review-Journal* research on, 117, 143; Sawyer shedding light on, 133; Sharpe, Robert, facing assault and, 83; strip clubs with, 180; Vice Section policing, 172; witnesses of, 104. *See also* prostitution

sex trafficking victims: Delgado, Angela, helping, 176; difficulty getting out by, 133–34; failed research letting down, 143; in-depth interviews of, 122; law enforcement not prioritizing, 172; as marginalized people, 103, 174; pimps faced in court by, 148; psychologist-patient communications of, 219n6; as survivors, xvi–xviii, 176–77; sympathy and compassion for, 39–40, 46, 144–45, 173–74; victim impact statement from, 146; violence ruling, ix; White call recommended by, 236n15
sexual activities, 109
sexual assault, 163, 237n19
sexual violence, xx
sex work, 179–80
Sex Worker Outreach Project-Las Vegas, 76
Sharks in the Desert (Smith), 97
Sharpe, Raymond (pimp), 70, 86, 215n6
Sharpe, Robert, III, 83, 105, 111, 219n8
Sheidlower, Jesse, 55
Silva, Cristina, 84–85
Sin City, 33, 115
Sisolak, Steve, 176
Six-Day War (1967), 55
Slave Hunter (television), 71–73, 75–77
slavery, white, 55

Smith, John L., 97
Snoop Dogg, 56, 211n10
Snow bunny, 173
social media, 239n34
"So Good, So Right" (song), 64
soliciting arrests, 113–14
Soulja Boy (rapper), 77
stabbing, of German, 174–75
statutory rape arrest, 212n17
Strength & Loyalty (album), 64
The Strip: dangers of, 4; of Las Vegas, 4; prostitution on, 4–5, 233n16; sex buyers arrested on, 115; sex soliciting arrests on, 117–18; soliciting arrests on, 113–14
strip clubs, 3, 6, 180
Suga Free (rapper), 19, 203
surgery, facial reconstruction, 137
surveillance, 46–47
Surviving Sex Trafficking (documentary), 176–77
survivors. *See* sex trafficking victims
SWAT team, 50
Sweet Jones (Beverly), 57, 205n2, 234n5

Take Care (album), 64
"Tell Me When to Go" (song), 173
Texas extradition, 131
Texas warrant arrest, 29–30
Thank Me Later (album), 64
throwaway people, 33

Thug Stories (album), 64
Tia. *See* Woodard, Tarnita
To Catch a Predator (television), 69
tourists, 34, 115
Tourist Safety Unit, 36
traveling services, by Delgado,
    Angela, 128–29, 133, 2318n4
Tresvant, Chanda, 237n20
Trick Baby (Iceberg Slim), 56
Trump, Donald, 98

UFOs (documentary), 89
undercover cops, 120, 130
undercover female officers, 227n19
upselling skills, 16
Usher, 63

Valentine, Shane, 110
Vegas Metropolitan Police
    Department. *See* Metro
the Venetian, 120, 228n7
Vice Section: corruption spec-
    ulation of, 110–11; Hoier,
    D., in, 39, 43–44; Hoier, D.,
    not trusting, 171–72; Knapp
    reporting on corruption of,
    107, 153–54; location of, 39; of
    Metro, 35; under microscope,
    83; more compassion from,
    46; prostitutes targeted by, 43;
    sex trafficking policed by, 172;
    sexual activities by, 109; victim's
    comments of, 236n15
victim impact statement, 146
Vigna, Vic, 28, 43, 137

Villani, Michael, 109, 226n10
violence: domestic, 138; Fleming's
    use of, 27, 155; Izadi's records
    of, 155; pimps using, 137; sex
    trafficking victims ruled by, xiii;
    sexual, xvii
Voy, William, 227n1, 229n14

wages, for women, 55
Walter Leitner International
    Human Rights Clinic, 76
Washoe County, Nevada, 208n5
welterweight fight, 29
Wheelchair Mike ("Big Mike"),
    225n9
White, Kevin, 107–8, 154,
    219n14; Fleming interviewed
    by, 86; Hoier, D., interviewed
    by, 84–87; Hoier, D., message
    from, 83–84; Joseph hung up
    on by, 161; Knapp's information
    source as, 90; Mally as infor-
    mation source for, 85; Mally's
    accusation about, 163–64;
    police corruption talk from, 86
white slavery, 55
white women, 21
wild animals, 14
winter coat, earning, 146
witnesses, of sex trafficking, 104
Wiz Khalifa (rapper), 67
women: equal wages for, 55;
    human rights of, 184; Mally
    employing, 162–63; Mally
    mentoring, 158; Mally

recruiting, 62; prostitution from desperation of, 180; sexual violence against, xiii; sex work by, 179–80; as undercover female officers, 227n19; white, 21. *See also* sex trafficking victims

Woodard, Tarnita (Tia): Delgado, Angela, meeting, 11–12, 15; Delgado, Angela, return request of, 133; as female lieutenant, 23; Joseph contacting Instagram account of, 166–68; Joseph manipulation attempt by, 160; Joseph meeting with, 158–61; Joseph's emails sent to, 241n39; on Mally's positive contributions, 158; Mally's road to redemption and, 157–58; Mally support sought by, 160–61; Mally working with, 165

work the carpet, 206n3

World Day Against Trafficking in Persons, 169

Wright, Tyree: Delgado, Angela, meeting, 135–36; Delgado, Angela, robbed by, 231n8; Delgado, Angela, savagely beaten by, 136–37, 176–77; felony convictions of, 138–39; felony indictments against, 137

Wynn, Steve, 97

Young, Bill, 114, 227n20

Yvette, Jacqueline, 167–68

Ziman, Daphna Edwards, 168, 240n37

ABOUT THE AUTHOR

Brian Joseph has worked as a newspaper reporter and investigative journalist for about twenty years, writing for the *Las Vegas Review-Journal*, the *Orange County Register*, and the *Sacramento Bee*, among other publications. In 2013–14, he was an investigative reporting fellow at the University of California, Berkeley, where he investigated privatized foster care for *Mother Jones* magazine. Brian is a graduate of the University of Missouri, Columbia, and the recipient of several journalism honors, including a George Polk Award. He lives in Las Vegas with his wife and daughter and their talkative orange tabby Nemo.